Doctors in Blue

THE MEDICAL HISTORY

OF THE UNION ARMY IN

THE CIVIL WAR

GEORGE WORTHINGTON

Adams

LOUISIANA STATE UNIVERSITY PRESS

BATON ROUGE

Louisiana Paperback Edition, 1996
05 04 03 02 01 00   5 4 3

Library of Congress Cataloging-in-Publication Data

Adams, George Worthington.
    Doctors in blue : the medical history of the Union Army in the
Civil War / George Worthington Adams.
        p.   cm.
    Originally published: New York : H. Schuman, 1952.
    Includes bibliographical references (p.) and index.
    ISBN 0-8071-2105-3 (pbk.)
    1. United States—History—Civil War, 1861–1865—Medial care.
2. United States. Army—Sanitary affairs. 3. Medicine, Military—
United States—History—19th century. 4. United States. Army—
History—Civil War, 1861–1865. I. Title.
    E621.A3   1996
    973.7'75—dc20   96-22219
                                                        CIP

TO MABEL

CONTENTS

THE AUTHOR HOPES HIS WORK WILL NOT ONLY HELP TO illuminate certain aspects of the Civil War, and the medical sciences of that period, but will also extend public understanding of continuing problems of military medicine.

The Civil War saw the beginnings of ambulance field work, the Army Nurse Corps and other organizations and practices now taken for granted. It highlighted such vexed questions as the proper relationship of line officers to medical officers, and of Regulars to "Reserves." An understanding of the origins of such questions may contribute to sane solutions in the days ahead.

The material in this book was first presented as a doctoral dissertation in history, at Harvard. For the sake of space and a more readable text the author has omitted footnote citations of his sources. Those who wish to pursue the subject further are referred to the somewhat longer and profusely documented version deposited in the Harvard Library.

The author is deeply indebted to Professor Arthur M. Schlesinger for his wise counsel and his editorial suggestions. He is also indebted to his father, the late Dr. Albyn L. Adams, and to Dr. Herrman L. Blumgart, Professor of Medicine at Harvard and Chief of Medicine at Beth Israel Hospital, Boston, who read the manuscript and offered criticism and encouragement. The kindness and cooperation of the staffs of the libraries in which research was undertaken are gratefully acknowledged. These include: Widener Library, Harvard University; the Boston Medical Library; the Library of the Massachusetts Historical Society; the New York Public Library, and the Army Medical Library at Washington.

Throughout the long period of preparation, the research and editorial services of the author's wife were invaluable. He is also indebted, for clerical assistance, to Elizabeth Starrett and Pamela Adams.

G. W. A.

Colorado College,
Colorado Springs

DOCTORS IN BLUE

1

The
Medical
Confusions
of 1861

IF WE EXCEPT THE TAIPING REBELLION IN CHINA, OF WHICH
little is accurately known, the great war of the century between
the Napoleonic Wars and the first World War, was the Civil War
in America, fought in the four years between 1861 and 1865.
In that war some 300,000 Union soldiers lost their lives. Confederate attacks account for only a third of these deaths; disease,
for the rest. There were 400,000 cases of wounds and injuries
and almost 6,000,000 cases of sickness. Startling as these figures
are, they nevertheless represent a great improvement over those
of the Mexican War, when ten men had died of disease for every
man killed by the enemy. Behind the sickness and mortality
statistics of the Civil War lie ignorance, stupidity, inefficiency
and jealousy. But behind them also, as the contrast with the
earlier war suggests, are to be seen earnestness, cooperative

spirit, and great strides of scientific knowledge which a later generation has all but forgotten.

The Army Medical Department entered the war unprepared. Its chief, Colonel Thomas Lawson, a veteran of the War of 1812, was over eighty. Seniority had brought him into office during the administration of John Quincy Adams and in the absence of any retirement law he had stayed on and on, concerned principally with pruning the budget. He considered the purchase of medical books an extravagance and is reported to have flown into a rage on learning that one army post owned two sets of surgical instruments.

Next to economy Colonel Lawson was most concerned over the military status of his corps. He is credited with having secured the passage of the act of 1847 which conferred army rank upon the surgeons. They had previously been called simply "doctor"; now they might be greeted as "captain" and "major." His subordinates thought him a martinet; and he would keep a man at a lonely post on the plains for as long as ten years before allowing a sixty-day leave of absence. The long Lawson regime may have been resented but its habits and ideas had seeped through the whole medical corps. At any rate the efforts of the Sanitary Commission, organized outside the Army, which sought to give advice and help were, in most cases, ignored or resisted.

The Medical Department personnel seems pitifully small when measured against the duties soon to fall upon it. Actually the medical staff, though under one per cent of the Army, was then considered large. In January, 1861, the United States Army numbered 16,000 soldiers. In the last year of peace it had averaged 13,531. Its medical staff was made up of the Surgeon General, 30 surgeons, and 83 assistant surgeons. Three surgeons and 21 assistant surgeons of Southern origin resigned to "go with their States," while five surgeons and eight assistant surgeons whose homes were in seceded states stayed on. Three assistant surgeons were dismissed for disloyalty. Consequently the corps began its war service with only 98 officers.

Headquarters consisted of the Surgeon General, two surgeons who acted as his "assistants," and two assistant surgeons whose work was mainly clerical. These, with the aid of only three clerks, administered the affairs of the bureau. However, the Quartermaster Corps had charge of the erection and equipment of military hospitals and the transportation of the sick and wounded, while the Subsistence Department had charge of supplies.

Surgeon General Lawson's parsimony is shown in his appropriations. In 1860 the bureau lived on $90,000, of which $27,000 paid for the services of civilian physicians serving in military hospitals under contract. In March, 1861, despite the imminence of war, Congress appropriated only $115,000. In all, $241,000 was made available before July 1, 1861, of which $194,000 was spent, mainly on medical stores.

On these small budgets the department cared for a surprisingly large number of sick—30,300 cases in 1859–1860, or an average of two illnesses per man for the year. Mortality was light, only 138 deaths during the year, with tuberculosis, and gunshot wounds received in Indian fighting, as the major causes.

Fortunately the Medical Department was not long left to its own devices. Public demand led to the creation of the United States Sanitary Commission, which was to act as a gadfly in stinging the moribund department into more effective activity. The Commission is said to have had its inception soon after the outbreak of hostilities in a chance sidewalk encounter, of two New Yorkers, the Rev. Henry W. Bellows, a prominent Unitarian minister, and Dr. Elisha Harris, a leading physician. Both were concerned lest the sanitary horrors of the Crimea be reenacted in America. With the support of a group of New York women a public meeting was called at Cooper Union, where a society was organized. It was known as the Women's Central Association of Relief.

Indicative of the customs of that time, the officers of this organization of women were all men. The organization began to collect articles likely to be of value to the sick and wounded. The ladies of the association were to meet weekly at Cooper Institute. By arrangement with Bellevue Hospital selected women enrolled in a special nursing course.

Wishing to know how they might best assist the Army, the officers of the association then sent a long list of questions to the Surgeon General at Washington. From the answer it was apparent that the Federal authorities regarded them as a nuisance and their questions as impertinences. They were told that the Medical Department was "fully aroused" and "fully competent." The Surgeon General pointed with pride to its work in the Mexican War as an example.

Other relief societies sprang up in New York City, some of them large and influential. A delegation representing the association and two other bodies was sent to Washington to see for themselves what needed doing. The delegation included Henry W. Bellows and Dr. Elisha Harris of the Women's Central Association; Dr. W. H. Van Buren, representing the "Physicians and Surgeons of the Hospitals of New York," and Dr. Jacob Hanson, of the "Lint and Bandage Association." Arriving in Washington on May 16, the delegation found new regiments kept standing in the streets, unfed for twelve to eighteen hours because their officers did not know how to requisition food and quarters. The volunteer surgeons did not know how to procure medicines. Every bureau of the War Department seemed to be in wild disorder. In the Medical Department, Surgeon R. C. Wood was acting in place of Colonel Lawson, who was slowly dying at his home in Norfolk. The delegation felt that the situation demanded the appointment of a sanitary commission like the one that had cleaned up the Crimea.

On May 18 they formally requested that the Secretary of War appoint a Sanitary Commission and proposed a number of immediate reforms. America, they declared, had the opportunity "to prevent the evils that England and France could only investigate and deplore." They emphasized that "a people's war" required organized popular participation. The proposed reforms included better examination of recruits, many of whom were obviously unfit; the training of cooks which the Women's Central Association of Relief offered to provide; the use of the several hundred women who had registered with the association as nurses in Army hospitals; and the hiring by the Medical Department of young medical men to dress wounds and perform similar services. These reforms seem mild now. They were revolutionary then.

The delegation won the Acting Surgeon General over to the idea of such a commission. On May 22 he recommended to Secretary of War Cameron the creation by the government of "a commission of inquiry and advice . . . to act in cooperation with the bureau." Dr. Wood went so far as to suggest that the proposed commission consist of a medical officer and five distinguished civilians, two of whom should be members of the delegation from New York. The men proposed were the Rev. Henry W. Bellows, D.D., Prof. Alexander Dallas Bache, LL.D., Prof. Wolcott Gibbs, M.D., Jeffries Wyman, M.D., and W. H. Van Buren, M.D. The Surgeon General's office, however, was not ready to relinquish its exclusive control over health matters within the Army. In a letter from Wood to Cameron, sent four days earlier, he had remarked that ". . . many advantages would accrue to the service were it (i.e., the proposed commission) strictly confined to detailed subjects of a practical nature."

The desires of proponents of the commission were modest enough. In their communication to the government, sent the same day Dr. Wood's letter was written, they asked no legal powers for the commission, but only the right to investigate and advise. They sought no grant of money, but thought they should be supplied stationery and office space. But the program proposed was ambitious—an investigation into the organization and methods of recruiting forces by the states; inquiries into diet, cooks, clothing, tents, camp grounds, transports, camp police and other matters of sanitary and hygienic interest; a study of military hospitals and of the possibilities of using women as nurses; inspection of the quality and procurement methods of hospital supplies; and consideration of ambulance and relief services.

Official Washington met these proposals with suspicion. President Lincoln, himself, could see no point in such an organization, fearing a "fifth wheel to the coach." But after some days of persuasion the government was won over, and the papers to create the commission were prepared. While they awaited the signature of the Secretary of War, Surgeon General Lawson died. He was succeeded at once by Clement A. Finley, a sexagenarian senior surgeon of the Army, who had served since 1818. Dr. Finley looked sourly at the proposed commission and yielded only to public pressure. On the understanding that the commission would "never meddle with regular troops," but would confine its attention to volunteers, he gave way and the order creating the United States Sanitary Commission was signed by Cameron on June 9 and approved by the President on June 13.

The commission received the broad powers of investigation and advice which its proponents had requested. They were further empowered, subject to the approval of the Secretary of War, to make their own rules and regulations. The order named twelve men, three of them soldiers, as the original commission: Henry W. Bellows, president; Prof. A. D. Bache, vice-president; Elisha Harris, M.D., corresponding secretary; George T. Strong, treasurer; George W. Cullom, U.S.A.; Alexander E. Shiras, U.S.A.; R. C. Wood, M.D., U.S.A.; W. H. Van Buren, M.D., Wolcott Gibbs, M.D., Samuel G. Howe, M.D., Cornelius R. Agnew, M.D., and J. S. Newberry, M.D. The civilian members were all distinguished in their respective fields. Dr. Wood was Assistant Surgeon General, Col. Cullom a member of General Scott's staff and Major Shiras an officer of the Commissary Department. Their war duties so occupied these military members that they had no opportunity for active participation in the work of the commission.

One of the first acts was the creation of the office of executive secretary, to which Frederick Law Olmsted was appointed. Olmsted was widely known as the author of *The Cotton Kingdom* and as the architect and superintendent of New York's Central Park. Much of what the commission was to accomplish was due to his energy and intelligence.

Mobilizing the Army surgeons

In the meantime a large army was mobilizing and had to be provided with surgeons. Eventually the Army was to have on its payroll more than 11,000 doctors, organized into seven distinct corps and arranged in a gold-braided hierarchy. But in the opening months there were only Regular Army surgeons, surgeons of State troops, and civilian surgeons working under contract.

The Regular Army Medical Corps could expand immediately by calling up doctors who had passed its examination but had not yet been appointed. The next scheduled examination, held on the day of Surgeon General Finley's appointment, brought 116 new candidates of whom 62 received appointment, 29 having withdrawn and 25 having failed to meet either the physical or professional requirements. In August another examination yielded 24 additional appointees. Another 110 doctors were added to the services when it was decided to have a new corps of "brigade surgeons" not attached to regiments. A special board met in August to examine 130 candidates for the new corps. The successful applicants included men who were to play a distinguished part in the medical history of the war. George H. Lyman of Massachusetts, who took first place in the examination, was later to be a medical inspector. Frank H. Hamilton of New York and John H. Brinton of Philadelphia, who ranked second and fourth respectively, were both professors in leading medical schools.

The first 75,000 volunteers furnished their own surgeons, without reference to Federal regulations, and some doubt was felt about their competence. In May 40 additional regiments were called, each of which was required to have one assistant surgeon commissioned by the governor of the State after an examination. This requirement was soon raised to one surgeon and one assistant surgeon. In practice it was frequently the colonel of the regiment who made the appointment and secured confirmation from some medical board. Some governors issued commissions without examinations; or an unqualified surgeon might have been commissioned before any kind of regulation was in force. Some colonels, protecting their own appointees, ignored the orders of the State Surgeon General or the governor and refused to receive a properly appointed man.

The States varied widely in their methods, and the competence of the appointees showed corresponding variations. "Plucking boards," both in the Eastern and Western theaters of war, had to rid the Army of some of the worst incompetents. According to the correspondent of the New York *Tribune* the Indiana regiments had an especially large number of such men, and he attributed the bad conditions in the Army of the Ohio to them. Even in the second year of the war the governor of Indiana sought to put through an appointee, without examination, whose sole qualifications were a term of service in the field as a hospital steward and one year of reading in a doctor's office. Wisconsin enacted a law placing the nomination of medical officers in the hands of the colonels, and made no provision for an examining board. The practice of recommending men who did not hold medical degrees, for appointment, was defended on the grounds that "neither in civil nor military practice . . . any more than in any other avocations of life, is scholarship the measure of practical ability."

Among the Western troops the surgeons of Ohio regiments stood out for their competence, their State having called for "thorough and trying" examinations. Among the Eastern troops the medical men of Massachusetts stood out. And Vermont not only insisted upon the strictest examination given in any State, but based the candidates' appointment as surgeon or assistant surgeon wholly upon his standing in the examination.

Late in June 1861, the editor of a leading medical journal complained: "We may estimate by hundreds the number of unqualified persons who have received the endorsement of these bodies (medical examining boards) as capable surgeons and assistant surgeons of regiments. Indeed, these examinations have in some cases been so conducted to prove the merest farce. . . . Whoever has examined the list of surgeons, passed by the different State examining committees, must have regretted to find so few names of eminent surgeons."

The situation was unsatisfactory but not drastic. After careful investigation Frederick Law Olmsted, of the Sanitary Commission, reported to the Secretary of War that conditions were "better than might have been expected." True, some "surgeons" had been found who had never seen an amputating knife until they received one as a government issue, but about seven-eighths of the appointees had proved "adequate," and about the same proportion had passed some kind of an examination.

The appointment of inferior medical men was partly responsible for one scandal—the farcical physical examination of volunteers. In his report to the Secretary of War, Olmsted wrote that hardly a single regiment had conducted a thorough medical examination and in 58 per cent of the cases the examination was a mere pretense.

The evidence came direct from the field. Fifteen to 20 per cent of the "three-months men" were reported incapacitated by disabilities suffered before entering the service, which should have been detected by the examining surgeon. Chronic cases were clogging hospitals needed for battle casualties. They included syphilitics and men between sixty and seventy years of age, many of whom had hernias and some who were epileptics. They were particularly numerous in the 61st N. Y. Volunteers; and the 5th N. Y. Cavalry was said to have eighty epileptics and hernia cases. Many of the volunteers, including one entire regiment, gathered at Washington had *never* been examined. At

Camp Dennison, Ohio, most of the sick were men who should never have been enlisted. Three-fourths of the men discharged for disability, who stopped at the Sanitary Commission "Home" in Washington, belonged in that category. The medical director of the Army of the Potomac reported officially that of 3,929 men discharged for disability in October, November, and December, 1861, 2,881 had had the diseases or defects for which they were discharged, at the time of enlistment.

The Army's regulations were not at fault. Imperfect as the prescribed routine for physical examinations seems to modern eyes, it would have uncovered most of the defectives had it been followed. "In passing a recruit," read a regulation, "the medical officer is to examine him stripped; to see that he has free use of all his limbs; that his chest is ample; that his hearing, vision and speech are perfect; that he has no tumors, or ulcerated or cicatrized legs; no rupture or chronic cutaneous affection; that he has not received any contusion, or wound of the head, that may impair his faculties; that he is not subject to convulsions; and has no infectious disorder that may unfit him for military service." It was also provided that a recruit, enlisted and examined elsewhere, be reexamined on joining his regiment.

The need for men, the ignorance of examining surgeons, the pleas of eager recruits and the pressure of "unscrupulous recruiting agents" led to scandalous abuses. Some surgeons merely looked at a recruit's legs and groin, then passed him; others did not have the recruit undress; one got through his task at the rate of ninety recruits an hour. At Chicago an examining surgeon was called out in the rain while a whole regiment paraded past him. He managed to tag "seven or eight obviously bad cases." So far as he knew, that regiment never had any further physical examination. The examination of the 33rd Ohio ". . . consisted of but little more than opening and shutting the hands, bending the elbows and knees, and rotating the shoulder-joint, with a casual glance at the teeth and eyes, and a question as to age and previous general health." How perfunctory these examinations were is indicated by the estimated number of 400 women enrolled as soldiers.

With disabled men pouring out of his army as through a sieve, General McClellan took remedial steps. The first was the War Department's General Order 51, August 3, 1861, requiring regimental surgeons to examine their men. Neglect of this order led to the supplemental General Order 104, December 3, 1861, which called attention to the alarming losses through discharges for disability and provided punishment for delinquent surgeons. Medical Director Tripler wrote dejectedly that the Army was apparently considered "a grand eleemosynary institution" for defectives whose townships would thus be relieved of the burden of supporting them.

One State which really grappled with the problem was New York, whose examining surgeons had also persisted in disregarding instructions. The State Surgeon General had the recruits reexamined by a special body of "inspectors" and of 47,417 men, accepted for the service, no less than 5,554 were weeded out in 1861. Even then the Surgeon General had to confess in his report for 1862 that ". . . this last call has not been without complaints coming back of unsound men enlisted."

Sick recruits and dirty camps of '61

Breakdowns of defective recruits accounted for only a fraction of the sickness which plagued the Army during the early months of the war. Conditions were so bad that in the early summer of 1861 some informed persons predicted that "malaria, camp fever and dysentery would within six months destroy 50 per cent of the volunteer army then assembling." Fortunately these predictions were not borne out. In his joy that they were not, Surgeon Tripler, medical director of the troops at Washington, later attempted by statistical exegesis to give the impression that the Army was unusually healthy. The sick list should be discounted, he said, because the captains had reported as sick any man who said he was sick. The Surgeons General of Massachusetts and Pennsylvania painted similarly rosy pictures. But the statistics of the Medical Department itself, as distinct from those compiled from the captains' reports, show a considerable amount of ill-health.

In May, 1861, about 30 per cent of the troops mustered in were on the sick list at one time or another. The prevalent affliction was "acute diarrhoea." Mortalities were light. Only twelve men, most of them typhoid patients, died, out of a muster of 16,161. In June the total sick rate continued about the same, with an increase of diarrhea cases and a sharp rise in measles cases, from three in May to 1,138 in June. Mortalities continued low.

Throughout July, August, and September the sick list averaged close to 30 per cent. Diarrhea was joined by "acute dysentery" as a major cause. Typhoid increased and remained the chief killer; but even in September, its month of greatest incidence, typhoid slew only a little more than one-tenth of 1 per cent of the men in the Army. As more and more troops gathered about Washington, at Cairo, and other river towns, the malaria rate rose steeply from approximately 3 per cent in August to more than 6 per cent in September. Measles held its own, proportionately, and was joined by mumps.

Medical Director Tripler would have been proud indeed had he known that statistics compiled in later years disclosed that while the Union Army, in the first year and a half of war, was to lose 2.01 per cent of its men by death from disease the Confederate Army would lose 3.81 per cent. Half again as many Confederates as Federals died of diarrhea and dysentery, while more than *five times* as many died of pulmonary diseases.

Within the Union Army there were wide disparities between the sickness and death rates of troops from different States, between troops in the East and troops in the West, and between commissioned officers and enlisted men. Using incomplete data for the first year of war the Sanitary Commission's actuary found the officers' sick rate to be 69 per thousand, as compared with 106 for enlisted men; the sick rate for Western troops was 161, as compared with 76 for Eastern troops; while the rate for the Army as a whole was 104. Mortality rates for the year averaged 53 per thousand, with disease accounting for 44 and battle causes for only nine. More officers were killed by the enemy than were enlisted men; while the latter died of disease at the rate of 46 per thousand as opposed to 22 for officers. Troops from the Middle States had a noticeably lower death rate from disease than did New Englanders, while all Eastern-ers with a rate of 32 per thousand did enormously better than Westerners, with a rate of 76. Regiments from the same region, camped side by side, sometimes showed wide variations. Among the Illinois regiments camped at Cairo in August, 1861, the sick rate ranged from as low as 29 to as high as 143 per cent.

As was later to be true of World War I, as well, "children's diseases" flared up wherever crowds of young recruits ap-peared. Measles, mumps, and scarlet fever struck down country boys who had never been exposed. Bad colds, sometimes ending in bronchitis or pneumonia, attacked those unaccustomed to a life of wet and exposure. Digestive ailments made life miser-able for those unaccustomed to a heavy and badly prepared diet.

The intestinal infections which were to kill and disable so many men tended to increase in virulence. Typhoid fever, which in the year 1861 killed 17 per cent of patients, increased in deadliness until 1865 when its mortality rate stood at 56. The high sick rate of the Army of the Potomac for "diarrhoea and dysentery," 640 per thousand in the first year of the war, rose to the extraordinary height of 995 per thousand the following year. The early cases in this category were so mild that the death rate in the East for that year was only 1.10 per thousand. In the West these diseases killed 9.56 per thousand.

Much of this resulted from violation of the laws of hygiene and sanitation, with ignorance and carelessness jointly respon-sible. Many men had difficulty adapting themselves to camp life; others suffered from improper food, clothing, and quarters. An inspection at Cairo, Illinois, in August revealed that no uniforms were being issued, while the insufficient blankets and underclothes received by the men were of inferior quality. An inspection of most of the forces in the West, made in November, disclosed that little of the clothing issued came up to regulation standards in weight and durability. New York physicians who inspected the troops at Washington in July found many of the tents and blankets inferior; regiments were notably unequal in their equipment and diet; and about a third of the regiments were badly demoralized. They suspected that in some regiments the colonel and the commissary were in league to defraud the men.

Army food was apt to be peculiarly hard on recruits, who did their own cooking. In urging that the Army use trained company cooks, a military surgeon of long experience declared that "beans killed more than bullets." An abrupt rise in the diarrhea rate of a command could often be observed immediately after the eating of bean soup. The soldiers fried everything. They would fry cakes of flour and water in bacon fat; they would frequently fry rice and beans; and they invariably fried their issues of beef. Such were the consequences that one surgeon reported having seen every one of the four hundred men in his charge at least once, for digestive ailments, within a period of three months. A medical officer, trying to save his regiment from "death from the frying pan," implored the men to put their meat on the end of a stick and toast it; but sutlers (men authorized to sell good goods to the soldiers) continued to do a rushing business in frying pans.

The recruits not only suffered from their poor cooking, but from their inability to make a ration last from one issue to the next. A New York newspaper reported that at Washington a soldier on parade had "sunk to the ground from weakness" because he had had no food for three days. Near-mutiny was rumored in a regiment which objected to its almost exclusive diet of that great army staple, fat salt pork.

No fresh vegetables were issued though "desiccated vegetables," a novelty detested by the volunteers, were sometimes offered them. Soldiers in the field, operating in an area where foraging was allowed, might supply themselves with vegetables at the expense of the enemy. But those in friendly territory had to go without, and suffer for it; or buy in the open market, paying from the "company fund," formed by the sale of a part of the regular ration issue. As only some 40 per cent of the troops had such a fund at their disposal, and as the fund idea seemed the only practical way to provide fresh food, butter, and milk, the Sanitary Commission inspectors encouraged it.

Secretary Olmsted of the Sanitary Commission reported that the army food at Washington was, on the whole, both plentiful and good. But he made many qualifications and a long series of recommendations. He called attention, particularly, to the fact that what sufficed for Regulars on the frontier might not do for volunteers in the East. He further pointed out that the volunteer's ration was "atrociously cooked and wickedly wasted." He took exception to beans and salt pork as staples, and recommended dried mutton and mutton soup as substitutes for the pork. The surgeons at Washington were united in condemning the absence of vegetables in the diet, and laid the prevailing diarrhea to that cause. It was suggested that potatoes be issued when possible, and that "mixed vegetables and dried fruits" be made a part of the regular issue, to add "to the cheerfulness of the army, and thus to its health."

The Sanitary Commission took as its most serious obligation the spread of information about proper sanitation and hygiene. In June it printed and circulated an excellent pamphlet, by two members of the committee on military surgery of the New York Academy of Medicine. In it the lessons of other wars were evaluated and the importance of cleanliness of camp and person were stressed. As early as May 15, volunteers were being asked by an enterprising publisher to buy a pamphlet on military hygiene, and before the year was out a full-length book on the subject was available to interested medical and line officers. Continuing to lend emphasis to this campaign of enlightenment, the Sanitary Commission brought out another pamphlet, written in a popular style; and from time to time pointed the moral by printing the inspection reports of its officers in the field.

Early in the summer Secretary Olmsted issued a *Circular Addressed to the Colonels of the Army*. "It is well known, that when a considerable body of men have been living together in a camp a few weeks a peculiar subtle poison is generated, the effect of which is exhibited in stiffness of muscles; sickness of the stomach in the morning; sudden and unusual looseness of the bowels; and subsequently by dysentery, and other endemic and epidemic diseases of a still more fatal character, such as camp fevers and cholera." Remarking that these dangers can be averted by strict cleanliness and proper preparation of good food, eaten at *regular* times, he placed responsibility squarely upon the line officers. The colonel, he said, should hold captains responsible for sanitation and hygiene in their companies; the captains should hold their subalterns responsible; and the subalterns should see that the noncommissioned officers made their squads keep clean.

So far as the promulgation of rules could help, the Army was cooperating. It was the rule in the army gathering at Washington, that every day the commander of each regiment or independent company should appoint "a police officer and a police party" to inspect the latrines, kitchens, and general cleanliness and good order of the unit. To encourage the army in its good work, the officers of the Sanitary Commission, augmented during the summer by the appointment of six distinguished physicians as Inspectors, visited camps and hospitals and took notes on what they found. It would seem as though, with all these sources of enlightenment and encouragement, the army had no excuse for the development of filth diseases.

But the sanitary crusaders ran headlong into the incorrigible "rugged individualism" of the American people. On reaching camp, recruits frequently let themselves go. Men who were so careless that they frequently shot themselves by accident could give little attention to the Sanitary Commission's ideas of camp cleanliness or to the advice of their medical officers. "It was a common subject of remark," wrote a surgeon, "that men who, but a few weeks before, occupied positions in society demanding cleanliness and care for personal appearance, now disregarded it, and either from apathy or laziness neither washed their persons nor the clothing they carried upon them."

Water was usually scarce, wrote another surgeon, and the recruit's surroundings dirty. Consequently "the necessity for cleanliness was by no means apparent." At all the training camps he was dismayed by "the slovenly, slipshod appearance of the clothing and accoutrements of the recruits, their filthy skins, uncombed hair, and matted beards." Even in regiments whose officers showed concern over cleanliness, men were not required to wash their feet, and sometimes not even their faces and necks. The visiting English novelist, Anthony Trollope, was left with a lasting distaste for the men of the Army of the Potomac by the squalor he saw in their camps.

There "some men were always sick, some muskets always out of order, some food was always indigestible to some men." The only conditions, apparently, that could be counted on, were filth, bad drainage, and drilling to the point of exhaustion. Many training camps persisted in their filthy ways far into the war period. In 1863 a Massachusetts colonel declared that a few weeks in barracks at New York City had "permanently diminished" the value of his troops 30 per cent. A medical editor agreed that those barracks "must be a more terrible ordeal to life than any exposures our armies have yet suffered upon the battlefield." Camp Sprague, New York, was described by the Sanitary Commission's inspectors as "a disgrace to the Empire State and to the National Government." The men, the grounds, the beds, and guardhouse and the hospital were deep in filth. A camp population varying from 1,400 to 3,500 had "more drunkenness than would be expected in an army of 100,000."

That training camps need not resemble slums was shown by Camp Butler, near Springfield, Illinois, chief mobilization center of that state. There cleanliness and good order brought the reward of low sick and mortality rates. Its 5,000 men suffered only three deaths in a three months' period, and its hospital averaged less than 30 patients at a time. The camps of two Illinois regiments located side by side near St. Louis offered a similar lesson in contrasts. One was clean and its sick list numbered six; the other was dirty, with a water supply "black and disgusting," and its sick list numbered 250 dysentery patients in two weeks. These 250 sick men were crammed into a filthy little hospital equipped to handle 25 patients.

The field army at Washington camped, for the most part, on well-selected sites, and was sheltered under fairly suitable tents. But most of the camps were dirty; clogged drains resulted in floods after each rain; and flies covered garbage left in the tents.

Most objectionable was the dearth of latrines and the reluctance of many men to use them. Some regiments had dug no latrines at all. The men of one such regiment had gone on for eight days "relieving themselves anywhere within a few feet of their tents." The usual "sink," as the army called it, was a straddle trench thirty feet long, into which fresh earth was supposed to be thrown once a day, but frequently was not. It was usually so malodorous and so befouled at the edges that soldiers often ignored it, despite orders. Dysentery and typhoid inevitably followed, and among the civil population as well. Washington was unusually sickly that summer of 1861, according to a local physician who said the city was "poisoned by the soldiers and everybody is ill."

The camps at Newport News, Virginia, were in much the same state while in the West conditions were, if anything, worse. Cairo, Illinois, from which the Union armies were to start down the Mississippi and up the Tennessee, was a veritable hellhole, a muddy, mosquito-infested point between the converging Ohio and Mississippi rivers. Garbage heaps and pools of fluid waste were everywhere. The men were "shockingly remiss" in their use of the poorly constructed and badly located "sinks." Within the town itself "masses of putrid offal, decaying bones, and dead dogs lay within eyesight . . ." of the best houses. The widespread diarrhea among the troops was attributed to the drinking of imperfectly filtered Ohio River water rather than Mississippi water, which was believed to be pure.

Cairo, until then a reasonably healthy river town, was now plagued with malaria and typhoid. Children's diseases ran wild through the army of farmer boys, who were utterly ignorant of personal care and led by officers who could not care for themselves. To Trollope, Cairo seemed "the most desolate of all the towns in America."

At Camp Dennison, mobilization center for Ohio, the men were sickening from a bad water supply. In Buell's army, to which many of them went, a Sanitary Commission rating made that fall commended five units out of thirteen for camp cleanliness, labelled four "medium" and condemned three. In one of Buell's regiments large numbers of men, refusing to use the latrines, were contaminating the slope leading to the small stream that served as its water supply.

Summarizing for the Army as a whole the Sanitary Commission, toward the end of the year, reported poor latrine arrangements for 20 per cent of the units, ineffective regulations for their use in 32 per cent; while in 35 per cent the men were permitted to urinate in the camp streets during the night.

As regards camp policing, i.e., general tidiness of the camp, the commission characterized 5 per cent as "admirable," 45 per cent as "fairly clean," 26 per cent as "negligent and slovenly," and 24 per cent as "decidedly bad, filthy and dangerous." In 23 per cent garbage disposal was poor and in more than 50 per cent horse manure was allowed to accumulate more or less indefinitely. But marked improvement was being shown, according to the report.

The correlation between the sanitary condition of the camps and the Army's high disease rates was understood. Surgeon W. S. King, medical director of the troops at Washington until mid-August, attributed his failure to improve conditions to his want of high military rank. He could not enforce orders issued to men of higher rank than his.

It became more and more obvious that bad discipline was the decisive factor. Officers of volunteers often had to try suasion instead of commands. Elective officers had an even harder time than those appointed from above in getting wayward boys to carry out sanitary regulations which they did not comprehend.

The Sanitary Commission transmitted resolutions to the President of the United States, calling for rigid military discipline. Laxity toward offenders against Army regulations was ". . . costing the country more lives by far than the bullets of the enemy . . ." and "a strict enforcement of the *Army Regulations* would do more to prevent disease than all that the Commission can recommend to be done by other means." It was decided to inform State governors of officers whose units were slovenly and disobedient.

On August 12, 1861, Surgeon Charles S. Tripler succeeded Surgeon King as medical director of the Army of the Potomac. In his first week in office he cleaned up the old Capitol prison in Washington, sent a special inspector to the camp of Pennsylvania cavalry, which had been reported as a nuisance, and moved the men encamped on the Arlington flats, a third of whom were sick with malaria, dysentery or typhoid. Pre-dawn drill was abandoned for a more reasonable hour and the men were to be served hot coffee before they began it—reforms suggested by the Sanitary Commission.

Improvement began to be noted. McDowell's division, which had had a sick list of 33 per cent in its camp on the flats in August, had only 9 serious cases of sickness among its 10,000 men by February. An inspector found marvelous improvement among certain divisions in the Army of the Potomac, the troops even being willing now to make use of the latrines. In 1862 it was noted in Massachusetts that recruits had become so sanitation-conscious that whereas "last year they rarely spoke of camp police; this year, this seems to be their principal topic of conversation."

But there was still room for improvement. When the first important battle, Bull Run, showed the Medical Department to be bungling and unprepared in ambulance and hospital work the members of the Sanitary Commission began an agitation for its reform.

2

Reformers

vs.

Regulars

THERE HAD BEEN A NUMBER OF MINOR ENGAGEMENTS DURING the first three months of the war but no major battle to test the Medical Department. On July 16, 1861, General Irvin McDowell led the Army of the Potomac, 30,000 strong, out of their slovenly camps at Washington toward Centreville, Virginia, 27 miles away, where a Confederate army was encamped.

At ten o'clock on the morning of Sunday, July 21, the Battle of Bull Run began. The troops had had no breakfast and were exhausted from hurried marching under the sun of an exceptionally hot day. Some had eaten no supper the night before, and had had little or no sleep. Reports that they were heavily outnumbered by the enemy had made them nervous. Nevertheless, they seemed to be winning until the afternoon, when the troops of Gen. Joseph E. Johnston reinforced the Confederate line. Forced back, the Union troops began the famous flight to

Washington, having lost almost 2,000 killed and wounded.

This battle tested the medical arrangements of the army and proved them wanting. There was no articulated organization and the chaos piled horror upon horror. At each mobilization point an officer had been designated by the Medical Department to act as "medical director" but without instruction as to duties, privileges and powers. Being attached to the personal staff of the commanding general, and subject to his orders, the medical officer had only such authority as his personal influence with his commander might win for him. He was the only possible co-ordinator of the battlefield relief work, yet was without authority to organize and direct the medical officers and stretchermen of the various regiments. As a result each regimental surgeon assumed responsibility for the men of his own unit only, while soldiers shot at a distance from their regimental surgeon might be left untended. Summing up Bull Run, Assistant Surgeon W. W. Keen, who found himself on his own all through the fighting, likened it to "the days when there was no King in Israel and every man did that which was right in his own eyes."

Medical Director W. S. King made some effort to direct the work of the surgeons, but found them, and the enlisted men subject to them, "loath to receive orders from a stranger." One surgeon refused to receive wounded into his regimental hospital because they were not members of the regiment.

Dr. King spent the day of battle riding over the battle ground with General McDowell. He attempted to compile a casualty list in his personal notebook. When he found surgeons badly overworked, he rolled up his sleeves and assisted them in operating.

A glaring defect disclosed at Bull Run, and all the other early battles, was the dearth and poor handling of the ambulances. The Army had been without ambulances until two years before the war, when a special board had recommended a four-wheel vehicle. This ambulance had been tested in expeditions on the plains; but the two-wheel ambulance which the Quartermaster Corps decided to issue in 1861 in the ratio of four to one of the four-wheeled kind had never had a proper test and proved most unsatisfactory. A great proportion of the few ambulances of any kind issued to the Army of the Potomac before Bull Run were used by the officers as pleasure or general utility vehicles.

At Bull Run the civilian ambulance drivers, hired for the occasion, took fright at the sounds of firing, whipped up their horses and left the field. Hundreds of wounded men were left to drag themselves to Washington if they could. Some of the ambulances were "captured" by fleeing soldiers who used them to speed their flight to Washington. The Sanitary Commission was unable to learn of a single wounded man having reached the capital in an ambulance.

Under the pressure of fear many wounded men performed remarkable feats in getting to the rear. A man who had just lost his arm by amputation on the field walked the 27 miles to Washington, and arrived the next day; another walked the distance with a large hole through both thighs and the scrotum; a third had a hole through both cheeks, a broken jaw and his tongue nearly off; yet another had bullet holes through both calves. All suffered intensely from thirst.

The reward for this amazing endurance was admission to one of the six hospitals located in Washington and its environs. When the war began the largest Army hospital had only 40 beds. The Medical Department had been busy during the months before Bull Run, improvising additional hospitals throughout the country, from hotels, seminaries and private houses. Many were filthy when taken over and most of them were criticized as inadequate in toilet and ventilation facilities. The administrative staff and attendants of those at Washington were reported as "so unqualified for their positions, that any civil hospital under such management would have been considered a disgrace to the science and humanity of the country." Dr. Tripler, who replaced Dr. King in August, disagreed, asserting that they were run by good men and were good hospitals. But even he found something lacking in their administrative routine.

They had, he wrote, "no system in reference to the admission or discharge of patients. Every regimental surgeon sent what men he pleased to the general hospitals without knowing whether there was room for them or not, and men were discharged from the hospitals with no means provided to insure their return to their regiments. It was not an unusual circumstance for sick men to pass the night in the ambulances, wandering about the streets from hospital to hospital, seeking admission."

The Sanitary Commission could then do little beyond publicizing its views on what was wrong with the Washington hospitals. It had been formed in an atmosphere of chilly disapproval from the seniors of the Medical Corps. It had encountered jealousy, "for its functions began in criticism, and criticism is ever disagreeable." Acting Surgeon General Wood had shown a desire to cooperate, and was proving a useful member of the commission. But from the day of his accession Surgeon General Finley had made any cooperation between the commission and the Medical Department impossible. The commissioners won the sympathy of generals and of many of the younger Army surgeons but Finley remained implacable. The thwarted commission was forced into a policy of independent activity and sharp criticism, using public opinion as a lever with which to bring about reform.

The chief block was the system of promotion by seniority. Olmsted wrote: "It is criminal weakness to intrust such responsibilities . . . to a self satisfied, supercilious, bigoted blockhead, merely because he is the oldest of the old mess-room doctors of the frontier guard of the country. He knows nothing and does nothing, and is capable of knowing nothing and doing nothing, but quibble about matters of form and precedent."

Its "elder-stateman" administration handicapped the medical bureau with faulty organization and rigidly conservative ideas. Years of penury had so inured the elderly officers to "doing without" that they kept stinting on hospital supplies, instruments, and books when money was available. The puny ambulance service was in charge of the Quartermaster Corps which limited its effectiveness by the same sort of penny pinching.

There was no system of general hospitals to which the sick and wounded could be sent. The hospital attendants were men temporarily detailed from the ranks, who knew nothing about their work and were returned to their regular duties before they could learn.

The campaign for Medical Department reform

Given an opportunity to ask Congress for additional facilities, the Surgeon General exposed his limited understanding of the situation. All he requested was 40 more medical officers for the Army, 50 young medical students, or "medical cadets" to serve as wound dressers, and the right to employ some civilian nurses in the general hospitals.

An attempt by the reformers to influence members of Congress to a more realistic view came to nothing. Feeling that Finley's "devotion to routine" and his "undisguised hostility" would wreck their plans for a healthier Army, the commission, at its meeting on September 12, 1861, voted to ask the removal or retirement of the Surgeon General and to press for remedial legislation.

This was the start of a long campaign. Late in September Bellows wrote to Secretary Cameron, complaining of the age and inefficiency of the medical director at St. Louis, whose appointment was another indication of the Surgeon General's poor judgment. An engagement at Ball's Bluff in October, where it was reported that a surgeon had been forced to fire at the ambulance attendants to make them function, was used as another argument for a trained ambulance corps.

Late in November the New York *Times* published a spirited defense of the Medical Department, charging the Sanitary Commission with trying to supersede the established authorities, and thus robbing the soldiers of the boon of having their welfare watched over by men of long military experience. The commission was working under cover in its campaign against Finley.

Anxious to maintain an appearance of harmony, it prepared a pamphlet in which it managed to express appreciation of the Regulars while pointing out the need for younger men.

In December the commission opened active agitation for legislation to create a corps of medical inspectors. Delegations of generals, physicians, and junior medical officers called upon the military committees of both houses of Congress, on the Secretary of War, and on Lincoln, on whom they urged their cause so strenuously that one of their number feared the President would have "painful recollections" of their "earnestness and pertinacity."

In December Finley made a decision which brought down upon his head the wrath of the powerful New York *Tribune*. The medical director of General Sherman's Port Royal expedition had asked that a hospital be built, and Sherman had so ordered. Finley countermanded the order on the ground that South Carolina's mild climate made a hospital unnecessary. In a scathing editorial the *Tribune* remarked that the Medical Bureau, instead of fighting "its natural and official enemies— typhus, malaria, and small pox, defective ventilation of tents, imperfect drainage of camps, and lazy regimental surgeons," was fighting the Sanitary Commission. The Medical Bureau, it held, "is not accused of mis-feasance or malfeasance, but of non-feasance. It seems to have done nothing since the war began. It is simply inefficient and inert, when inaction is the gravest of official misdemeanors."

But the poor showing of the Medical Department was part of a generally grim picture. Simon Cameron's regime as Secretary of War was saturated with the spirit of spoils politics. When in mid-January Cameron, sent to Saint Petersburg as ambassador, was replaced by Edwin M. Stanton, it was felt that only good could result. The Sanitary Commission's conferences with General McClellan had led to the drafting of a Medical Department reform bill in which President Lincoln himself showed interest. This bill, introduced in the Senate by Henry Wilson of Massachusetts on December 10, was in the hands of the Military Affairs Committee at the time of the Stanton appointment. The new Secretary's backing of the bill was looked for by the Sanitary Commission. When on his third day in office Secretary Stanton visited the Sanitary Commission rooms to hear their views, there was rejoicing.

The proposed bill represented a compromise between reformers and the Army conservatives. It provided for a Surgeon General, a Sanitary Inspector General and a number of Sanitary Inspectors, all of whom would be appointed on merit, with a higher military rank than heretofore and all under sixty years of age. The commission believed that desirable changes could be effected without further legislative action by active, intelligent men appointed to the new offices created by this bill.

After the measure had undergone considerable alteration by its sponsor and by committees, Secretary Stanton exerted his influence for the kind of bill the commission wanted. He had become convinced, he said, of "an urgent necessity of reorganizing and remodelling the Medical Bureau."

Congress passed the reorganization bill, which was signed by the President on April 16, 1862. Though, as time went on, it became evident that this measure was insufficient, the great improvement in the administration of the Medical Department was obvious.

Surgeon General Finley was removed from office, and the medical director at St. Louis, about whom Dr. Bellows had complained, was also removed. A few days later the administrative authority of the Surgeon General's Office was enhanced in a general order empowering it to transfer medical officers and hospital stewards from one hospital to another.

The Sanitary Commission then had to decide what candidate to back, if any, as the new Surgeon General. Relations between the Commission and Asst. Surgeon General R. C. Wood had always been good, and it was understood that Dr. Wood had obtained "about as good as a promise" from President Lincoln that he should have the appointment. But the commission felt that a younger man was needed for the difficult job of reorganizing the medical system. Impressed by the work of William Alexander Hammond, an assistant surgeon in the Regular Army, they decided to back him.

Dr. Hammond's Army rank was an example of the evils of the seniority system. Despite eleven years of distinguished service he was virtually at the foot of the list. He had entered the Army Medical Corps after a year of hospital work in New York. During his years of service on the frontier he had put some of his observations into an essay on food that had brought him first prize in an American Medical Association contest and had been translated into French and German. In 1860 he had resigned to accept a professorship in the University of Maryland, which he had given up, together with a profitable practice in Baltimore, to reenlist in the Army. The length of his previous service and the brilliance of his qualifications were bureaucratically ignored. He was entered at the bottom of the list of assistant surgeons.

Some of Hammond's friends who had been pressing the Surgeon General to grant him a rank commensurate with his experience and talents, brought his name up before members of the Sanitary Commission. One ventured to suggest him for Finley's place. Hammond happened to be a friend of General McClellan, then the patron saint of the sanitarians, and this, too, was in his favor. Early in March he was reporting to the commission on the filthy state of some of the hospitals, and a pamphlet he prepared for the commission was useful in their agitational work.

The vexed career of Surgeon General Hammond

The rivalry of Hammond and Asst. Surgeon General Wood was now in the open. Each was telling the commission what a fatal mistake the appointment of the other would be. A campaign of letters, delegations of physicians, and appeals by the commission on Hammond's behalf bore fruit. On April 25, 1862, he received the appointment, and Dr. Wood was reappointed Assistant Surgeon General. It was a severe setback to the seniority ring. Their champion, that "fine gentleman" Finley, had been forced out of office to be succeeded by an "ambitious and arrogant" young man. In one stride a mere professor had stepped over the heads of all the ranking Army surgeons from captain to brigadier general. But the seniors were to have their revenge.

The effects of the new appointment soon became evident. In the fiscal year 1862, toward the end of which Hammond came in, the Medical Corps failed to spend even its meager budget of $2,445,000. In the following year under Hammond appropriations demanded by him reached $10,314,000 and its expenditures came to $11,594,000. Hammond spent more on refrigeration in one year, than the total expenditures of the department in 1860.

Hammond began to replace certain medical directors, with younger men "not quite so thickly incrusted with the habits, forms and traditions of the service." Of these new administrators many of whom were to win laurels in the field, the outstanding figure was Jonathan Letterman, who was promoted from assistant surgeon to medical director of the Army of the Potomac. In his letter of instructions to Letterman the Surgeon General explained the new department policies. Red tape was out; efficiency and results would be all that counted. Letterman was given carte blanche to "order" any supplies he might need from the medical purveyors at Washington, Baltimore, Philadelphia, and New York, whether or not the supplies were listed in the official army supply table and regardless of form. If additional nurses or physicians were needed Letterman might employ them on the spot, without special authorization.

The battles of 1862, particularly Manassas (second battle of Bull Run), demonstrated the need of a better ambulance service. After the bloody horrors of Manassas, where some wounded men were left on the battlefield for a week, Surgeon General Hammond demanded War Department authorization to form an ambulance corps. The proposal was vetoed by both Stanton and General Halleck.

Without waiting for their conservatism to give way Medical Director Letterman, acting under the authority of General Mc-Clellan, organized ambulance services for the Army of the Potomac. His system worked so well that it became the model of the world's armies for the next two generations. However, hindrances remained which could be only dealt with by legislation. For some time the Letterman system was restricted to the Army of the Potomac.

Hammond who had received Stanton's promise that an order would be issued conferring additional powers on him, persisted in his requests for remedial legislation. Public opinion, spearheaded by the Sanitary Commission, finally led Congress to create an ambulance corps, based upon the Letterman experiments, for all the armies in the field. In operation during the last year of the war the ambulance system elicited widespread admiration.

The large scale warfare also proved that two medical officers per regiment were not enough. A greater number of surgeons was called for.

After six months in office General Hammond had formulated his plans sufficiently to offer the War Department a long list of desired reforms. He stressed the need of a special hospital and ambulance corps, and asked for more regimental and staff surgeons, authority to appoint more medical cadets and employ additional civilian physicians for service in general hospitals. An act of July 2 had changed the title of the "brigade surgeons" to "surgeons of volunteers" and had raised their number to 320 men; 300 more were requested. The medical staff of each infantry regiment had been raised to three men by the July act, and it was proposed that the cavalry and heavy artillery regiments receive a like increase, and that an assistant surgeon be assigned to each light battery of artillery, units which were now without medical officers. An increase of executive personnel by another Assistant Surgeon General, two more Medical

Inspectors General and eight more Medical Inspectors was also asked.

General Hammond's next suggestion had the long-range view of bolstering the scientific attainments of the Medical Corps. He proposed establishing a great graduate school of medicine in Washington where the medical officers of the Army could be kept in touch with advances in the science. It was to include an Army medical museum, whose pathological and surgical exhibits would be contributed by the surgeons in the Army hospitals, and an Army medical school operated in connection with a general hospital. After the war this central hospital was to serve as a permanent center of clinical instruction.

Other far-reaching proposals challenged the Army's traditional administrative setup. The Surgeon General demanded that his department take over from the Quartermaster Corps the control of the ambulances, the medical supply trains and the construction of military hospitals. The Medical Department, he said, should follow the example of the Navy in establishing and operating its own pharmaceutical laboratories. A part of the appropriations for the relief of disabled soldiers should be used to establish a permanent "home." Medical directors on the staffs of the commanders of army corps should receive an increase in rank and pay.

In raising the question of increased rank and pay for officers other than Medical Inspectors, General Hammond opened a controversy which was to agitate the medical profession to the end of the war. Except for the Surgeon General, the Assistant Surgeon General, the Medical Inspector General and the Medical Inspectors, all the full surgeons in the Army were held to the rank of major. As they saw their line-officer associates going up the ladder of promotion, these majors developed a rankling sense of injury unassuaged by the grant of increased rank to Quartermaster Corps officers in 1862. The lowliest of regimental "saw-bones" and the medical director who gave orders to hundreds of surgeons, held the same rank and drew the same pay.

It was observed that the Army could not attract the best qualified men if there were no possibilities of advancement. The sanitary scandals of the French Army in the Crimea were attributed
to the refusal of line officers to take orders from medical officers
whom they outranked. "If the purely military portion of the
service chooses the standards of the middle ages, when barbers,
farriers, and sow-gelders . . . constituted the medical staff of
armies," said one surgeon, "they ought not to complain when
they have the misfortune to fall into the hands of medical officers of a quality and character little superior to the leeches of
the days of Charlemagne."

Congressional reaction to the demand for higher rank was a
bill, by Senator Hale, to abolish such military rank as the surgeons had already acquired. The Military Affairs Committee
scotched the bill, but its author, ignoring the storm of protest
from the surgeons sought to revive the idea the next time a
Medical Department measure appeared in the Senate.

The first of Surgeon General Hammond's proposals to receive
Congressional consideration was the request for two additional
Medical Inspectors General and eight additional Medical Inspectors. Senator Wilson presented the measure, which he wisely
named "a bill to facilitate the discharge of disabled soldiers and
the inspection of convalescent camps and hospitals."

The bill encountered the usual difficulties. Senator Grimes,
who seems always to have been ready to sabotage a Medical
Department measure, offered an amendment making all three-
year volunteers eligible to the Federal bounty, but withdrew
it in the face of objections. A good deal of the debate was taken
up with criticism of the Medical Corps' slowness in discharging
disabled men. Senator Clark remarked: "It is harder to get
Dives out of hell than to get one of these men out of their hands."
Senator Fessenden, observing sarcastically that the way to improve the Army "always seems to be to give somebody more
rank and pay," succeeded in getting the section providing for
the two additional Medical Inspectors General stricken out.

In defense of his bill Senator Wilson argued that 10,000

men now in hospitals would be unable to serve again and must be inspected by properly qualified authorities to avoid frauds against the government. Inspectors had to have the rank of lieutenant colonel to enforce their orders upon the majors who commanded the hospitals. Finally, with an added provision that the Inspectors must see to it that the men they ordered discharged actually were discharged, the bill passed, and became law on December 27, 1862.

When another of the Hammond proposals reached Congress, in January, 1863, the Senate economy-bloc offered lengthy objections. This new bill, also introduced by Wilson and approved by the Military Affairs Committee, provided that medical directors of army corps and the senior surgeon in the Surgeon General's Office be promoted to lieutenant colonels; that the cost of a soldier's hospital rations be raised from 18 to 30 cents a day; that 300 officers be added to the corps of staff "surgeons of volunteers" along with ten medical storekeepers and "as many medical cadets as the Surgeon General may deem necessary," and that the rule forbidding the promotion of an assistant surgeon before five years service be removed.

It was explained that the Medical Department had observed great improvement in patients fed on a better diet than the 18-cent ration provided; but the Senators seemed to feel that this would deplete the treasury. Senator Fessenden expressed himself pleased with a provision "which did not propose to improve the lot of the wounded by raising the rank and pay of doctors," but otherwise the proposition found little favor. The plight of hospital patients, it was suggested, could be laid to thieving hospital personnel rather than to insufficient appropriations.

The attenuated bill that was passed provided only (1) that the Surgeon General might prescribe, with the approval of the Secretary of War, all such articles of hospital diet as he might see fit (but with no extra appropriation); (2) that 50 surgeons and 250 assistant surgeons be added to the number of surgeons of volunteers; and (3) that all these new commissions lapse at the end of the war.

In February, 1863, the Senate considered a law to provide a professional cook for each Army company, give $10 a month pay to hospital matrons, and add tobacco, at cost, to the ration. What little time the Senate devoted to the bill was squandered in debate over the morality of encouraging men to use tobacco. Wilson testified that medical inspectors reported the Army's greatest need to be "tobacco at a reasonable price." The bill passed the Senate but was buried by the House. The Army's health received no further consideration during the rest of Surgeon General Hammond's term. Improvements had to be made within the existing legal framework.

The Senate's debates give the impression that the legislators were badly informed and were, perhaps justifiably, suspicious of all medical officers. Slurs against all things medical were abundant with practically no balancing compliment. Active interest by the lawmakers appeared to be limited to whether or not their constituents would be eligible to appointment to the new offices.

The projects for an Army medical school and an ambulance corps were defeated by War Department opposition. Stanton objected that since classes would meet in the evening students would in all probability cut them and go to the theater. Consequently Army surgeons were forced to perfect their learning upon the battlefields. To bring his corps into touch with recent scientific developments, Surgeon General Hammond spent his own evenings preparing a textbook on military hygiene and sanitation, and collaborating with one of his officers on a manual for hospital stewards.

He also ordered the collection of specimens in the field for a medical museum. Under his direction a system of accurate case-cards, to be attached to the wounded before they were evacuated to the rear, was instituted. Later in the war, when this proved impossible for surgeons under battle conditions, detailed case reports made up at each general hospital were substituted. Another important change was a new classification of diseases adapted from the one used by the British Army which incorporated recent medical advances. Still another indication of Hammond's progressive spirit was his establishment of a "microscopical department" at his headquarters.

He also carried on a gigantic program of hospital building, of the "pavilion" type which represented the advanced ideas of the time. In 1863 he issued a completely revised version of the Medical Regulations, embodying improvements in organization suggested by war experience. Such work was facilitated by the allotment of 25 additional civilian clerks early in 1862 so that it was no longer necessary to use hospital stewards, who were pharmacists, as clerical help.

One of Hammond's reforms was to outrage a large proportion of the medical profession and deprive him of their sorely needed support. In May, 1863, the surgeons of the Army were startled to receive a Medical Department circular removing calomel and tarter emetic from the supply table of the Army. The use of calomel, the circular explained, "has so frequently been pushed to excess by military surgeons," that the only way to deal with it was to banish the drug, "the melancholy effects of which have exhibited themselves not only in innumerable cases of profuse salivation, but in the not infrequent occurrence of mercurial gangrene." As for tarter emetic (another preparation of mercury), it was dropped because diseases could be treated without it. "No doubt can exist," Hammond concluded, "that more harm has resulted from the misuse of both these agents, in the treatment of disease, than benefit from their administration."

The shocked horror with which these pronouncements were received by many medical men can be understood only in the light of the inter-professional controversies of that time. The first half of the 19th century had been a period of heroic dosing with calomel, especially by physicians in the South and West, some of whom would give a dram of the drug every hour. Salivation was sometimes the object of the dosage; sometimes it was an accidental effect. The unfortunate salivating patient would present a miserable picture with "the tongue protruded out of the mouth, the face greatly swollen, and the saliva flowing out at the rate of from a pint to a quart in twenty-four hours." A frequent complication was the loss of teeth, and, in extreme cases mercurial gangrene, which would rot the soft parts of the mouth and cheeks, causing them to fall out "a putrid mass."

In reaction the Thomsonians, one of the "sects" of the time, opposed all mineral drugs, the Hydro-Therapeutists recommended therapeutic bathing, the "Botanics," favored roots and herbs, and the Homeopaths advocated tiny doses. All joined in the anti-mercurial camp. Many "Allopaths," or physicians of the conventional school, had also denounced the reckless prescription of calomel, while continuing its moderate use. Most of them disliked the "faddists" of their day as much as their successors dislike the chiropractors and naturopaths of ours. In issuing Circular No. 6 Hammond offended surgeons who prided themselves on their discreet use of calomel, and evoked the wrath of all who were opposed to the "faddists" and who thought their chief had become the patron of quacks.

The ensuing "calomel war" may have aided in ultimately checking the misuse of the drug, but the immediate benefits were slight. Circular No. 6 was disobeyed or disregarded; its principal result appeared to be that Hammond, already disliked in influential Army circles, was delivered into the hands of his enemies.

Relations between the Surgeon General and Secretary Stanton were deteriorating. Stanton had thwarted Hammond's plans for an ambulance and hospital corps and for an Army medical school, but the greatest friction seems to have been over the appointment of the medical inspectors. When the inspecting corps was authorized in April, 1862, the Sanitary Commission and the Surgeon General, acting upon request of the Secretary of War, had submitted a list of candidates, recommended on a merit basis. Few of these received appointment, and it developed that Senators had been asked to designate the new inspectors. As finally constituted, the corps consisted of four officers from the

Regular Army, appointed without consideration of seniority and therefore resented by the older Regulars, and four new-comers whose appointments were widely believed to be based on neither seniority nor merit.

The man chosen as Medical Inspector General was Thomas F. Perley, a person of no military experience, whose "name was not familiar to medical circles." Having neither professional nor Army reputation he was quite naturally put down as a poli-tician, and his administration of the sanitary inspection of the Army was criticized. His work was said to be distinguished by its "imbecility" which rendered him unfit to use the good re-ports turned in by his staff.

Though Congress had been persuaded to authorize the ap-pointment of eight additional inspectors, as a pressing immedi-ate need, Stanton delayed making the appointment for seven months. Once again, he divided the commissions between four officers recommended on a merit basis by Hammond and four who had political influence.

In August, 1863, Perley was succeeded as Medical Inspector General by Joseph K. Barnes, a Regular Army man then acting as personal physician to Army officers and War Department offi-cials resident in the capital. His chief qualification, apparently, was his friendship with Secretary Stanton. Having opposed Stan-ton on so many matters, and irritated him with protests, and having lost the support of many of the organized physicians who had helped to get him into office, Surgeon General Hammond should not have been surprised when in November, 1863, he was ordered away from Washington and Col. Joseph K. Barnes was named Acting Surgeon General.

The news first reached Hammond as a rumor, while on an inspection trip in Tennessee. He also learned that he was being "investigated" by a group of civilians, headed by a personal enemy. Under the circumstances he demanded trial by a court-martial. When the court convened he was formally charged with "conduct to the prejudice of military discipline" and "unbecom-ing an officer and a gentleman."

Space precludes consideration of the flimsy evidence pre-sented to back up these charges. A court made up of docile offi-cers, though it refused to accept some of the specifications and modified others, found the defendant guilty of ungentlemanly conduct. That rang down the curtain on the military-medical career of William Alexander Hammond.*

The *Tribune's* correspondent had thought the trial a fair one. But the field surgeons in the Army of the Potomac were reported to believe that the Surgeon General was "the victim of a clique inimical to him," an opinion shared by the *Boston Medical and Surgical Journal.* To the Sanitary Commission people he was a martyr. An important postscript to the trial was added in 1865 when Surgeon Cooper, whose evidence had been crucial, re-marked to a colleague: "Now, Doctor, I will tell you, in the late trial it was Hammond's head or mine, and I saved mine." The Regulars who did not want to be reformed, the elders who did not want young men promoted over them, the politicians who did not want to wrestle with idealists, had won a victory.

No doubt Hammond's personality played a part in his down-fall. He impressed people as irritable, tactless, and pompous. An admirer, closely associated with him, has described him as "impulsive," and as "not always wise or prudent," but certainly more sinned against than sinning. In view of the haste with which the Medical Department had to be renovated, it was probably inevitable that any active Surgeon General would affront many subordinates.

The old-guard's victory had long-lasting effects. As the older men began to get the important posts the best young men tended to leave the service. There was an end of new ideas, and after 1865 a partial relapse into ante-bellum lethargy. The Depart-ment slumbered until the sudden crisis of the Spanish-American War rudely awakened it.

* For an excellent and extended account of the trial, see Louis C. Duncan, "The Strange Case of Surgeon General Hammond," *Military Surgeon*, LXIV (January, 1929), pp. 98–114, and (February, 1929) pp. 252–267.

The

Barnes Regime

and the

Army Surgeons

JOSEPH K. BARNES, THE SURGEON GENERAL WHOSE FORMAL appointment was made in August, 1864, had then been in charge for almost a year. His reputation is based on the establishment of the Army Medical Museum and the Army Medical Library (both conceptions of the previous administration) and the publication during the post-war years of the first volumes of the *Medical and Surgical History of the War of the Rebellion,* the original impetus for which had come from General Hammond.

Administrative routine varied little from the Hammond regime. In the spring of 1864 the Assistant Surgeon General, transferred to Louisville the previous October, was given practically viceregal powers over medical department activities in a widespread western area. It was felt that the distribution of supplies and the provision for hospital accommodations in that region might be better attended by a resident official.

The spreading war fronts brought corresponding increases in departmental expenses. In the year 1863–1864 total expenditures were $11,025,000, of which $9,000,000 went for medicines and supplies. The following year expenditures reached $20,489,000, of which $15,200,000 went for medicines and supplies. The hospital payroll jumped from $437,000 in 1863–1864 to $949,000 in 1864–1865; the outlay for artificial limbs rose from $34,000 to $126,000. The Surgeon General could finance his activities in the last year of the war only by securing a $3,251,000 deficiency appropriation and by anticipating the appropriation for the following year to the extent of $6,000,000.

An old problem reappeared with the arrival of contingents drafted for service in the winter of 1864. Defectives had burdened Grant's army in 1862 when a Sanitary Commission inspector had been struck by the large number of old men suffering from degenerative diseases occupying the hospital beds in the Department of the Gulf. These had been weeded out but numbers of the new recruits were found to be in deplorable condition.

The reasons for this were the provisions for quotas, bounties, and substitutes in the conscription system of the time. Paid substitutes, or poor men seeking bounty payments, hid their disabilities from the examiner. In a town that had not filled its quota with volunteers, and wished to avoid a draft, the selectmen would sometimes persuade the examiner to be lenient.

The Medical Department regulations providing for re-examination of all men within three days before they reached their units could soon eliminate the unfit, but the process was wasteful. The problem was to eliminate them at the recruiting points. It was proposed that physical examinations be given by experienced medical officers, capable of seeing through deceptions. The draft act of March, 1863, provided fine and imprisonment for examining surgeons derelict in their duty, but with such little effect that a year later more defectives were inducted than in any period since 1861.

The Provost Marshal General's Office helped examiners in

January, 1864, by specifying the disabilities to watch for. *
But anxiety to meet quotas brought defectives South in such
large numbers that in August the War Department finally issued
a remedial order, which might well have come years earlier.
Army surgeons were sent to recruiting centers in every State to
check on the work of the State-appointed examiners. There was
little complaint after these men began their work.

Many of the "defectives" whose breakdowns were to embar-
rass the Army, suffered only from youth, or in some cases
extreme age. Conscription began at the age of twenty; consequently boys in their teens, lured by the fife and drum, formed
the chief supply of substitutes for drafted men. According to
statistics based upon the affirmations of more than a million

* These included: Imbecility; insanity; epilepsy; paralysis and "decided atrophy of a limb"; organic diseases of internal organs "which
have incapacitated the man for laborious activity in civil life"; "developed" tuberculosis; cancer or aneurism; extensive skin diseases; permanent physical debility; scrofula or secondary syphilis "which has so
seriously impaired his health as to leave no doubt of the man's in-
capacity for military service"; chronic rheumatism; total loss of sight
in right eye; partial loss of sight in both eyes (nearsightedness does not
exempt) ; total loss of nose, or deformity so great as to obstruct respira-
tion; decided deafness; deformities of jaw that seriously impede masti-
cation or speech; dumbness, well proven; total loss of tongue; stammer-
ing, "if excessive and confirmed"; total loss of all front teeth, the
eyeteeth and first molars; tumors or wounds of neck that impede res-
piration; excessive deformity of the chest; hernia; anal troubles; old
and ulcerated internal hemorrhoids, (external hemorrhoids do not
exempt) ; total, or nearly total loss of penis; incurable organic stricture
of the urethra, "in which the urine is passed drop by drop," ("recent
or spasmodic stricture" does not exempt; bladder stone; confirmed or
malignant sarcocele; hydrocele if complicated with organic disease of
the testicles; loss of hand or foot, incapacitating wounds; incapacitating
fractures, dislocations or anchylosis; loss of right thumb or any two
fingers of same hand; club feet or loss of big toe; varicose veins of leg,
if serious; chronic ulcers. No one reading this list will feel that the
Army was making it difficult for people who wanted to enlist or be
accepted as conscripts. Any army that will accept men with secondary
syphilis and incipient tuberculosis would seem to be welcoming the sick
with open arms. The fact that the protests from the field concerned men
who could not meet even these low standards is striking.

soldiers, their age at enlistment averaged twenty-three. The 133,475 boys who professed to be eighteen constituted the largest single age group in the Army. Only 97,000 claimed to be twenty-one, the second largest age group. It is reasonable to infer that many of the supposed eighteen-year-olds were actually younger. Approximately 4,000 who gave their age as sixteen or younger, had been accepted though the minimum legal age was eighteen. Even without discounting any statements of age the Army had the strikingly large proportion of 29 per cent who were twenty or younger. Boys of thirteen and fourteen were continually trying to enlist, and 457 who professed those ages were actually on the muster rolls. Yet it was generally agreed that men under twenty were a liability to the Army through their inability to withstand hardship.

Whole regiments might show high sick rates because they had not been sufficiently trained and conditioned before being sent to the front. Every state except Wisconsin committed the error of continually forming new, raw regiments instead of sending new recruits as replacements to regiments already in the field, where they could have the guidance of veterans. Added to their high sick rate was the comparative ineffectiveness of new regiments in battle. As early as July, 1862, the Sanitary Commission urged a reversal of this policy, pointing out the advantages of the replacement system and attributing the high induction rate of defectives to the pressure that officers of a new regiment would place upon the examiner to fill the ranks.

A problem, already encountered during the Hammond administration, became urgent during that of Barnes—recruiting an adequate number of qualified surgeons, and keeping them once their value had been increased by field service. Half the army surgeons at Nashville in March, 1862, were reported absent, sick, or resigned. Since the troops disliked being treated by civilian physicians who were Southern sympathizers, the situation was serious. Resignations and long leaves of absence were common. A division medical director in the Army of the Potomac wrote in January, 1863, that more than half of his division staff were away, some for more than a year. Newly recruited Army surgeons were generally young and inexperienced, and often of inferior quality. The best men usually took the examination for "surgeons of volunteers," offered by the Surgeon General's Office, and were assigned to staff or general hospital duty.

Resignations were spurred by the findings of examining boards, or by the apprehensions of some surgeons that they would be disqualified on re-examination. After the opening of 1863 these boards worked with such efficiency that few incompetents were left by the spring of 1864.

Feeling that maintenance of an adequate medical personnel required a positive as well as a negative approach, Letterman had urged advances in rank and pay. Balked in this by Congress, various expedients to please the surgeons were tried. Surgeons in the field were permitted to transfer to general hospital duty, which meant an end of campaign hardships, the opportunity usually of living in a northern city, and, strangely enough, better compensation. In theory field surgeon and hospital surgeon had the same rank and pay: the difference was in their allowances for quarters. The field surgeon was assigned part of a tent while the hospital surgeon received from $40 to $60 a month as "commutation of quarters." An economical man could rent a cheap room and pocket the difference. The rush to hospital service withdrew many able men from the field armies, but at least it kept them in the service.

A new opportunity, which appealed particularly to the surgeons of the three-year regiments mustered out in 1864, was that of taking a contract as "acting staff-surgeon." This brought no increase in rank or pay, but it provided the use of a government horse, and, as a Federal appointment, greater dignity. Such a surgeon might be assigned to any type of service.

The vexed question of higher rank and pay for medical officers was settled in February, 1865. In his annual report for 1864 Surgeon General Barnes requested "brevet" promotions equal to those of line officers. This would have meant titular promotion but no real advance in Army rank. But a bill calling for full equality of Medical and line officers, sponsored by the persevering American Medical Association and backed by the Sanitary Commission, was already before Congress. A law was enacted which conferred the temporary rank of colonel upon all medical directors of field armies and medical directors of departments which contained at least 4,000 hospital beds; and temporary rank of lieutenant colonel to medical directors of army corps and of departments with less than 4,000 beds. Volunteer surgeons were to receive two-thirds of these choice appointments. Passed so near the end of the war, it is impossible to tell how well it may have operated as an inducement to retain ambitious surgeons.

So vast was the demand that by April, 1865, more than 12,-000 doctors had seen service in the field or in hospitals. They had been organized into seven bodies, as follows:

(1) Surgeons and Assistant Surgeons of the U.S. Army. This was the regular Medical Corps, composed of men in service when the war began and such additions as Congress had authorized. Once the war was under way they were used for staff duty.

(2) Surgeons and Assistant Surgeons of Volunteers, the former "brigade surgeons," created by Congress to supplement the work of the Regulars in staff duty. There were 547 such commissions issued.

(3) Regimental Surgeons and Assistant Surgeons, commissioned by State governors rather than by the President. This, the largest Army category, numbered 2,109 Surgeons and 3,882 Assistant Surgeons.

(4) Acting Assistant Surgeons, U.S. Army. These were the great majority of the "contract" surgeons, who held no commission but received the pay of first lieutenants. They numbered 5,532 and were employed chiefly in northern general hospitals, where many engaged in civil practice as well.

(5) Medical officers of the Veterans Corps.

(6) Acting Staff Surgeons.

(7) Surgeons and Assistant Surgeons of Colored Troops. These received Presidential commissions, but were assigned to Negro regiments and were ineligible for staff positions.

The first and second categories were intended for staff duty; the fifth and sixth were bait to retain officers toward the close of the war; the seventh was made necessary by a special situation. The burden of giving medical care to the troops, therefore, fell upon the regimental medical officers and the contract men, the former providing care in the field and the latter in the general hospitals. The regimental medical staff had been fixed by Congress as one surgeon and two assistant surgeons. It was the duty of the State authorities to provide the proper number for each of its regiments and to provide replacements for men who had resigned. The Federal government tried to provide enough contract surgeons to maintain a ratio of one hospital surgeon to each hundred cases. As the war went on, and as the load increased, it grew harder to secure good men in adequate numbers. The absence of thousands of surgeons had made private practice too lucrative for such as remained at home.

The States thus found themselves in a dilemma. With strict examinations they might not secure enough surgeons; if they were lax they might fill the Army with incompetents. A few Western States chose laxity and issued commissions without any kind of examination. In Illinois, on the contrary, a lobby of leading medical men secured a policy of strict examinations. New York's examination system was deliberately lenient, its surgeon general being a firm believer in the "large practical experience and sterling moral worth" of the numerous rural medical men, out of touch with recent advances, who would be "lost to the service" were the examinations more exacting. Ohio tempered its strict examinations with "private" examinations when it needed men urgently, and by relaxing its rule requiring candidates for commission as assistant surgeons to have had five years practical experience since graduation. A Danbury doctor believed that Massachusetts forfeited the services of many excellent practical surgeons by overly minute and theoretical examinations.

Qualifications and effectiveness of the army surgeons

Under Surgeon General Hammond applicants for Federal commissions were given searching examinations which demanded knowledge of the latest developments in sanitation and hygiene. An examination given by the Army Medical Board in the fall of 1862 began with an oral interrogation, from one to two hours long, testing the candidate's knowledge of history, geography, zoology, literature, natural philosophy, and languages. A three-hour written examination followed in which seven or eight questions had to be answered from each of the following "branches": surgery, anatomy, practice of medicine, pathology, physiology, obstetrics, medical jurisprudence and toxicology, materia medica, chemistry and hygiene. Quite a number failed to survive these examinations, and in the summer of 1862 the members of the examining board were informed by the Secretary of War ("the dreadful Mr. Stanton") that more candidates must be passed or the board would be broken up. They acted upon this advice, and to the subsequent surprise of their chairman the service was found not to have suffered. The passing of such examinations did not seem to correlate with actual performance.

In evaluating the Civil War surgeons many allowances must be made. Judged by modern standards, the best of them were deplorably ignorant and badly trained. But in comparison with the older generation of practicing physicians of their own time they appear in a better light. Nearly all had diplomas from medical schools, while as recently as the second quarter of the century most American practitioners had been office-trained. This must be considered a mild distinction, based on the theory that any diploma is better than no diploma, for American medical schools were never worse than in the middle years of the nineteenth century. The standard medical course was two years of nine months each, topped off with a term of service as assistant to an active practitioner. The second year was usually given over to a repetition of the first year's lectures. In neither year was laboratory or clinical instruction given real attention. In many States dissection was legally prohibited. The backwardness and poor equipment of even the better schools is illustrated by the fact that the Harvard medical school had no stethoscope until 1868, thirty years after its invention, and no microscope until 1869. Its catalogues failed to mention these instruments until those years. Many schools were mere diploma mills, living upon the fees of their students entering practice in a society which had not even set up a State licensing system for its own protection.

Had the schools represented the most advanced knowledge of their day they could have given their students only the merest beginnings of modern scientific medicine. The long debate between "rational medicine" and empiricism, between deductive knowledge and experimentalism, was ending in a qualified victory for the latter. In Europe, with France taking the lead, modern medicine had just come to birth during the first half of the century. The post-mortem investigation of local pathological lesions, combined with careful clinical observation, proved the key which was to make possible accurate diagnosis and understanding of disease. When scientific medical statistics were introduced, and used in conjunction with the findings of the pathologists, medical men began to feel that the ground was firm beneath their feet. The work of Pasteur and Koch in bacteriology was to shed a great light on the causes for diseased tissues that had been explored by the pathologists; antisepsis in surgery as pioneered by Lister was to make great surgical triumphs possible. Both however came too late to affect the ideas and methods of the men who had to do the medical and surgical work of the Civil War.

The time lag between Europe and America in medical ideas was due to various causes: the width of the Atlantic Ocean, the vast distances and frontier conditions of much of the United

States, the poverty and inadequacy of the American medical schools. Pathological investigation had been dependent for its success upon the invention of the achromatic microscope, yet not even the headquarters of the Army Medical Department had one until 1863. The clinical thermometer was hundreds of years old and its use was being urged by the French medical schools, yet there were not more than twenty thermometers in the Union Army. Auscultation and percussion, the procedure by which the physician sounds the patient's thorax for internal conditions, was a great scientific attainment of 1800–1820 in Europe, but only the better educated American surgeons practiced it during the war, and its adjunct, the stethoscope, was a novelty even to them. The hypodermic syringe was used by some surgeons, but the majority continued to "dust" morphine into wounds, or administer opium pills. The ophthalmoscope, by which the inside of the eye may be examined, had been invented in 1851, yet few "could use it in our army ten years later," and even fewer were acquainted with the laryngoscope invented in 1858. The large number of practitioners professing the medical cults, based on some monistic theory of disease or of treatment, is a further indication of the lag.

Consequently the presence in the Army of numbers of backward and incompetent medical men should not occasion as much surprise as the presence in equally large numbers of earnest, intelligent surgeons anxious to make good their educational deficiencies through foreign books, and capable of advancing science by the use of the clinical opportunities the war opened up for them. Brilliant young men like W. W. Keen and J. S. Billings appeared. Keen who entered the Army after only one year of medical school, made such use of his opportunities that by the end of the war he had won international reputation as a neurologist; Billings, who entered soon after graduation, made his war experience the basis of one of the great reputations in American medicine.

The volunteer doctors and the Regulars were critical of each other. The volunteer considered the older Regulars arrogant.

Most had started as young men above the average in talent; but in peacetime, their long tours of duty on the lonely plains, and lack of any spur to ambition after their one examination for promotion tended to lower their standards, weaken their professional interests and fix them in stagnant routine. This "vegetable existence" of the Regular surgeon offered little of the stimulation that civilian practice afforded. Part of the resentment of the volunteers came from their having to take orders, a discipline for which they were unprepared. The fact tha. the high administrative posts were virtually monopolized by the Regulars, whom they considered their professional inferiors, embittered the antagonism of the volunteers.

The Regulars, in their turn, pictured the volunteer as an intractable subordinate hard to break in, who ignored orders and upset routine by inattention to forms and reports. Many of the volunteers were considered poorly trained and guilty of many mistaken diagnoses. Western volunteer surgeons were considered especially poor by Easterners; but Medical Inspector Lyman, Easterner, denied this emphatically. Brinton, a Pennsylvania medical professor who became a medical director in the West in 1861–1862, was at first appalled by the Westerners, but later asserted that he had misjudged them, and that "their hearts were good and they were professionally zealous." Though defective in surgery, they were judged, by a Sanitary Commission inspector, as good average country practitioners.

It would have been remarkable indeed not to find some incompetents and even scoundrels in an aggregation of some thousands, appointed by more than a score of independent political agencies. These were spotted by reports to medical journals and civilian physicians on inspection tours. The Sanitary Commission denounced only a small percentage as incompetent. Rating the medical men of 200 regiments at the close of 1861 the commission's inspectors found only 2 per cent "incompetent" and 13 per cent of "doubtful competence," while 64 per cent were reported "as having discharged their duties with creditable energy and earnestness."

The two fields in which volunteer surgeons were most likely to be found wanting were operative surgery and the then vague and "modern" department called "sanitation and hygiene." Large numbers had had little or no surgical experience before entering the Army. Their wants in this respect were solved by a division of labor between physicians and surgeons.

The prevailing ignorance of preventive medicine was remedied by the study of European works and by distribution of the thousands of pamphlets by the Sanitary Commission. The Medical Department during the Lawson-Finley reign contributed nothing to this offensive against ignorance. But in 1863 Surgeon General Hammond's textbook was issued to all the surgeons of the Army.

Officers of the Sanitary Commission praised the eagerness and enthusiasm of the volunteers but found them wanting in practical matters. They would often neglect to provide "food, buckets, cups, vessels of any sort, and water of any sort." Doctors, nurses, and philosophers, it seemed, were "much easier to be had . . . than men who would be able to keep an oyster cellar or a barber shop with credit."

In defense one volunteer surgeon pointed out that they might at least claim the distinction of being the only class of volunteer officers with practical experience in their work before the war, and the only group who had to take an examination before being commissioned. The ignorance of the unexamined line officers often proved a hindrance to carrying out sanitary measures. "The general idea seemed to be," wrote Medical Director Tripler, "that it was the duty of the doctor to physic every man who chose to report sick and to sign such papers as the colonel directed him to sign. To superintend the sanitary condition of the regiment, to call upon the commanding officer to abate nuisances, to take measures for the prevention of disease was in many instances considered impertinent and obstrusive. . . ."

Professional zeal was manifested by the formation of many Army medical societies. Medical Director Brinton's impression of the "uncouth" qualities of his Western subordinates was soon tempered by the enthusiasm with which they flocked to the society he organized at Cairo, in 1861, at whose sessions they engaged in "prolonged discussions." A similar society, formed in a New York brigade early in 1862, opened its doors to any medical students working in the hospitals or with the ambulances. They met once a week, read papers and discussed such problems as "the position of the medical staff and their attendants during an engagement," "the advantages of primary vs. secondary amputation," and "conservative surgery." The Sanitary Commission's chief hospital inspector attributed the excellent condition of the Washington hospitals in the fall of 1862 in part to the new spirit that had come over the hospital staffs with the formation of the Army Medical Society, started under the auspices of Frederick Law Olmsted, which had held its early meetings in the Sanitary Commission's rooms. The hospital surgeons at Baltimore also had a society in 1862. At Suffolk, Virginia, the director lured his surgeons away from the line officers' poker games by setting up a dissection-laboratory for pathological exploration, which he kept supplied with Negro corpses.

Throughout the war the doctors were subjected to character attacks by newspapers and by civilians generally. Because patients in hospitals often received rough fare despite the collections of delicacies organized by the Sanitary Commission, surgeons were often charged with appropriating these gifts for their own tables, or selling them for profit. A few authentic instances of panic stricken surgeons deserting their patients under fire set off a great deal of malevolent gossip.

Drunkenness was the commonest charge against the surgeons. Women nurses were particularly prone to call attention to "drunken carousals" and resulting neglect and mistreatment of patients by surgeons and one case reached the Senate floor. A writer who claimed that sick rates were high in regiments with "drinking surgeons," and low in those cared for by teetotalers, took the position that the Army should commission no officer who used liquor. He claimed that generals had "more than once" told him of surgical damage inflicted by "the knife of a tipsy operator," a claim that found support in the report by a hospital surgeon of an amputation case in which the patient bled to death because "the operator was too drunk to take up the arteries."

Nevertheless, in more than two years of service, a highly reputable surgeon in the Army of the Potomac saw only one drunken surgeon, and another observer reported having seen only one during his year in the Army. It was the belief of Dr. Elisha Harris, of the Sanitary Commission, that medical officers were more temperate in their drinking than any other kind of officers. He excused the excessive drinkers on the ground that they were so exhausted from unbroken days and nights of work that "stimulants" were needed to keep them going. Nervous exhaustion seems a sounder explanation than inherent viciousness or deliberate neglect. Walt Whitman, who had unrivaled opportunities to observe surgeons during his years as a hospital visitor in Washington, judged all but a few of them excellent men.

An occasional complaint about a drunken surgeon came from soldiers in the ranks, but for the most part they criticized their medical officers for other defects. An English traveler wrote that surgeons were considered incompetent and inhumane, an opinion to which other sources give color. John D. Billings, who for his part thought the surgeons fine fellows and efficient doctors, admitted that they were generally considered quacks. A frequent complaint was that they inflicted unnecessary pain by their rough probing or dressing of wounds and that they neglected the sick. Distrust of their surgeon was often manifested by the men by throwing away the medicines prescribed for them.

Some doctors tried to meet the soldiers' criticism by using gentler methods; but the more common reaction was the counter-charge that men who complained were malingerers frustrated by the surgeon in their knavish attempts to escape duty, or malcontents irked by a hospital discipline which was for their ultimate good.

Sometimes soldiers liked their surgeons, and gave public demonstration of their regard. A surgeon of the Army of the Potomac, visiting a general hospital in Philadelphia which contained many of his former charges, was cheered as he toured the wards. And one day, at a large field hospital, all of the amputation cases able to walk formed ranks, and marched in review past the doctors' quarters, giving loud cheers for their surgeons. The astonished doctors thereupon "returned the cheer with a tiger." Some of the soldiers who sat down in later years to write their memoirs spoke affectionately of surgeons, or of some surgeons; but faultfinding and complaint were more frequent.

Civilian volunteers: blessing or nuisance?

A class of battlefield surgeons unmentioned by soldiers of the line, but who made a very bad impression upon the uniformed medical officers, were the civilian volunteers who came flocking down South, after major engagements, to lend a hand with the operative work. Medical men were exempted from the draft and this may have led to mixed motives. Adventure, and an opportunity to get surgical experience may have joined with patriotism to bring them to the battlefields.

Massachusetts had sent out small delegations of able operating surgeons to the Southern coast in February, 1862. They had been sent upon the requests of General Burnside and Medical Director Frank Hamilton. When the Peninsular campaign got under way in the late spring, requests for larger delegations were made by the Secretary of War. Similar requests to the Surgeon General of New York were met by a specially organized auxiliary corps, formed in the realization that two surgeons per regiment would not be sufficient for big battles. The civilian surgeons were provided transportation, tents, horses, and the opportunity to buy commissary's rations.

This extemporized civilian service soon showed grave defects. In their lack of organization and discipline, and specific responsibility, the civilians were merely in the way. They sat about doing nothing, or went sightseeing. They refused sick care because they were surgeons and had come for the express purpose of operating. The New York *Tribune* reporter, at the second battle of Bull Run, said many had refused assignments to Washington hospitals, insisting upon their right to "cut and carve" on the battlefield. The Surgeon General was reported as having sent away 2,000 of them, with their return fare paid by the government. The military surgeons' distrust of the civilians was deepened by their behavior on the bloody field of Antietam, in September, 1862. They were charged with performing needless operations merely to perfect their technique, and with wandering off from work that might prove fatiguing or uninteresting. One military surgeon posted an armed guard over his patients to protect them against civilian meddling, after he had seen one of the visitors cut away a soldier's bandages, inspect the wound, and, finding it "uninteresting," walk away leaving the patient unbandaged. On the other hand, a medical journal charged that at Antietam the civilian surgeons "were treated with indignity, and snubbed by surgical goslings of the army," with the result that they had no desire to return to the front.

After Gettysburg had once more demonstrated the flaws of the "civilian-auxiliary" system, Surgeon General Hammond secured the cooperation of the State governors in an improved plan. Each State formed a reserve surgeons corps, whose members would be vouched for by the governor and would come in answer to a telegram. The real improvements of the new plan lay in its remaining provisions: every reserve surgeon was to have the pay of a contract surgeon while away from home (most of the earlier volunteers had been unpaid); he must serve a minimum of 15 days unless released by the military authorities; and he must consider himself subject to the orders of the Medical Department. This program answered the very real need of an emergency personnel.

The one campaign in which the new "reserve surgeons" seem to have been used in large-enough numbers to attract any attention was Grant's spring campaign of 1864, when the great battles of the Wilderness, Spotsylvania, and Cold Harbor sent tens of thousands of wounded men into the field hospitals within a few weeks. A month after the campaign opened 194 "reserve surgeons," 42 contract surgeons and 775 nurses and medical students, gathered from sixteen states, were serving in the hospitals at Fredericksburg, medical base of the Army of the Potomac. Even then "a great lack of physicians" was reported by a newspaper correspondent. No crop of scandal stories followed the performance of the civilian surgeons in this campaign.

The medical cadets, the young students who would sometimes "come down to the front in all the glory of gold-lace, inexperience, and bottomless assurance," were likewise suspected of thinking more of improving their surgical skill than of benefiting their patients. However, their true function was to act as wound dressers and ward helpers, for which they sometimes won praise.

Regimental surgeons, living and working side by side with fighting men, sometimes turned from their work of mercy to "grab a gun" and play a martial role. Caught by his medical director, and reprimanded, one replied: "I'm all right Doctor, I have done all the surgery of this regiment, and I have fired forty-five shots, by God!" Even the surgeon who stuck to his trade underwent the hardships and many of the dangers that threatened the soldiers of the line. With 42 of its officers killed in battle, and 83 wounded, the Medical Department proudly claimed that its casualties were higher than those of any other staff corps. In addition to these battle casualties the Medical Corps lost 290 officers through death by disease or accident, and four died in Confederate prisons. The number of those who sickened and resigned, only to die at home, or who carried with them for years the curse of chronic invalidism, will remain forever unknown.

4

Beginnings

of an

Ambulance

System

ONCE AN ARMY HAS TAKEN THE FIELD NO MEDICAL FUNCTION IS more important than care of the wounded. The injured must be gathered, transported to dressing stations, given surgical attention, and fed and cared for. They must be hospitalized within the army's lines or evacuated to some general hospital outside the combat area. The successful performance of these functions demands intricate organization, vast stores of goods, and a trained personnel. In 1861 all of these were wanting. After the bloody campaigns of 1862 administration reached a workable basis, an efficient ambulance system had come into being in the Army of the Potomac, and the replacement of regimental hospitals by better brigade or division hospitals had begun. These good beginnings were carried forward throughout 1863 and 1864, and by 1865 American ambulance and field hospital systems had become models of their kind.

The appointment of a medical director for each army, the first and most obvious organizational step, took place before the Battle of Bull Run. But the anarchy that ruled on that ill-starred field showed how much more was needed. The task of bringing order out of chaos was entrusted to Surgeon Charles S. Tripler, who replaced Surgeon W. S. King as medical director of the Army of the Potomac on August 12, 1861.

Dr. Tripler faced many problems. New regiments, arriving from the North, brought volunteer surgeons to whom Army methods and Army reports were mysteries. The sick and wounded, not in regimental hospitals, were scattered helter-skelter through the improvised general hospitals in Washington. A public scandal that developed over the gruesome conditions in a hospital at Cumberland, Maryland, was the first knowledge Tripler had of its existence. He had received no reports from it and had not even been informed that troops were stationed at Cumberland. There were no subordinate administrators through whom he could issue commands; no hospital inspectors; no provision for the training of hospital and ambulance personnel.

Since the new "brigade surgeons" were competent medical men and most of them had been at Bull Run and presumably had some idea of what was needed, Tripler decided to fix certain administrative responsibilities upon them. Each was to make sanitary inspections of the brigade's camps, maintain its medical supplies, transmit the weekly morbidity reports of the regimental surgeons, and supply casualty reports after an action. Each was further charged with the duty of drilling the bandsmen (regimental musicians) and hospital details (ten men from each regiment) in their duties as stretchermen, and was responsible for the organization of a field hospital and its surgical personnel at the time of an engagement. In the spring of 1862 the inspection of hospitals within Tripler's department became a special function of officers appointed for the purpose. Since a medical director (usually a regular or a "brigade surgeon") had been appointed to the staff of each division commander, it may be said that a fairly comprehensive administrative system had been set up before the Army of the Potomac moved south in March, 1862, to begin the Peninsular campaign. (So called from the York Peninsula on the Virginia coast near which the Confederate capital, Richmond, was situated.)

This was the system which, with some variations, was establishing itself in the other Union armies and was to remain, almost unchanged, throughout the war. In time divisional medical directors overshadowed chief surgeons of brigades in the medical hierarchy, and were in turn overshadowed, when army corps were formed and corps medical directors appointed. The Surgeon General, at the top of the pyramid, exercised control through instructions to the medical director of each army or military department. He was kept informed through the reports of these officers and kept check on them through the inspection reports of the medical inspectors created by the act of April 16, 1862.

The faulty ambulance work and the pathetically inadequate field hospitals of most of the battlefields of 1862 bear witness that the medical-administrative system was far from perfect. For this there were numerous reasons. No system can rise superior to the men who administer it, and in the Army no staff corps can work effectively without the cooperation of the line commanders. The Regular Army surgeons who held most of the ranking medical directorships were frequently without administrative talent and often of a stubbornly conservative cast. They were hampered by the ignorance and inexperience of the volunteer regimental surgeons, many of whom were insubordinate and undisciplined. They were further hampered by unclearly defined and divided authority. The regulations provided that a division medical director, "after consultation with the quartermaster-general," had the authority to dispose his men for battle and to set up a field hospital, but only the medical officers, hospital stewards, and nurses of the division were under his command. He had no control over the ambulances and their crews, who belonged to the Quartermaster Corps. The other duties and powers of the medical directors and the chief surgeons of brigades were "never specified or defined by law or general orders —and were only assumed as natural suggestions attaching to the ranking of staff officers, and extended to a general supervision of the affairs of their respective commands."

Happy was the medical director who served with a general inclined to accept suggestions and delegate full authority! McClellan supported both Tripler and Jonathan Letterman who succeeded Tripler. Grant cooperated with John Brinton, his medical director in 1861. Many generals however were at cross-purposes with their medical staffs. During Don Carlos Buell's command of the Army of the Ohio the Medical Department was "merely tolerated . . . as an unpleasant necessity." The general resented the detailing of any men for hospital service since he believed that "the Medical Department should be self-sustaining—that the sick should care for the sick." Serious clashes between medical and line officers continued as late as 1864 in the Department of the South, where the medical director was not only denied needed details of men, but saw his ambulance horses requisitioned as cavalry remounts.

These difficulties must be remembered when the battlefield-relief activities of the Medical Department are considered. From the notably poor ambulance work during the Peninsular campaign in the spring of 1862 the casual student might conclude that Tripler had done nothing to mend the flaws exposed at Bull Run. But as we have seen, he had ordered that the bandsmen and ten detailed men from each regiment be drilled in stretcher work and had fixed responsibility for this upon the chief surgeons of brigades, and he had worked hard to secure an adequate number of ambulances from the Quartermaster Corps. Had the brigade surgeons fulfilled their responsibilities, and the regimental surgeons carried out the brigade surgeons' orders, an ambulance corps of sorts would have existed.

The number of ambulances available in the Army of the Potomac continued inadequate through most of 1862. On the assumption that four-wheeled vehicles were best for slightly wounded men and two-wheelers for the seriously wounded, one four-wheeler and five two-wheelers had been allotted per regiment. Tripler regarded this number as fantastic. An army of 100,000 men would have an ambulance train twenty-five miles long, consisting of six hundred vehicles. He asked for 250 ambulances which he considered sufficient, only to find that the quartermaster's shops could not meet even the reduced demand.

The situation was complicated by the rapid disappearance of the vehicles issued. Of 228 two-wheeled ambulances delivered to the Army between July 1 and October 1, 1861, 119 were out of service on the latter date. Many had broken down; others had simply vanished. The breakdowns demonstrated the need for a more rugged vehicle, while the disappearances might be accounted for by the Army's defiance of orders in using ambulances as cabs and light trucks. On special orders from General McClellan, the medical director managed to cut down these illegal practices. Breakdowns were solved by the virtual abandonment of the two-wheelers, which had not only proved too light for Army use but too uncomfortable for the sick and wounded who nicknamed them "avalanches." Leaving one of these vehicles with each regiment, Tripler turned the remainder back to the Quartermaster Corps.

The regiment was the traditional unit of medical treatment and hospitalization. After the first year of the war this gave way to a more rational organization under the impact of the great battles of 1862 and 1863. The British Army had clung tenaciously to the regimental hospital during the Crimean War, on the argument that the patient does best with the doctor he knows, and that surgeons must not be robbed of authority over the men in their own regiments. Brigade hospitals had finally replaced regimental in the Crimea, and American experience was to follow the same course. It proved difficult, under battle conditions, to get the wounded to their own regimental hospitals; it multiplied the supply issues; and by confining each regimental surgeon to his own hospital, it often wasted his talent and had awkward consequences. It remained a convenient means for tending the moderately sick and the slightly wounded; and, as the greater proportion could be so classified, apparently the majority of cases were treated in the regimental hospitals.

They varied in size according to the sick lists. They might be housed in tents, dwellings, churches, or even cow barns. Regulations allowed every regiment three "hospital" tents, one "Sibley" tent and one "common" tent. The "hospital" tent was a white wall-tent, fifteen by fourteen feet, and eleven feet high in the center, with side walls four and a half feet high. The "Sibley" was a large, conical affair, resembling a tepee, while the "common" tent was simply an inverted "V" of canvas. But tents were not always available and many hospitals were otherwise sheltered. And, men accustomed to more solid shelter did not always take kindly to tents.

These little hospitals were good or bad according to the intelligence and sense of responsibility of the regimental surgeons in charge. There was suffering in many because the surgeon did not know how to draw supplies, or how to husband those he had drawn. The Army custom was to issue drugs and other supplies at fixed intervals and in fixed quantities, which meant that a regiment sometimes had an oversupply while at other times it lacked the commonest necessities. Then there was that great Army mystery "the hospital fund" which volunteer surgeons found hard to understand. It was supposed that a sick man ate less than his normal ration and the surgeon was expected to keep account of the difference. This provided a fund which could be used to buy delicacies, when obtainable.

From time to time during the war, and especially during its first year, outsiders made horrified inspections of some of the worst regimental hospitals. Inadequate supply and filthy conditions provoked most of their criticisms which were usually summed up in the epithet "pigsties." In some hospitals the only nurses available were convalescent soldiers, hardly able to drag themselves about and without any training. Clara Barton found a prostrate fever patient in a regimental hospital at Washington whose socks had not been removed for six weeks. "His toes," she wrote, "were matted and grown together and are now *dropping off at the joint;* the cavities in his back are absolutely frightful."

The Sanitary Commission however was able to assure the public that these were the exceptions. At the end of 1861 the commission's inspectors classified 105 regimental hospitals as "good," 52 regiments as "indifferent or tolerable" and only 26 as "bad." They found thirteen regiments without hospitals. The belated appointment of hospital inspectors for the Army of the Potomac in November, 1861, brought improved conditions. And the excessive reliance upon regimental hospitals was ending. Before the spring campaign opened, Dr. Tripler, despite lack of any provision for it in the regulations, issued an order creating the first brigade hospitals in the East. This halfway measure yielded to legal scruple by organizing the new brigade hospitals as aggregations of regimental hospitals. Their commissioned and enlisted personnel remained on the regimental rolls. Regimental hospitals continued to play a big role in the Army of the Potomac as late as the battle of Antietam, and lasted into 1864.

In the field, the lives of regimental medical officers usually alternated between short frantic periods of overwork and slack periods when their duties occupied them less than an hour a day. During the lulls the medical high-point of each day was "sick-call," when men who sought excuse from duty were paraded before the doctors by the first sergeants. In many regiments this diagnosis was made by the assistant surgeon while the surgeon called on the bedfast and attended sick officers. At the diagnosis it was decided whether the soldier reporting sick should be put in the regimental hospital, excused from duty but allowed to remain in quarters, or assigned to light duty. These were among the most important of the medical officers' powers. In theory at least, a whole regiment might be excused from duty, and everyone, officers included, came under the surgeon's command. Or he might exercize his power in another way; he could discharge his patients and order them to the battle line. But no surgeon had a right to separate a man from the command by sending him to a general hospital; nor had he a right to dismiss a man from the service; rights that some surgeons claimed.

When a battle impended it was the surgeon's duty to select some building or site for his "depot," or field hospital, at a "safe distance" in the rear. "Safe" meant beyond the range of the enemy's artillery, or about a mile and a half to two miles. The regimental hospital detail of ten men and the band, about 25 in all, would be divided, some assigned to the field hospital as nurses, the remainder accompanying the troops as stretcher-men. While waiting for the wounded to arrive the hospital staff would make their preparations. The hospital steward would open the medical chests and lay out surgical supplies, opiates, and bottles of whisky. The men detailed as cooks would heat water, prepare tea, or coffee, and soup, and put sponges to soak.

The assistant surgeon, accompanied by an orderly carrying a hospital knapsack filled with emergency supplies, went with the stretcher bearers to establish a "primary station," just outside musketry range. There first aid was given and the regimental ambulances loaded. Another of his duties was supervision of the stretchermen so far as his location and circumstances permitted. The stretchermen were supposed to cover the field and give no excuse for a soldier to leave the line in order to escort the wounded to the rear. When they found a wounded man incap-able of walking—many wounded could and did walk—the stretchermen would carry him to the primary station, using a practiced pace to hold the patient's suffering to a minimum. There the assistant surgeon, with the help of his orderly and usually of a hospital steward, would give him liquor to counter-act shock, and administer first aid with an equipment consisting of pails, basins, sponges, lint, and bandages. The treatment was usually limited to a tourniquet and bandages. The patient would then be put in one of the regimental ambulances and taken to the field hospital.

There the seriously wounded would go at once to the operat-ing table for detailed examination and, if found necessary, for an operation. If the army was stationary, the patients might lie in the field hospital until they recovered or died. The more usual procedure was to evacuate them within a few days to a general hospital, at the army's base or to the North.

Field relief remained much the same throughout the war, though increasing in extent and improving in management, housing and supplies. During the early battles of 1862 most field hospitals were regimental hospitals and the operations were performed by regimental surgeons, at much needless suffering. There was a gradual evolution toward larger hospitals. Some brigade hospitals appeared during the Peninsular campaign, in the East, and at Fort Donelson, in the West. By the end of 1862 division hospitals were the rule in the Army of the Potomac, and in 1863 these were often clustered together in corps hospitals. The surgical specialization that this made possible, and the improved supervision vastly bettered the lot of the sick and wounded.

The deficiency of the battlefield medical work is largely to be attributed to the untrained and usually inferior men assigned to nursing and stretcher work. The only man permanently assigned to the surgeon, and supposed to have some knowledge of his work before appointment, was the hospital steward. A warrant officer, he ranked above the first sergeant of a company. He was supposed to have a knowledge of practical pharmacy. He must "take exclusive charge of the dispensary, must be practically acquainted with such points of minor surgery as the application of bandages and dressings, the extraction of teeth, and the application of cups and leeches, and must have such knowledge of cooking as will enable him to superintend efficiently this important branch of hospital service." Naturally, this office became the special haven of druggists, medical students, and would-be medical students. There was no prescribed system of examination for such appointments until 1864, when a candidate had to appear before a board of three medical officers.

Conditions would not have been so bad if the prewar regulations had been continued. These permitted the surgeon to select his own men "with the approval of the commanding officer."

The men could then be removed *only at his request,* "or for mis-behavior, or other special reason, which the commanding officer shall report to the adjutant-general." But the revised regulations of 1861 dropped the removal clause, and all the nurses of a hospital, who were now picked by the company captains instead of the surgeons, could be suddenly withdrawn. In the early days of the war, some captains refused to detail anyone, or designated men who were physically weak or notorious for their "determined worthlessness as soldiers."

The regimental musicians were ex-officio members of the hospital detail. As the scrubbing of blood soaked floors and dragging out the wounded under fire have nothing to do with music it is not surprising that many lacked skill or interest in the work. It was charged that they "proved utterly worthless in bringing off the wounded, behaving with the utmost cowardice, and required more persons to watch and see that they did their duty than their services were worth"; that they were "averse to labor or danger, and habitually insubordinate." When a field hospital came under fire they would disappear. By 1864 some divisions of the Army of the Potomac had given up using musicians in the hospitals, sending them to the front. In other divisions the medical authorities persisted in their attempt to subdue the artistic temperament, and continued to find them "rather an encumbrance than a help."

Observers reported that the men detailed from the line, who together with the convalescents did much of the field-hospital nursing, were hardly better than the bandsmen. Some proved drunkards. Others deserted when most needed, in order to avoid capture. They were further charged with neglecting and mistreating their Union patients, and preferring to nurse Confederates, whose conversation they found more interesting. Being combat soldiers, they were subject to capture by the enemy who might thus strip a hospital of its entire nursing staff. As for the convalescents, who oftentimes had to do most of a hospital's nursing, they were glaringly unfitted for the work by their weakness.

Many soldier nurses, however, behaved with conspicuous bravery under fire. Some became such excellent assistants at the operating table that they were called upon to do the work of assistant surgeons. And some won commendation for their gentleness and kindness. While this was reported it had to be admitted, however, that even the kindly ones did not keep the wounded clean and were usually too ignorant or too weak physically to be worth much as nurses. The need for a special hospital corps, enlisted for nursing only, became increasingly obvious.

Nursing of sorts was also done by nondescripts, inside or outside the regulations. During the Peninsular campaign 50 "contrabands," as runaway slaves were called, were obtained from the Quartermaster Corps for hospital work. Though useful to "carry wounded and pass lemonade," they proved inferior to detailed soldiers. At Gettysburg the need was so pressing that paroled Confederate soldiers were used, and turned out to be friendly and efficient nurses. Sometimes a father who had rushed to his son's bedside, or a brother in the same regiment, would be allowed to come into the field hospital to nurse his relative. Commissioned officers were the only category of patients who could count on being reasonably well served. Each officer in hospital could use his orderly as his personal nurse.

Mistaken notions of Clara Barton and her work have fostered the legend that women nurses played an important role on Civil War battlefields. Many served in general hospitals in the North, or well to the rear, but the number who functioned in field hospitals was never large. Here and there a regiment had brought with it a "vivandiere," or a "matron"—really a washerwoman —who would make herself useful in caring for the wounded after a battle; but generally the nursing in field hospitals was done entirely by men. Regularly enrolled women nurses were supposed to serve only in general hospitals, although a few were allowed to supervise the light-diet cooking and perform some nursing duties in field hospitals.

However, every great battle attracted a certain number of

free-lance women nurses and "reliefers" to the front. They appeared on the York peninsula during McClellan's campaign there, but were soon ordered to leave. A delegation, one of whom was the "Cairo Angel," served for a time at Savannah, Tennessee, after Shiloh. "Mother" Bickerdyke, an able and picturesque woman, was invited by General Sherman to work in his corps hospital at Chattanooga, where she was the only woman nurse. The Gettysburg holocaust brought numerous Northern women, who served in the field hospitals for several weeks, and the government even permitted Southern women to come to Gettysburg to tend their wounded. Clara Barton was a one-woman relief-agency rather than a nurse. She visited numerous battlefields, and helped either by temporary nursing or by distributing the relief goods she had collected. Like the majority of these women, she was a "volunteer," received no pay or allowances, had no official standing and was free to leave the Army when she chose.

Medical lessons of the Peninsular campaign

Having spent almost nine months in organizing and disciplining the large Union army gathered about Washington, General George B. McClellan took the field in March, 1862. His plan was to land a seaborne expedition on the York peninsula of Virginia, and march from Fortress Monroe upon Richmond. The first big battle was fought at Fair Oaks at the end of May. After a lull, a bloody series of engagements was fought from June 26 to July 1. During the Seven Days' Battles, the Army of the Potomac withdrew from the vicinity of Richmond to Harrison's Landing on the James River.

This campaign should not have presented any medical problems. The lines of communication on land were short. The Navy's command of the waterways kept communication open with the North. A railroad and ships were available to evacuate the sick and wounded. But bad teamwork, poor preparations and dearth of ambulances, food, tents, and supplies made the medical work a mess.

The army left the Washington area with 177 ambulances instead of the 250 its medical director considered essential. One regiment began the campaign with a single small, two-wheel vehicle, which promptly broke down. An entire brigade could not locate an ambulance to convey a sick colonel. Toward the end of the campaign an army corps of 30,000 is reported to have had ambulance transportation for only 100 men. Many regiments left their sick and wounded in farmhouses, or "dying houses," along the way. The retreating army left large numbers of its wounded behind to become captives of the Confederates.

Despite an attempt to cluster regimental hospitals together as brigade hospitals, so strong a hold did the old regimental practice keep on many surgeons that they wasted time and effort hunting for disabled members of their own regiments. Wounded men who made their way to the hospital of another regiment found themselves unwelcome because they complicated the food problems, food issues being made on a regimental basis. The quartermasters and commissaries, who were responsible for the transportation and issue of food, failed to provide enough food, cups, spoons, tents, and practically everything else.

Much of the trouble may be attributed to Medical Director Tripler's decision to keep the sick with the army, and his failure to prepare suitable base hospitals. There was a large toll of malaria, typhoid, dysentery, and other serious diseases. Tripler, not wishing to see the army depleted, kept them with the army instead of evacuating them, with the result that the hospitals were clogged when the battle casualties descended upon them.

Other than the fact that some of the field hospitals at Williamsburg were so badly placed as to come under fire, there seems to have been little complaint about them. Despite the ambulance shortage the lines of communication to the "landings," where the hospital ships lay, were so short that there was little difficulty in evacuating the seriously disabled. But the field hospitals were already crowded when the Battle of Fair Oaks poured its more than 3,000 wounded into them. When the Seven Days' Battle added 8,000 more conditions became frightful.

The army's base at the time of Fair Oaks was White House Landing, on the Pamunkey River. It was transferred to Harrison's Landing, on the other side of the peninsula, when the army retreated. It was at these points that the hospital boats, which had evacuated the wounded from Yorktown and Fortress Monroe, received the wounded from Fair Oaks and the Seven Days' Battles. A nondescript evacuation hospital was set up at each of the two Landings, following neither precedent nor plan. They were extremely bad. At the hospital at White House Landing there were five surgeons, one steward and no nurses when the 4,500 sick and wounded from Fair Oaks began arriving. The situation would have been desperate indeed had not the Sanitary Commission cut all red tape and rushed in large quantities of relief goods.

The situation was made worse by the condition of the arrivals. Many had had no surgical attention since leaving the front. One trainload of 300 had been packed side by side on the bare floors of the cars and had been without food for three days.

The embarkation of the disabled at White House and at Harrison's Landings began a new chapter of errors. The Quartermaster Corps was responsible for transportation, and had provided and equipped the steamers to be used as hospital ships, and was responsible for their operation and management. But the vessels were filthy, ill provisioned and lacked hospital equipment. They were therefore put under the temporary management of the Sanitary Commission, which provided whatever doctors, nurses and equipment it could assemble for the emergency.

The feeling was widely held that the Medical Department, and more particularly Medical Director Tripler, had let the Army down; that the medical aspects of the campaign had been quite as unsatisfactory as had been the campaign as a whole. In response to Olmsted's request a medical inspector had been dispatched to White House in June, and Secretary Stanton had sent a civilian physician to conduct a "private investigation." On July 4, 1862, while the difficulties of caring for the wounded from the Seven Days' Battles were still at their height, Dr. Tripler was replaced by Jonathan Letterman, whose ideas on field organization for the Army were ultimately to be extended to all the Union forces.

Tripler was not as inept as was thought. One may agree with his own judgment, contained in his final report as medical director, that his administration had been neither "a complete success nor a very decided failure." His long list of reasons for failure are reducible to two: (1) faulty cooperation of other departments of the Army in furnishing transport and supply; and (2) military ignorance and lack of teamwork displayed by the volunteer surgeons and line officers. These are undeniable but the unhappy Tripler's epithets hurled at his Sanitary Commission and volunteer critics,—"sensation preachers, village doctors, and strong-minded women,"—suggest the arrogance which provoked defiance rather than commanded obedience among his subordinates. His sneer that "the army was, perhaps, unfortunate in having a medical director who supposed it was assembled to make war, and that cartridges were more indispensable than bed quilts," only emphasizes the ability of other medical directors to provide for the wounded without causing any dearth of cartridges. His suggested medical-administrative system was good; but he was not the man to head it.

The medical showing was even worse when the second Battle of Bull Run was fought at the end of August. Letterman spent July and early August in the preliminary organization of what was to become an effective field relief system; but he was not destined to be present at the second Bull Run, and ambulance men trained by him formed only a portion of the force there.

Hoping to bring victory by a change in generals, Lincoln had brought General John Pope from the West. With an improvised force called the Army of Virginia, he was to attack Lee's army from the north. Outmaneuvered by Lee and Jackson, this army was forced to give battle, August 29 to September 1, on the old

Bull Run battlefield, where it was heavily defeated despite re-inforcement by two corps from the Army of the Potomac.

Almost incredible anarchy characterized the field relief work at this battle. There was no organized ambulance system except in the two corps from the Army of the Potomac; there were not enough ambulances. The best-equipped of the three corps in the original Army of Virginia had a total of 45 ambulances and carts instead of the scheduled 170. In the maneuvering many had broken down and had been abandoned before the battle opened. The reinforcements from the Army of the Potomac were even worse off. They had been embarked at Harrison's Landing in such haste and with such limited ship-space that the majority of the ambulances were left behind. Whole divisions were with-out ambulances.

McParlin, the medical director in charge, made poor use of what he had. Instead of setting up division or corps hospitals, he established one large field hospital, leaving the regimental hos-pitals to act as dressing stations. Located some miles from the nearest railroad point, this hospital was unsuitable as an evacua-tion depot. Furthermore, it was seven miles from the front on the first day, imposing a harrowing ride for the ambulances. This was soon made worse by the destruction of bridges. Since regi-mental medical men stuck with their regimental units, the large hospital was understaffed. At the end of the first day, the pa-tients had not been evacuated from the field hospital to make room for the thousands to come. This stupidity was compounded by an opposite stupidity. When the fighting was over and no new patients were to be expected, the wounded, many of whom could not be moved without harm, were evacuated "with a dogged indifference to consequences."

The Confederate victory added further complications. A large proportion of the wounded had been left on the field over which the Confederates had become the masters, as well as over a num-ber of regimental hospitals crowded with other wounded. On September 1, Medical Inspector Richard Coolidge, who had been sent out from Washington the day before to take control of Medical Department activities, succeeded in arranging a truce. He found Lee's medical director, Dr. Lafayette Guild, courteous and friendly, and it was agreed that the Union wounded be paroled, and might be cared for by their own surgeons until they could be taken through the lines. The Confederates restored to the Union surgeons the greater part of the captured medical supplies and agreed to share captured blankets equally; but Lee had little to offer in the way of foodstuffs and would not permit an enemy supply train to enter his lines.

Three days after the battle some 3,000 wounded men still lay where they had fallen, most of them unfed and practically all without surgical attention. Two days later they still numbered 600. The last convoy of wounded, some of whom had lain six or seven days before being picked up, left the field September 9, three days later. One of these unfortunates had been given water by the Confederates, but had gone without food for six days and seven nights. They had lain through alternating thunderstorms and blistering sunshine, suffering immeasurable agonies. Many reported "Killed in Action" must have died lingering deaths, victims of faulty organization.

The handling of the wounded was fatally slowed down by the villainous conduct of the civilian teamsters hired by the Quartermaster Corps to drive the army's ambulances. Practically every one of them ran away. Responding to the continued and desperate calls for ambulances and supplies, the Surgeon General procured a troop of cavalry which commandeered vehicles on the streets of Washington, to the number of 140 hacks, 40 omnibuses and numbers of beer and delivery trucks, and other vehicles. Government clerks and other civilian volunteers were added to the civilian surgeons arriving from everywhere in response to Secretary Stanton's pleas, and a mighty relief force started out for Centreville and the battlefield. But the drivers were of the same stamp as the earlier deserters. The vehicles carrying supplies were known to include liquor. In the darkness many of the drivers eluded the cavalry escort, broke into the liquor boxes, and turned back to Washington. Because the drivers of some of the hacks were persuaded to do their duty a few reached the battlefield. Even these, along with drivers of additional wagons and ambulances which came out on September 6 and later, behaved abominably. They refused to give water to the wounded; they refused to assist in putting them into the ambulances; they were impudent to the medical officers; they stole blankets and provisions from the scanty stores; some even went through the pockets of their helpless passengers.

From this "frightful state of disorder," Surgeon General Hammond drew the proper deductions. The Army must have an ambulance corps; and the Medical Department, rather than the Quartermaster Corps, must have control of the ambulances and the medical transport. He reminded Secretary Stanton of the plan already submitted and killed by General Halleck; and he humbly urged that some plan be put through before the army had to face its next big battle. But much blood was to color the Southern grass and a vast amount of agitation by outraged civilians was to ensue before the army got more than an approximation of Hammond's requirements.

Meanwhile Lee, taking instant advantage of his victory at Bull Run, moved rapidly northward into Maryland. The Army of Virginia was united with the Army of the Potomac, under General McClellan's command. Hurrying northward, the advance guard made contact with Confederate forces in the passes over South Mountain on September 14. The brisk engagement there would have seemed a big battle earlier. Three days later the main forces of the two armies met on the banks of Antietam Creek, near the village of Sharpsburg, in the battle which caused September 17, 1862, to be known as "the bloodiest day in American history."

Jonathan Letterman had charge of medical activities. Antietam was his first battle, but his administrative talents and his good fortune were considerable. The Medical Department's performance on that field showed real improvement. The greatest piece of luck was that Antietam was a Union victory and the field hospitals were in Union hands. Hardly less fortunate were good weather, good roads and the fact that the Sanitary Commission was able to furnish large quantities of goods to make up for shortages. The medical director's administrative talents were shown in the intelligent organization of his ambulance forces, the foresight with which he tried to improve the supply situation, and the smoothness with which he evacuated the wounded to general hospitals.

Had events moved less swiftly Letterman might well have displayed a perfected field-relief system at Antietam. Early in August he had persuaded McClellan to issue a general order creating an Army of the Potomac ambulance corps. Through a delay in receiving the printed copies of the order it was not put into effect until shortly before the army left Harrison's Landing for Alexandria. Under it the ambulances were taken away from the regiments and organized into corps and division units, to be manned, drivers and all, by soldiers chosen by the Medical Department, and drilled by line officers especially selected for the purpose. The training had shown its value in the fine performance of those few Army of the Potomac ambulance men who had had ambulances to drive at Bull Run. In the short period between Bull Run and Antietam only a beginning could be made in applying the Letterman idea in that part of the army which had formerly been Pope's. Fortunately, the trained ambulance men received additional rolling stock. Some of the ambulances left at Fortress Monroe when the army sailed were recovered. With 200 new ones received just before the battle the total was 300, or one ambulance to each 175 men.

Despite insufficient training of a part of the ambulance force, and despite the fact that the new ambulances arrived too late for proper organization, the battlefield was cleared fairly quickly. All the wounded had been removed from the right wing by two o'clock in the afternoon of the day after the battle and those from the left wing by that night.

Letterman was fully convinced of the advantages of division hospitals, but lacked the time, the tents and the separate personnel to try them out at Antietam. Regimental hospitals were

ordered to merge into divisional units "so far as practicable,"
—an order ignored by the majority of surgeons. Seventy-one
separate field hospitals were set up, most of them in houses and
barns.

The load placed upon these little hospitals was enormous, for
in addition to the 10,000 Union wounded they had to care for
some 4,000 Confederates. Fortunately, Letterman had anticipated
a major action and had supplies on the way from Washington,
Alexandria, and Baltimore. Railroad delays postponed their
prompt arrival, but with the Sanitary Commission to fill the gap
there was little serious suffering.

Realizing that the field hospitals must be cleared if their personnel were to be free to move with the army, the medical director arranged for the evacuation of the wounded to general
hospitals. For those patients too seriously injured to stand transportation he established two field hospitals, in which some 600
men were left. Others were returned to the lines. The rest—some
8,350—were transported to Frederick, where 2,500 wounded
from the September 14 fighting were already established in
improvised general hospitals. The ambulances were kept busy
almost constantly in this evacuation, which was carefully
planned. Many men with arm wounds walked the twenty miles
to Frederick. The ambulances moved on fixed schedules, stopping at Middletown, halfway to their destination, where an army
relief station gave food, drink, and attention to the passengers.
At Frederick those patients who could stand a railway journey
were laid on straw in freight cars and started out for Washington, Baltimore, and Philadelphia hospitals.

The men who could not bear the additional travel were hospitalized at Frederick, which soon became so crowded that two
large tent hospitals, accommodating 1,000 men between them,
had to be set up. It was these tents, and the well-ventilated cow-
sheds used by some of the field hospitals at Antietam, which
taught the Army of the Potomac medical men what they regarded as one of the leading lessons of the war: that surgical
cases treated out-of-doors showed lower mortality and shorter

recovery rates than those treated indoors. It was a lesson generally heeded later in the war.

The Medical Department's Antietam experience gave it reason to feel that it was making progress. However, field hospitals and the surgery performed within them showed need for improved organization; and it was to them that Dr. Letterman turned his attention in October of 1862.

Field relief in the West: 1862

Meanwhile, the Western armies were going through the same stern education in the realities of war, learning from the same mistakes. They had the great advantage, during 1862, of fighting most of their battles on or close to the banks of the Mississippi, the Tennessee, or the Cumberland, which facilitated the evacuation of the sick and wounded. This was offset by the much wider area of operations which complicated communication problems, and by an even greater scarcity of equipment than in the East.

A visitor at Cairo, Illinois, in the spring of 1861 was shocked not to find a single ambulance in the place. He saw a small military expedition sally into enemy territory without a stretcher for the removal of its wounded. On July 1, 1861, Henry W. Bellows, after visiting Cairo and a number of other camps in Ohio, Illinois and Missouri, reported: "We saw no ambulances in any Western camp, and no stretchers." By August at the Battle of Wilson's Creek, Missouri, two ambulances were in service. Since 40 per cent of the 3,000 men were casualties, it took nearly a week to transport the wounded to hospitals. In November, seven months after the war began, the troops massed at Cairo had come into possession of two ambulances. Each regiment now had two stretchers. No unit had undertaken to drill its future ambulance details.

It was this force at Cairo, under General U. S. Grant, which effected the comparatively bloodless capture of Fort Henry on the Tennessee early in February, 1862, and a few days later, after a three-day battle, seized Fort Donelson, the great Confederate fortress on the Cumberland. Fortunately, the ambulance and hospital supplies had been augmented, and the intelligent use of them by Medical Director H. S. Hewitt, a volunteer surgeon, helped to offset a cold spell and the staff's inexperience. The medical organization at Fort Donelson was, at least in outline, a forecast of that which the Army of the Potomac would evolve through months of bitter experience. The regimental hospitals were merged into four field hospitals, three in buildings and the fourth in tents. Dressing stations were maintained close to the battlefield by each regiment. The ambulances, formed into brigade units, shuttled back and forth between the dressing stations and the hospitals.

The plans were good, and they were well executed, but heavy suffering was caused by a fall of temperature to five above zero, heavy casualties in some regiments, and the fact that the enemy controlled for a time a part of the field upon which many Union wounded were lying. In a half day of fighting the 11th Illinois Infantry lost 330 of its 452 effectives; one of its companies, 57 strong, lost 10 killed and 23 wounded. According to one of the injured the Confederates stripped the dead, and even some of the wounded, of their clothing. Left on the field all night this witness' hair froze to the ground. Another man lay on the field for two days; when the stretchermen reached him they had to chop him out of the frozen earth.

The Donelson wounded spent four or five days in the poorly supplied field hospitals and then were removed by steamer to Cairo, Mound City, St. Louis, or Paducah. Hurriedly converted by private relief organizations or the State governments, these river boats were poorly equipped and poorly managed and passage on them was a trying experience for the wounded. Later in the campaign they were much improved.

After evacuating his wounded and resting his men, the triumphant Grant marched his army southward. Disposal of the disabled, during the army's march, worried the new medical director, Surgeon Robert Murray of the Regulars. With only two ambulances per regiment and the sick list mounting, sick and wounded men were being left behind in every village along the way. Supplies were so short that suitable medicines and dressings could not be left for their use. Some patients had to be left lying on a floor, without food or bedding. This was the penalty for carrying on a war of movement at a distance from a base. The only answers were general hospitals deep within the South, or a railroad or steamer hospital service in constant contact with the army. Later both were tried; but in the spring of 1862 these deserted sick men could only grit their teeth and endure.

If the field relief work at Fort Donelson can be termed a qualified success, that at Shiloh can only be called an unqualified failure. Early in the morning, April 6, 1862, Grant's troops were surprised by a terrific Confederate attack. Neither Grant nor his medical director had expected a battle. Furthermore, the brave beginning in medical organization which Dr. Hewitt had displayed at Donelson seems to have been neglected by his successor. In theory there were brigade ambulance trains and brigade field hospitals; but under the hammer of circumstances the medical organization fell apart into regimental units, each struggling to do something in a battle turmoil which came close to anarchy. The military situation was so desperate that the men detailed to the medical department were returned to the ranks, forcing the surgeons "to depend for hospital attendants wholly upon the panic stricken crowd who had ignominiously deserted their colors and fled to the river for protection."

The enemy pushed the Union forces back two miles and captured a large part of the camp, including the regimental hospitals and their equipment. Supplies having been short even before the battle, these losses were serious. The wounded got themselves to the rear, or were brought by friends glad of an excuse to leave the fighting, or they lay where they fell. A few volunteer women nurses went about on the edge of the fighting, trying to help the wounded. They tore up their skirts and used grass and leaves for wound dressings.

With the help of the Army of the Ohio, which arrived that night, the troops recovered the lost ground the next day and recaptured much equipment, and began to do something for the thousands of wounded who had been lying there since the day before. With chaos reigning, it was Dr. B. J. D. Irwin of the Army of the Ohio who conceived the idea of commandeering enough tents from infantry regiments to create a huge field hospital accommodating 2,500 patients. This celebrated hospital—the first field hospital entirely under canvas—was elaborately organized into administrative sections of 125 beds, each subdivided into four wards. Three medical officers, one senior and two junior, were assigned to each section. This tent hospital anticipated a trend which would not begin in the East until after Antietam.

In the meantime the Army of the Tennessee, Grant's force, had set up a large field hospital at Monterey, Tennessee, and was preparing to evacuate its wounded to the North. The plan was duly carried out by a large fleet of river boats, whose equipment and organization showed that the lessons of February had been heeded. A whole fleet of large vessels was outfitted and operated by the United States Sanitary Commission and the Western Sanitary Commission of St. Louis, on the understanding that the government would pay for their rental and furnish ordinary commissary stores while the two commissions would supply surgeons, attendants and such other stores as were necessary. Others of the boats were operated by the Medical Department itself, a triumph over the Quartermaster Corps. All this was to provide a strong contrast to the impending Peninsular campaign. The vessels sent by governments of certain Middle Western States were for the most part well-equipped, but made trouble by refusing to transport wounded from other States. In 1863 the Medical Department took over the floating hospitals of the two commissions and discouraged the further use of State-controlled boats.

During the six months after Shiloh the Army of the Tennessee, using brigade ambulance trains and brigade field hospitals, fought no battle of sufficient dimensions to put its medical system under strain. The Army of the Ohio was not so fortunate. At Perryville, Kentucky, in October, it fought an engagement which, from the medical standpoint, was, if anything, worse conducted than the one at Shiloh. One explanation was the failure of the general to cooperate with his medical director.

In September the Confederate General Braxton Bragg invaded Kentucky, and sent a shiver of fear through the populous cities of the Ohio Valley. To head him off before he reached Louisville, General Don Carlos Buell led the Army of the Ohio on a rapid march northward from Tennessee. As speed was of the utmost importance, most of the medical and hospital wagons were left behind.

The Army of the Ohio was peculiar in having almost no Regular Army surgeons to occupy its administrative posts. It had no regularly organized ambulance and field hospital system. Finally, its commander is said to have withheld information which would have assisted in the medical staff's battle preparations. The results were disastrous. Since there were no hospital tents, the 2,800 wounded occupied every house in the village of Perryville and every farmhouse for ten miles around, making it difficult to attend them properly. With no more medical supplies than the surgeons could carry on their persons, many wounds were not dressed for days. Since all the wells in Perryville were dry, the patients were dirty. The only foods available were the army field rations of hardtack and salt pork, virtually inedible to invalids. Eventually Medical Department and Sanitary Commission supply trains brought relief. At the end of the month General Buell was replaced by Gen. W. S. Rosecrans. He proved as interested in the Medical Department as his predecessor had been bored. Under him the force, now known as the Army of the Cumberland, was to develop a more effective field relief system.

5

Improvement

in

Field

Tactics

TO THE TWENTIETH CENTURY MIND NO STAFF TROOPS OF AN ARMY seem more necessary than the ambulance and hospital corps. It now seems odd that the North should have gone to war with the unspecialized field-relief system, or lack of system, that cost such misery at Fair Oaks and Bull Run. It also seemed odd to some persons then. They agitated for an ambulance corps from the summer of 1861 until Congress gave them an approximation of what they wanted in 1864, exerting continuous suasion and pressure on military men and politicians.

The idea of a specially enlisted ambulance corps seems to have first been conceived by the surgeon of Duryee's Zouaves. On July 3, 1861, he advertised for twenty men for such a "corps" for his regiment. Apparently nothing came of it. On July 15 a volunteer surgeon, B. A. Vanderkief, presented a well-conceived plan for a divisional ambulance organization to the

Surgeon General. It differed from the later Letterman plan in only one essential: medical officers were to be in command rather than line officers, a feature definitely in its favor. It too was stillborn. After the first Bull Run the worried Sanitary Commission officers began a series of conferences with General McClellan looking toward an efficient ambulance service. The general seemed cooperative and the commission decided to ask the War Department for authority to enlist a special corps of nurses in place of the men detailed to hospital duty, and to propose the formation of an ambulance "regiment" for the Army of the Potomac.

In October F. L. Olmsted of the commission was conferring with the Secretary of War on this plan. There was talk of organizing a great ambulance corps of 12,000 men, to serve the whole Army and not the Army of the Potomac alone. But by December nothing had been done, and possibly to avoid further straining the relations of the Medical Department and the commission, Olmsted left the ambulance corps unmentioned in his published *Report to the Secretary of War*.

Dr. Finley was still Surgeon General and the Medical Department was still floundering in the pre-Hammond quagmire. There were no good foreign examples to follow, and the whole question might well have seemed to the authorities one where caution rather than speed was desirable. The French, who had had the most experience with a specialized corps, had left it in the control of quartermaster officers. The French service was hardly an ambulance corps at all, for when the hospitals were full, the ambulance personnel found all their time taken up by hospital nursing. The British had experimented with a special corps in the Crimean War but had staffed it with pensioners too old and too feeble for the strenuous work, and the scheme had been dropped.

The horrors of the Peninsular campaign under Tripler's makeshift ambulance system have been described, and Letterman's attempts to improve matters in August of 1862. Meanwhile, William A. Hammond, the new Surgeon General, was pressing the War Department to adopt a comprehensive scheme for the whole Army. On the eve of the second Bull Run he submitted his proposal for an independent body organized on the basis of six ambulances, six drivers and twelve trained stretcher-men per regiment. For reasons unknown it was pigeon-holed by Secretary Stanton at the insistence of General Halleck, his chief military adviser.

At this juncture the greatest champion of ambulance reform, Dr. Henry I. Bowditch of Boston, entered the lists. His zeal was born of personal grief. His son had fallen wounded upon the battlefield, "and it is believed *no one connected with* an Ambulance Corps ever approached him there." Despite a serious abdominal wound Lieutenant Bowditch was brought off the field on a horse. When an ambulance at last reached him it was without water, and its driver would procure none. Young Bowditch died of his injury, and his father went into battle against the War Department's apathy. He never ceased his efforts until the Ambulance Corps Act of 1864 was on the statute books.

Dr. Bowditch opened his campaign with a visit to Surgeon General Hammond, who told him of his own repeated attempts to stir the War Department to action. As a civilian, Bowditch could do many things that would have been insubordinate in a surgeon general. He laid siege to General Halleck, who admitted that Stanton had left the ambulance corps matter up to him, and finally conceded that if General McClellan would write a letter asking for an ambulance corps he would consider that "sufficient to decide the matter of expediency." With Olmsted's approval Bowditch then called on McClellan, who was most co-operative. He unhesitatingly signed a letter giving it as his opinion that a specially enlisted and specially trained hospital corps should be established for the whole Army.

The triumphant Dr. Bowditch, returning to Washington, called upon Stanton with two co-workers, a Mr. Pierce and a Mr. Welles. The Secretary of War promised to do exactly as Halleck might direct. He cheered his hearers by stating that he was willing even to authorize a draft on the Treasury, since he believed

Congress would undoubtedly sustain any "humane proceeding." But when Pierce called on Halleck he was coldly received. After reading McClellan's letter the general merely remarked: "Well, Mr. Pierce, you will please now send in your propositions in writing." When the shocked Pierce rejoined that, at the general's request, he had already sent in well-written propositions three times, he was "sternly" told: "Send in your propositions in writing, Sir," and the interview was over. Convinced now that the "faithless" Halleck deserved "the curses of all humane men," Dr. Bowditch turned his attention to promoting his ideas among the public.

Almost at once the influential *American Medical Times* offered strong editorial support, pointing out that even the despised "rebels" had a system of permanently detailed ambulance men, chosen because of their qualifications. In December the Boston Board of Trade offered its support, following the *Boston Medical and Surgical Journal* which had presented the arguments for an ambulance corps as early as October. Another medical journal of national circulation, the *Medical and Surgical Reporter* of Philadelphia, had come out against the existing system, directing its fire particularly at control of the ambulances by the Quartermaster Corps.

Before the ambulance corps question reached the floor of Congress again the Medical Department was tested by the two bloody engagements of December, 1862: Fredericksburg in the East and Stone's River, or Murfreesboro, in the West. Had they been as badly handled as earlier battles the ambulance bill might have had better treatment from the Senate.

Dr. Letterman improves Eastern field methods

The Peninsular campaign had shown the need for an ambulance corps; an ambulance organization had been worked out in August; it had functioned fairly well at Antietam; and now, Letterman, Medical Director of the Army of the Potomac, by drilling and improved details, was perfecting it as far as was possible with men detailed from troops of the line. The battles of 1862 had shown at least a temporary failure of stores in emergencies. Letterman reorganized the supply system on a divisional basis, thus getting away from the waste and confusion of regimental issues. The battles had also shown that regimental hospitals meant administrative confusion and bad surgery and that administrative assistance for the army and corps medical directors was essential for proper coordination and supervision of their work. By assigning officers to serve as medical inspectors under himself and his corps medical directors, Letterman mended this latter flaw.

On October 30, 1862, he set up a system of division hospitals and provided for division of labor among the medical officers attached to each. Under the old system operations were performed by any surgeon who felt like trying his hand at them; and anybody or nobody kept the necessary records and administered the hospital supplies. Under the new plan one assistant surgeon of each regiment conducted a dressing station at the front; the remainder of the divisional medical staff gathered at the hospital. There one officer was assigned to keeping records; another to supervising food, shelter, clothing and bedding; others functioned as wound dressers. About one in fifteen was a member of the surgical "team" that performed operations. When the new system was first tried, at Fredericksburg, there was heartburning because everyone wanted to be an operator. Nearly a year later many regimental medical men still considered the division-hospital system a slur upon their capacities. But the tests of battle showed it to be a major advance in military medicine.

The weeks of inaction that had proved so valuable for perfecting the Army of the Potomac's ambulance and field organization had convinced President Lincoln of McClellan's unworthiness for high command. Eight days after Letterman's field-hospital circular was issued McClellan was replaced by General Ambrose Burnside, whose rashness was to set off his predecessor's caution. On December 13, 1862, Burnside ordered a frontal assault on Lee's Army of Northern Virginia, intrenched on the low hills south of the little town of Fredericksburg, Virginia. The formations sent into the attack lost almost 1,200 killed and 9,000 wounded in the single day's action, but failed to open the road to Richmond.

Letterman's renovated ambulance corps gave a good account of itself. The ambulances crossed the Rappahannock with the troops. When the fighting began "the stretcher bearers pushed forward even to the skirmishers, and . . . their zeal in the performance of their task was unparalleled in the history of this war." Surgeons on the field agreed that the wounded were taken to the hospitals with great speed and efficiency, though certain nonmilitary persons disputed these claims. Walt Whitman wrote that he had talked to a man who lay on the cold, December ground for two days before he was picked up, and a "female" nurse reported a number of men who had remained there for "several" days.

The same disparity characterizes judgments on the field hospitals. The medical officers were pleased with what seemed to them a brilliant achievement in hospital management; the Sanitary Commission's agent applauded; and the *Tribune* correspondent reported that "the best possible care" was being given the wounded. But Clara Barton did not like what she saw, and Walt Whitman deplored the lack of cots, the stacks of severed arms and legs, and the filthy state of the patients.

The other great December battle was fought at Stone's River, near Murfreesboro, Tennessee, December 31 to January 3. There the Army of the Cumberland lost some 12,000 men, or more than 25 per cent of its strength. The medical staff, which had won no laurels at Perryville, seem to have acquitted themselves well. There was no fixed ambulance organization for the whole army, but one of its corps, the 14th, had an ambulance and field hospital organization approximating Letterman's and the ambulance men of the other corps also won praise.

Early in February, 1863, the House of Representatives passed an ambulance corps bill embodying the ideas of the Sanitary Commission and Dr. Bowditch. It provided for the special enlistment of 10 to 12,000 men, and the commissioning of 4 to 500 new officers as noncombatants to serve wholly under the Medical Department. The bill had General McClellan's approval; but with Secretary Stanton and General Halleck thumbing it down as "impractical" it died in committee.

A month later Surgeon General Hammond tried to influence all the armies to adopt Letterman's Army of the Potomac ambulance organization. A circular letter describing it was sent to the medical administrative officers, in the hope that they would persuade their respective commanding generals to institute it.

Meanwhile the medical organization of the Army of the Potomac was being brought to new heights of efficiency. After Fredericksburg the morale of Burnside's disheartened troops, encamped once more on the north banks of the Rappahannock, was raised by a new commander, "Fighting Joe" Hooker, one of the unfortunate Burnside's loudest critics. Hooker showed poor generalship as a campaigner but he knew how to build the health and spirit of his men. He gave them furloughs, added vegetables to their ration, and in other ways showed interest in their welfare. Under him the ambulance details were drilled daily and Dr. Letterman was enabled to set up huge tent hospitals capable of caring for 8,000 patients. These hospitals were located at Acquia Creek, Potomac Creek, and Brooks Station, from which evacuations could conveniently be made. They were organized by divisions, but grouped together to make a corps hospital with one medical officer in command of all. The system was further improved by the detailing of a line officer to act as quartermaster and commissary of hospitals.

When these dispositions met their test at the Battle of Chancellorsville in the opening days of May, Confederate victory made for a mixed result. There seems to have been no difficulty in caring for the 8,000 men brought into the division hospitals, but the 1,200 left on the field when the army retreated, or captured in the advance depots, suffered considerably. Many lay in thickets for two or three days before being found by the stretchermen. Some were burned to death when exploding shells set the pines on fire. Those in the captured hospitals were well treated by the Confederates, but a shortage of supplies was felt during the ten days before their exchange. It is hard to see how the Medical Department could have improved its service at Chancellorsville. The lesson of that battle was simply that it pays to win a battle and to retain command of the field.

The contending armies rested during the remainder of May. In June, Lee moved northward for the invasion of Pennsylvania, pursued through the blazing summer heat by the Army of the Potomac. On July 1, 2, and 3 the two armies fought the epic Battle of Gettysburg. There Dr. Letterman commanded a magnificent organization of 650 medical officers, 1,000 ambulances, and close to 3,000 ambulance drivers and stretchermen. The ambulance and stretcher work approached perfection despite the huge number of wounded removed from the field and taken several miles to the field hospitals. Each night the day's casualties, except for a few beyond the picket lines, were recovered and taken to the rear. By the morning of July 4, 14,000 Union wounded had been removed, and in the course of the day a few hundred more were brought in under the fire of enemy snipers.

The field hospitals at Gettysburg failed to earn the compliments bestowed upon the ambulance corps. The medical supply trains were inexplicably detained within the army's lines some miles from Gettysburg, which helps account for the scarcities at the hospitals in the first days after the battle; but the chief explanation was the unprecedented and overwhelming number of the disabled. To the enormous total of 14,500 Union men were added more than 6,000 Confederates. Before the first rush of battlefield surgery was finished the army moved south in pursuit of the enemy. Since another big battle was expected, Letterman left only 106 medical officers out of his 650 to care for the 21,000 patients. This meant approximately 300 patients per doctor, and since only a third of the medical officers were operating surgeons, this meant some 900 cases each.

For six days only beef and hardtack were available, but then the army supplies arrived along with supplies brought in by the civilian commissions, which had already helped to relieve scarcities at the field hospitals. Many "corps hospitals" (the division hospitals being so grouped) were moved out of the woods into the sunlight, where their patients were immediately benefited. Others, which had been without hospital tents, acquired them. Still others were put in buildings in Gettysburg where nearly every house formed a hospital ward. In these surroundings, and eating the chicken broth, the mutton soup, and the craved-for fresh vegetables prepared by the Christian Commission and other "relief ladies," the Union wounded began to improve despite lice and flies.

The Army of the Potomac had lost as many men in one battle as an army might be expected to lose in a campaign. Fortunately it was not destined during the remainder of 1863 to fight any engagement which placed the least strain on its ambulance corps and field hospitals. The only developments were administrative. The Letterman ambulance system reached its full development on August 24 with the issuance of General Order 85, which made the army corps the normal ambulance unit and laid down further details for the management of the ambulances. The system was a makeshift, but its performance at Gettysburg had shown it to work. The Medical Department had the right to examine the men offered for the ambulance detail, and reject those they considered unfit. Separate insignia, inverted green chevrons for the mounted sergeants, of whom there was one for every three ambulances, and a single green chevron for privates of the corps gradually developed *esprit de corps.*

Early in January, 1864, Jonathan Letterman ceased to be medical director of the Army of the Potomac. He had organized an ambulance service which was being cited as a model for the other field armies; he had reorganized the medical supply system; and had moulded an efficient division field hospital organization. He was relieved at his own request which, coming at the time when the reforming Surgeon General Hammond was being driven from office by the "old guard" suggests that Letterman, a reformer too, immolated himself upon the funeral pyre of his chief.

The medical services of the Western armies met even severer tests in 1863. In the spring and early summer Grant's Army of the Tennessee fought a brief campaign of maneuver and conducted the successful siege of Vicksburg. Rosecrans' Army of the Cumberland worked its way over the Cumberland Mountains to Chattanooga, only to meet a shattering defeat at Chickamauga in September. Under the command of G. H. Thomas, the Army of the Cumberland redeemed itself in November when, joined with the Army of the Tennessee commanded by W. T. Sherman they won the victory at Chattanooga which opened the way for the drive on Atlanta the following year. Since the Western armies were campaigning in Louisiana, Arkansas and elsewhere at the same time, they faced far greater administrative and communications problems than the Army of the Potomac.

The earlier fumbling and divided management of the Medical Department administration in the West had given way, before the end of 1862, to a smooth and harmonious system centered in the office of R. C. Wood, the Assistant Surgeon General, first established at St. Louis and later at Louisville. As the 1863 campaigns were about to open, such difficulties as there were centered around Dr. H. S. Hewitt, medical director of the Army of the Tennessee, an intelligent and well informed, but conspicuously tactless administrator. Grant answered an inquiry of Surgeon General Hammond: "It is a great question whether one person in ten could be so well taken care of at home as in the army here." Nevertheless the irascible Dr. Hewitt was replaced by Surgeon Madison Mills.

On March 30, 1863, only five days after the Surgeon General's message extolling the Letterman ambulance system, it was adopted for the Army of the Tennessee; and on April 8 the divisional hospital system was also adopted. Thus reorganized, Grant's medical troops seem to have experienced no difficulties during the campaign of maneuver which preceded the siege of

Vicksburg. The siege presented none of the problems of pitched battle and no strain was placed upon either the ambulance or the hospitals. The hospital arrangements reflected Grant's annoyance with the evacuations of the disabled northward, which had followed each of the major battles of 1862. To maintain control over the sick and wounded, so that he could use those discharged as fit, as replacements, he had the slightly injured cared for in the division hospitals at Millikan's Bend, close to Vicksburg. The more serious cases were sent to Memphis (where general hospitals capable of handling 5,000 men had been set up), in three river steamers assigned the Medical Department as hospital transports. When the State of Ohio attempted a raid upon the field hospitals, intending to take the Ohio wounded back to Ohio, as had been done the year before, its agents were stopped by an order of Secretary Stanton himself, forbidding them to take a single soldier unless accommodations were lacking at Memphis.

Eastrond, improper location of the hospitals and the lack of a well equipped supply base made Chickamauga one of the worst medical failures of the war. The battlefield lies some twelve miles southeast of Chattanooga, from which it is separated by the small mountain range called Missionary Ridge. Medical Director Perin located his "corps hospitals" at Crawfish Springs, to take advantage of its plentiful supply of good water needed for the water-dressings used at that time. But this was some three miles south of the nearest, or right wing of the Union forces, and had Missionary Ridge between them and the army's base at Chattanooga, exposing the hospitals to capture by the enemy.

On September 19, the first of the two days of battle, things went badly. Congestion on the single road between the battlefield and Crawfish Springs slowed down the ambulance traffic. This was complicated by the northward shift of the fighting, which increased the travel distance by about a mile. Nevertheless the 4,500 wounded had been removed by midnight. The next day the fighting moved further north, and the hospitals were bombarded, the Confederates claiming that they had mistaken the red hospital flags for "battle flags." Despite frantic efforts to remove the injured to Chattanooga many were left upon the field, where they were captured along with the patients of the Crawfish Springs hospitals.

When the smoke of battle cleared, General Rosecrans' unwisdom in risking a major battle without a suitable advance supply base was manifest. Railroad communications with Nashville were cut by the enemy, shutting off relief from that direction and putting the hospitals in and about Chattanooga in a serious plight. Surgeon Israel Moses, ordered to prepare hospitals for 3,000 men the day before the battle, had found supplies and shelter available for only 500. During the battle 4,000 patients poured in upon him and soon the number rose to 7,500. Every house and shed in town was full, and makeshift tent hospitals were set up outside the town, whose frequent changes of location intensified the confusion and suffering.

Medical Department affairs were conducted so smoothly at the subsequent series of engagements called the Battle of Chattanooga (Nov. 23, 24, 25, 1863), that little was ever put down on paper about them.

The Ambulance Corps Act of 1864

On December 23, 1863, just a month after the battle around Chattanooga, a new ambulance corps measure was introduced in the Senate by Senator Henry Wilson of Massachusetts, chairman of the Military Affairs Committee. That committee's adverse report on the House bill of the previous session had failed to still the clamor for ambulance legislation. Medical societies continued to present memorials. Massachusetts passed a monster petition whose first signer was Governor Andrew. As Wilson's bill was being introduced, propagandist articles were in press in two important magazines, supporting the type of organization urged by Dr. Bowditch in his pamphlet, *A Brief Plea for an*

Ambulance System, and for which Greeley was thundering editorially in his *Tribune.*

The reformers wanted a specially enlisted corps, under Medical Department control, its ambulances and supply trains no longer subject to the Quartermaster Corps. The New York *Tribune* admitted that the Letterman system as used in the Army of the Potomac represented a real advance, but held that its unequal performance among the different army corps of that force showed the need for a uniform plan for the whole Army.

To fend off charges of mere humanitarianism, Dr. Bowditch and his comrades-in-reform emphasized the practical military value of their ideas. A "real" ambulance corps would strengthen the Army in two ways: it would save the lives of soldiers, who would later return to duty; and it would obviate any necessity for soldiers leaving the ranks to escort wounded comrades to the hospital. The first claim was the more difficult to prove; but the second touched on a scandal. Dr. Bowditch told of seeing a wounded soldier escorted off the field by eight sound men—four to carry the stretcher and four to relieve the bearers when they wearied. Forty men left the battlefield of Gettysburg to carry General Dan Sickles the twenty-five miles to Westminster, Pennsylvania. Together with the tendency of men whose wounds were hardly more than scratches, to leave the field, this often meant serious depletions of strength at critical battle points.

The Wilson ambulance corps bill fell short of the Bowditch ideal but constituted a real advance. It was a compromise of the reformers with the War Department and the generals. In effect, it gave statutory basis to the Letterman system and extended it to all armies. Under it there was no special enlistment and detailed men were still the only personnel, but the Medical Department was assured the right to choose and examine the men to be assigned. The Quartermaster Corps still controlled the ambulances and horses as part of the Army's transportation system, but their use for any other purpose than carrying sick soldiers and, in emergencies, medical supplies, was prohibited.

Persons other than ambulance corps men were forbidden to assist the wounded from the field.

The bill was supported by the advocates of an ambulance corps, and after a few inconsequential changes by the Senate, passed both houses and became law on March 11, 1864. At last the Army had a legally constituted ambulance service which it probably would not have had but for the civilian reformers, led by Dr. Bowditch. The principles of the Letterman plan and the Ambulance Corps Act of 1864 formed the basis of the ambulance organization of most of the armies of the world down to World War I. The German system used in the War of 1870 was a "close adaptation" of ours, and the American surgeon J. Marion Sims was decorated by France for having introduced it into the French Army during that war.

With the exception of Clara Barton's, opinions on the ambulance and field work of the Union army in 1864 were highly laudatory. Writing in 1871, an Englishman ventured the opinion that "In the last year of the war the American soldiers were treated better than ever soldiers have been treated before or since." Thomas A. McParlin, medical director of the Army of the Potomac, was so pleased with the work done in the Wilderness campaign that he found it possible to compliment even the Quartermaster Corps for its "perfect cooperation." Nevertheless there is considerable evidence of preventable suffering during the summer campaign of 1864.

This is partly attributable to that unfortunate section of the Ambulance Corps Act which, by making the number of ambulances dependent upon the size of a regiment, lowered the number available for the Army as a whole. The force which crossed the Rapidan on the night of May 3, 1864, had some 20,000 more men than the army at Gettysburg, but 400 fewer ambulances—1,000 at Gettysburg and only 600 at the Wilderness. This discrepancy was made worse by the constant movement of the army in May and June, 1864, which put a greater strain on the vehicles. But the principal troubles arose from the appalling numbers of wounded.

Grant was determined to push head-on against the Confederate army, grinding Lee down with the attrition of superior numbers, and holding him too closely engaged to send reinforcements to Georgia, where Sherman was driving a wedge between the seaboard and the Gulf States. As a result the Medical Department had to evacuate 46,000 seriously wounded and 11,000 sick men between May 4 and July 31. The number of injured almost equals the total wounded in all the Army of the Potomac's battles from Bull Run through Fredericksburg.

This had not been foreseen in the Medical Department's preparations. Resiliency and adaptiveness, however, marked the department's struggles with circumstances. A special order of April 12 had improved the organization of the medical staff: surgeons-in-chief of brigades and divisions were designated by the army commander, "thus rendering their position to a great extent independent of the caprices of brigade and division commanders." The medical director had formed a personal staff consisting of an assistant medical director, two inspectors, a purveyor, an assistant purveyor, and a statistical officer.

Realizing that the seriously wounded could not be cared for close to the battlefield during a campaign of movement, McParlin set up at Fredericksburg a "depot," or evacuation hospital, which could be moved further south to keep it near the troops. The various divisions' hospital trains were instructed to follow immediately behind their respective divisions. Half the ambulances of each division's train were instructed to follow their division, the remainder moving with the general supply train, which at the Wilderness was only 5 miles behind the troops, not 25 as at Gettysburg. But as events were to show, there was not enough of anything. The number of ambulances had been reduced; the supply train had been cut in an effort to free the army's movements; even the number of doctors proved insufficient.

During the early spring the 60 officers and 2,300 men of the ambulance force were busy with drills, and with attempts to improve their equipment by repairing harness and installing spare parts in the vehicles. It was a much improved ambulance corps which crossed the Rapidan. But the great Battle of the Wilderness, fought on the old Chancellorsville field, May 5-7, tested it severely, and when Grant swung around to the southeast for the mighty slaughters at Spotsylvania Court House on May 12 and at Cold Harbor on June 1-3, the system all but broke down.

At the Wilderness it was difficult to find many of the wounded in the dense growth. As at Chancellorsville, the woods caught fire burning 200 wounded to death. But most of the injured were gotten into the division hospitals quickly. When it was decided to evacuate the serious cases to the depot hospital 7,000 patients had to be carried to Fredericksburg. Five days later, at Spotsylvania, another great battle was fought with many of the ambulances still evacuating men from the Wilderness.

An innovation at Spotsylvania was the first serious attempt to enforce the rule, hitherto ignored, that no one should leave the field except under the care of the ambulance corps. Under General Meade's orders a provost guard of cavalry followed along behind the infantry, driving the stragglers and wounded ahead of them, even using their sabers at times. Only those too badly injured to walk escaped this pressure. Since the stretchermen were inadequate to carry the 6,000 wounded, and the distance to the dressing stations was unusually long, and some of the stretchermen proved cowardly and negligent, this measure had unfortunate results.

The new restrictions upon the number of ambulances also proved unfortunate. The army was in motion and the wounded had to be sent to Fredericksburg, but many of the ambulances detached after the Wilderness had not reported back. From the Quartermaster Corps the Medical Department got hundreds of clumsy vans, supplemented by 56 spring-wagons used for staff-officers' baggage. The standard four-wheel ambulance had been criticized for its crudities: it lacked rollers to ease the loading of the wounded; had no head cushion, and its springs were stiff. But compared to an army wagon it was luxurious. The movements of these wagon- and ambulance-loads of wounded over the corduroy roads were marked by the screams of tortured men, some of whom begged the drivers to shoot them. Patients who had to endure that agonized ride to Fredericksburg did not do well. They proved more subject to bone infections, secondary hemorrhage, broken adhesions, and "prostration of the vital power."

The situation worsened toward the end of May, when the army moved down to the North Anna and Cold Harbor. Grant's insistence on keeping the slightly wounded with the army meant a strain on the ambulances, which were now picking up additional loads of sick men and sunstroke cases. Appeals to Washington for additional ambulances met some response, enough being sent to bring the army's total up to 800; but many were old and defective, and their civilian drivers proved to be of the same stamp as those who had disgraced themselves at the second Bull Run. On May 20 the *Tribune's* correspondent cited the number of wounded with the army as the reason why Grant had not been able to move south and make contact with Butler's Army of the James. Removal of the depot hospital on May 30 from Fredericksburg to McClellan's old base at White House shortened the lines of communication.

When the division hospital trains pulled out to follow their divisions in the Wilderness campaign, they left behind them the best field hospitals the army had ever known. In the winter camp at Brandy Station, hospitals had been gaily decorated bowers, resembling "pavilions built for some rural fete," where men lay on real cots and basked in the warmth of fireplaces while they consumed such delicacies as jellies and canned fruits. Even Walt Whitman, who had been so shocked by the field hospitals of two years before, found them good. Now the division hospitals were launched upon a fierce campaign in which equipment had to be held to a minimum. Under the circumstances, the service they maintained was good; and the organization worked out was superior to anything that preceded it. The last vestige of the regimental hospital was cast aside when regimental hospital wagons were abolished, to shorten the wagon train.

The brigade operating team, headed by the chief surgeon of the brigade as principal operator, was all that was left of the brigade medical organization. The Letterman division-hospital system, with a few improvements, was what remained. A typical division hospital train consisted of fourteen army wagons and four medical wagons, their contents being twenty-two hospital tents and the medical supplies and surgical equipment which would ordinarily be sufficient for the care of the 7,000 to 8,000 men in the division. In the summer of 1864 a small detail of medical officers and attendants would set up three or four hospital tents at the end of each day's travel. At this "Ambulance hospital," as the innovation was called, the slightly wounded who were being kept with the army, the sunstroke cases and the men who fell sick during the day received care. Those needing more than minor attention were evacuated to the depot hospital. During battle the full division hospitals would be set up; the divisions of an army corps grouped their tents together; the four operating teams, composed of three men each, would prepare for action. Since experience had taught that field hospitals must not be crowded with old cases, all but the slightly disabled were usually out of the division hospitals and on their way to the depot hospital within forty-eight hours after the battle. At the dressing stations only rough dressings, whisky and opium pills were to be had; at the division hospitals more thorough examinations were made and emergency surgery was undertaken; but a large proportion of the operations were postponed until the patient could reach the comparative security of the depot.

The division hospitals performed their limited function well, and after the first few weeks of the campaign were able to offer their patients ice, lemons, and nightclothes. But the performance of the depot hospital, especially during the first few days after the Wilderness, left something to be desired, and excited the shocked criticism of some of the civilian volunteers who flocked there to serve as doctors or nurses. Tents, food, and supplies were wanting, but above all military surgeons and attendants. McParlin was able to furnish only 40 men to attend the 7,000 Wilderness-wounded set down by the ambulance men in an old warehouse, the "receiving hospital" where some lay for days waiting for the overworked surgeons to get to them. Other patients were distributed through hundreds of houses and buildings in the town. Many of these crowded and ill-smelling "wards" were in charge of inexperienced civilian volunteer doctors and nurses, who did not know how to draw even the inadequate ration then available.

McParlin's original intention had been to evacuate most of these patients to northern general hospitals after their first needs had been seen to. This was blocked by a lack of ambulances. There were not enough to carry more than a tenth of the men the nine miles to Belle Plain, where they could be put aboard hospital steamers. The railroad to Acquia Creek was unguarded, and was considered unsafe. Army wagons were called into service to carry groaning and swearing patients to Belle Plain, while groups of the "walking-wounded" were marched there. After Clara Barton had aroused her political friends in Washington, the Quartermaster General came down to Fredericksburg and directed the opening of the rail service to Acquia Creek. As the Spotsylvania wounded were now being added to the already overflowing wards, it was a great boon that the evacuations could begin in volume on May 22. Within a few days affairs were running smoothly, so smoothly that the eminent civilian, Dr. W. T. G. Morton, could find only praise for the depot hospital. On May 28 all the wounded had been removed from Fredericksburg, and the staff and equipment of the hospital were embarked for White House.

During its two weeks under its 300 tents at White House the depot hospital served wounded from the North Anna and Cold Harbor without difficulties. The daily, and sometimes hourly, ambulance trains from the front brought men who were sent north by hospital boat as soon as they were able to travel.

Between June 12 and June 16 the Army of the Potomac

crossed the James River to assault Petersburg, considered the strategic key to Richmond. The new base of the army was set up on June 20 at City Point, a bare nine mile from Petersburg, with which it was connected by railway. Its location on the James River made it accessible to shipping. After the attempt on Petersburg on July 31 failed, the two stalemated armies resorted to something like the trench warfare of the first World War until the following April 2. The soldiers occupied trenches and dugouts, and kept their heads down.

In such a war medical arrangements were simple and benefited from the stability of the lines. The wounded man had his first dressing in a carefully located advance station, protected by earthworks or logs; an ambulance, from a sheltered divisional ambulance picket, carried him the short distance to the railroad, where he was laid on a bed of straw in a freight car and sent off to City Point. Unless his wound could not be expected to heal before some months, or a change of climate seemed desirable, he would remain there until he recovered and could return to his regiment.

The City Point depot hospital, a merger of five corps hospitals, was not much to boast of during its first two weeks, the staff being too busy to keep it clean. But it quickly became the outstanding field hospital of the war, well equipped for 6,000 patients and capable of caring for 10,000 during a warm-weather emergency. Although there was a depot head, the functioning administrative unit was the staff of each corps hospital which, in turn, was subdivided into division hospitals. At first the depot hospital was housed solely in tents. But log houses, or "pavilions," fifty feet by twenty feet, were built in anticipation of cold weather. Ultimately the entire establishment consisted of 90 such pavilions and 324 hospital tents. Descriptions of the equipment sound fabulous. There were 6,000 iron beds; two steam engines pumped the water for a camp water system; the streets were graded and lined by "corduroyed" sidewalks; "contrabands" operated a steam laundry capable of handling 6,000 pieces a week. On dusty days a sprinkling cart laid the dust; and two fire engines were ready to fight fires. The hospital's planning was well nigh perfect except for the latrines. These were open ditches, and even in the opinion of a man of 1864, located too close to the tents. Swarms of flies were mentioned, along with the incidence of typhoid fever. But mosquito nets were hung on frame works over the beds and the latrines were treated with sulphate of iron, without which the typhoid might have been worse.

Each corps hospital had its dispensary, commissary storehouse, general and special diet kitchens, convalescent dining room and Sanitary Commission station. In each division hospital (there were ordinarily three divisions in a corps) one medical officer had charge of food and shelter, an "executive officer" transmitted and saw to the execution of orders, and three "prescribing surgeons" treated the patients. Records and reports were the duty of a surgeon called the "Recorder." Although contract surgeons were used to some extent in 1864, the regimental medical men were not withdrawn from the hospital and ordered to accompany the troops until March, 1865.

The food seems to have been unusually good and plentiful. A supposedly typical dinner consisted of "roast beef, nice boiled potatoes, fresh butter, good bread, and tomatoes. . . . For dessert: lemon and cranberry pie, water melon, ice cream." This diet was made possible by the stationary front beside a navigable river, the liberality of the relief commissions, and the tax on newspaper vendors and sutlers, which General Meade imposed in February, 1864, to raise additional funds for hospital food and comforts. Of the $20,000 which this tax had brought in by November the lion's share went to the purveyors for hospitals; the rest was divided between the medical directors of independent commands, and the corps medical directors.

Some criticism was levelled in 1864 at the transportation of the wounded northward. Hospital steamers were frequently commandeered by the Quartermaster's Corps for nonmedical uses and returned in bad condition. The Surgeon General finally persuaded the Secretary of War to issue an ironclad order forbidding such withdrawals, even by General Grant himself. Surgeon General Barnes consented to Grant's use of the well equipped hospital steamers only when he realized that his refusal would delay Grant's crossing of the James River a fortnight. Barnes then used ordinary transports to remove the Wilderness-Cold Harbor wounded to general hospitals.

The result was considerable discomfort for the wounded. The food, which could be prepared only in large caldrons, was poor; and other equipment was deficient. On one vessel a single urinal had to serve for all the patients. In the absence of any basins for washing wounds a tin cup from the engine room had to be used, and men were later seen drinking from it. But after the hurried evacuations from Acquia Creek, Belle Plain, and White House conditions improved. Once the base was established at City Point four "fine" hospital steamers called regularly. With two which plied to Fortress Monroe enough bed space was available so that ordinary transports were seldom resorted to. These boats operated under a Medical Director General of Transportation at Philadelphia, who was kept informed of the number of available beds in the various general hospitals and could direct a ship, accordingly, to Washington, Point Lookout, Annapolis, Baltimore, Philadelphia or New York.

The railroad transportation of the Medical Department in the East continued to be crude down to the end of the war. The hospital trains from Petersburg to City Point in 1864 were made up of freight cars whose floors were covered with straw. The ride was mercifully short, but when men began to be sent into the depot hospital from as far away as Burkesville, Virginia, such transport, aggravated by inefficient loading and handling of the trains, caused suffering. Early in 1865 real hospital cars, similar to those in the West, were used in these runs to City Point; but they were reserved for the worst cases and were too few in number to make any perceptible change.

Western campaigns: 1863–1865

In the West, in the Army of the Tennessee, although the Letterman system, promulgated in March, 1863, had been even more generally adapted than in the Army of the Potomac, complaints continued to be made of the abuse of ambulances and hospital tents by the quartermasters. In the Army of the Cumberland there was a considerable medical lag behind the other large armies. Dr. George Cooper, its medical director, tried hard to bring his force into line with the best Eastern practice.

Early in the campaign of 1864 Cooper reorganized the ambulance system, put the supply system on a brigade basis and created a real division-hospital scheme to replace the so-called "divisional system," which was merely a cluster of brigade hospitals. He was much annoyed by the reluctance of the colonels to comply with the provisions of the Ambulance Corps Act for detailing to the Medical Department men of its own choice. Another difficulty was the weakness of the horses and mules which pulled its ambulances and supply wagons. These animals had come so near to starvation while Chattanooga was isolated that they never fully recovered their strength.

The military operations of 1864 were such as to facilitate the evacuation of the sick and wounded to general hospitals. From May until September, General Sherman, starting from the vicinity of Chattanooga, led the combined Armies of the Tennessee, the Cumberland, and the Ohio down the line of the Western and Atlanta Railroad, to Atlanta. His two principal field armies had different ways of meeting the problem of caring for the many sick and wounded which the battles and vitamin deprivations of this campaign produced. The Army of the Tennessee gave initial care in its division hospitals, then sent patients to a series of evacuation hospitals where they recovered or waited to be sent north. Down to the end of June, that is, during the first two months of the campaign, the 15th Army Corps had sent sick and wounded to such hospitals at Huntsville, Alabama, and Resaca,

Allatoonce Pass, and Rome, all in Georgia. By June 30 many of the sick left at Huntsville had rejoined their regiments.

A novelty, contributed by the Army of the Cumberland, was a "travelling general hospital" which followed the army down the railroad, serving the same function as the Army of the Tennessee's hospitals, but keeping all the sick and wounded together until they were either evacuated or returned to duty. This great hospital of 100 large tents, equipped for 1,000 patients, won praise for its excellent administration and the comparatively high quality of its food, the latter made possible by the appointment of a special commissary and the assistance of the Sanitary Commission. It cared for 15,500 wounded and 43,000 sick. Of these 1,200 died, 26,000 were sent north, and the remainder returned to their units. The hospital was established for varying lengths of time at six places in Georgia: Ringold, Resaca, Big Shanty, Marietta, Vining's Station, and Atlanta.

The systematic evacuations of the wounded by railroad were probably the most interesting medical feature of the Atlanta campaign. These represented an evolution in hospital transportation which had been going on in the West since the first year of the war. Although two specially fitted hospital cars were put in service by the Western Sanitary Commission in Missouri in October 1861, credit for the first regularly operated hospital train belongs to Dr. Elisha Harris of the Sanitary Commission. During the emergency after the Battle of Perryville, in the fall of 1862, the commission utilized a car in which some of the more seriously wounded could be brought to Louisville. In it thirty litters were suspended from rubber "tugs" which took up the jolts of railroad travel. Some "invalid chairs" were also provided, and a pantry was furnished with medicines, utensils, beverages, food, towels, socks, and blankets. At least one of these cars for reclining patients was attached to a "hospital train," staffed and controlled by the commission, which regularly operated on the Nashville-to-Louisville run throughout most of 1863. In August, 1863, this facility was supplemented by a Medical Department train, prepared by Medical Director

George E. Cooper of the Army of the Cumberland upon orders of General Rosecrans. The car "invented" by Cooper suggests the standard Pullman. An arrangement of slats converted ordinary day-coach seats into "lower berths." Litters hanging from braces attached to the side walls formed "uppers." It was a train made up of two of these cars, some passenger coaches, and a number of freight cars fitted out with beds, that ran to Stevenson, Alabama, in the hectic weeks after Chickamauga to evacuate the half-starved wounded of that battle.

The mortality among men transported by hospital train was so very low in 1863 that additional cars of an improved model were prepared for 1864, and the Army of the Cumberland took over the management of those previously in the hands of the commission. General Thomas was especially considerate to the new service, assigning his best engines, rolling stock and engineers to three trains that ran from Nashville to the front. To notify enemy patrols or train wreckers, the smokestacks, cabs, and locomotive tenders of the hospital trains were painted a glaring scarlet, while at night three red lanterns were hung beneath the headlight. Morgan and Forrest, the Confederate cavalry leaders, were said to have given orders to let the trains alone. At any rate, they were never wrecked or captured.

While Sherman's army was fighting its way to Atlanta, the wounded were, for the most part, quickly and efficiently evacuated to northern hospitals. There were, however, two emergency periods, when the regular hospital trains could carry no more than a fraction of the sick and wounded. The first was after the Battle of Resaca in the middle of May, 1864. The other and more drastic case was immediately after Kennesaw Mountain at the end of June, when military necessity dictated the prompt removal of several thousand patients to Chattanooga. After a harrowing ambulance ride of eight miles these men were laid upon the straw-covered floors of freight cars. Ordinarily a twelve-hour journey, the trip took thirty-six hours, and the men arrived badly chilled, unfed, and demoralized.

Since the accompanying surgeons could attend their patients

only when the train was on a siding, many wounds had had no attention. A nurse had been assigned to each car, but being unsupervised, some neglected their charges. This kind of transportation had to be used again, but under better conditions. "Feeding stations" operated by the Sanitary Commission had proved valuable along the road from Chattanooga to Stevenson, in the post-Chickamauga period. Similar stations were set up along the Western and Atlanta Railroad at Kingston, Dalton, Deckard, and a number of other stops. Thus food and attention were made available even for those slightly wounded who later had to ride in freight cars.

There is little to say about the medical field service of the other Western armies in 1864–1865. The battles of Franklin and Nashville cost relatively light casualties, and there is no record of ambulance or field-hospital difficulties. A major deficiency in ambulances, complicated by the death from starvation of most of the horses and mules, marked the operations of the Army of the Frontier in Texas. In contrast, the expedition which took Mobile, Alabama, in 1865, was said to be "very nearly perfect" in its medical equipment and organization. Relations of the Quartermaster Corps and the Medical Department were so harmonious that, for once, there was no dispute over who should give orders to the ambulance train.

The last great operation of the Western forces was Sherman's "March to the Sea." Before leaving Atlanta on November 16, 1864, Sherman had purged his army of every sick or ailing man. He made a harmless cut in the size of the medical supply train, by ordering that tent flies, rather than complete tents, be carried for the division hospitals. There was an ample provision of ambulances, 600 for an army of 60,000, although, had any battle been fought, with the army isolated from its base, ambulances and supplies might have proved inadequate. There was no fighting of any consequence, however, and it was an exceptionally healthy army that arrived at Savannah on December 10, the men having had fresh food all the way. While the army was on the move one ambulance followed each regiment, while the rest, along with the hospital wagons, accompanied the division train. The relatively few sick and wounded (less than 2 per cent of the force) could be transported in the ambulances with room to spare and were cared for at night in a few tents set up by each division hospital. When the march northward through the Carolinas began, the sick were left in corps hospitals at Savannah, to which additional sick were sent as long as the army remained within reach.

From the military standpoint, important services were rendered in 1864 by the Army of the Shenandoah, under General Philip Sheridan, which ravaged the valley of Virginia, and was merged with the Army of the Potomac in the spring of 1865. But its medical organization calls for comment only on two instances. One is that the Ambulance Corps Act made a great difference in its efficiency, correcting a most chaotic field relief system. The other is the establishment of the largest hospital under a single unified control in any Union force during the entire war. This gigantic collection of tents, housing 4,000 patients, was set up at Winchester after the Battle of Cedar Creek on October 19, 1864. As the surgeon commanding it found himself so immersed in paper work that he could carry on no ward inspection, the experiment can hardly be called a success.

The Army of the Potomac's 1865 campaign was over almost as soon as it began. The only real battle was Five Forks, a small affair compared to those of the previous years. The campaign's wounded numbered only 5,000. But, despite the army's experience and greater preparation, it had fewer ambulances than at any time in the previous two years, and this shortage created some difficulty during the march to Appomattox.

Anticipating the possibility of a real campaign, Medical Director McParlin had increased the size of the depot hospital at City Point by 1,000 beds. These were not needed, and the medical demobilization of the Army of the Potomac began with an order on April 30, 1865, to reduce the size of the depot from 7,000 to 2,500 beds. The 1,000 patients remaining on May 4 were moved, along with the depot, to Alexandria where after four weeks the few remaining sick and wounded were distributed to general hospitals, and the depot discontinued. On the last day of June, the Army of the Potomac passed into history.

In the years since Bull Run the Medical Department's field service had evolved from a buzzing confusion to an orderly system. Something approaching a trained Hospital Corps had replaced frightened musicians as stretchermen and callous teamsters as ambulance drivers. Field hospitals had progressed from tiny regimental affairs, through brigade and division units, to the smoothly working corps hospitals of 1864–1865. The designation of certain surgeons as operators had done a good deal to improve surgical technique, though even after this reform there was much criticism of wartime surgery.

6

Wartime

Surgery

THE REPAIR OF MANGLED BODIES AND TREATMENT OF WOUND infections are the primary concerns of wartime surgery. Because the surgical advances of the Civil War were few and of limited consequence, our interest centers on war surgery as representative of the art during a peculiar transition period. Anesthesia had come in the eighteen-forties; thus, operations, hitherto forbidden by the shock and sensibilities of patients, were now possible. But the revolutionary modern techniques of antisepsis and asepsis were not to come until the decade after the war. Consequently the surgical meddling and experimentation which anesthesia had invited were paid for in an appalling ratio of wound infections accompanied by an even more appalling mortality rate. Caught between the desire to exercise their art and fear of the infections that were almost sure to follow, the surgeons of a whole generation were placed in a quandary. From this dilemma the war tended to release them, though controversies continued to rage as to whether the conscientious surgeon should amputate or should attempt to save a limb at the risk of infection. For the most part, wartime operations were not elective: the patient's body was already opened—by Confederate lead—and the doctor *had* to become a surgeon, cutting, sawing and messing about in the wound, and wrestling as best he could with the suppuration and "fevers" which followed. This provides an interesting but tragic chapter of surgical history.

The nature of the surgery in any war will be determined in good part by the methods and weapons of combat, and particularly the size, shape, and material of the projectiles. The typical Union wounded man would be hit in an arm or leg by a soft lead bullet of conoidal shape fired from a musket. The chances were seven to one that he would live, though he might go through a dangerous and uncomfortable period of infection and might be discharged with a useless or a missing limb. One of the curious things about the Civil War was the small number of men injured by other than small arms. A table of all reported wounds, classified according to cause, shows 94 per cent to have been bullet wounds, 5.5 per cent to have been caused by artillery fire, torpedoes and grenades, and less than .4 per cent to have been inflicted by saber or bayonet. In contrast more than three-fourths of all gunshot wounds in the first World War were caused by shellfire.

At the Battle of the Wilderness there were 250 cannon in action on each side yet Dr. W. T. G. Morton was astonished to find only 12 cases of shell injuries in the Fredericksburg depot hospital. In view of the considerable hand-to-hand fighting in that battle it is even more surprising that only 6 out of the 7,302 recorded wounded were injured by sword or bayonet.

Wondering at the few artillery wounds incurred at the Siege of Yorktown, a surgeon answered for himself the obvious question, "Of what use are cannon?," by reflecting that troops under artillery fire became demoralized. Although bayonet wounds in the Union army were fewer than in European conflicts, that weapon never seems to have sent many men to the hospitals in any war. Pondering this question in 1918, Dr. Harvey Cushing concluded that the bayonet in the hands of a merciless infantry-man, determined to take no prisoners, killed more than it injured. This may have been true in World War I, but not apparently in the Civil War. Corpses of men killed by the bayonet were rare, and conspicuous by their "peculiarly contorted" look. That Americans don't like cold steel is very likely the answer. Surgeon J. T. Calhoun, who gave it, explained that bayonet charges were mainly matters of morale: either the charging line breaks and streams back or the defenders take fright and run on seeing the points of the bayonets.

Bullets, then, were the overwhelming cause of Civil War battle wounds, accounting for approximately a quarter of a million patients, of whom 14 per cent died. Of the 144,000 cases where the type of missile could be ascertained the conoidal ball (Minie ball) caused 108,000 wounds, the old-fashioned round ball 16,000 wounds, and shell fragments 12,500. Cannon balls were responsible for only 359 cases, and explosive bullets for 130.

The musket balls of that day made far worse wounds than modern steel-jacketed cartridges. The old lead bullet, traveling at low velocity, readily lost shape on impact, frequently lodged in the tissues, often carried with it particles of clothing and skin, and almost invariably left an infected wound. The round ball was slightly less dangerous than the conoidal one, as it might sometimes glance off a bone, instead of shattering two or three inches of it; but each ball made a large wound, which, if the bullet spread, presented a violently lacerated appearance and a track enlarged out of all proportion to the caliber of the projectile. The modern bullet, in contrast, travels at such high velocity that it is sterilized by heat, and being steel-jacketed does not change its shape, but drills a neat, aseptic hole through tissue and bone alike, usually passing completely out of the body. If the soldier is not killed at once, he will suffer less pain than his

Civil War prototype, will bleed less, and his wound will be less likely to become infected.

Considering the difficulties of chest and abdominal operations in the preantiseptic era, the Union soldiers may be considered lucky in having received 71 per cent of their wounds on arms, legs, hands or feet, and only 18 per cent on the torso. This may be accounted for by the tendency of soldiers to take cover behind trees or breastworks. Injuries of head, face, and neck represented 10.77 per cent of all gunshot wounds; on the torso, chest wounds were almost three times as frequent as abdominal wounds.

Some 44,000 men were reported "killed in action." One investigation showed that 82 per cent of the corpses on a portion of a battlefield showed wounds of the head, chest or neck. Only 5 per cent showed wounds of the extremities, and the blanched appearance of the 12 per cent hit in the abdomen indicated that an artery had been penetrated. A large percentage of the "killed-in-action" category must have bled to death.

The Union doctors were average in their education and experience. So far as surgical preparation and experience were concerned they were therefore unsatisfactory. Specialization of function had not yet advanced to the stage where surgical practice as a specialty was common. The Medical Corps contained many men with little or no surgical experience, but with an eagerness to acquire it, which they did "at bitter cost to many a wounded man." The young assistant surgeons, many of them recent graduates, attracted the most criticism for their misguided zeal for experiment. But experienced surgeons also experimented. Such dangerous attempts as disarticulation of the hip joint were tried; and a Dr. Peter Pineo at Gettysburg attempted a resection of the head of the humerus—an operation performed only twelve times before the war, and then always in a fixed hospital.

But the men who tried to treat gunshot wounds without ever having done so before, and to perform amputations without ever having seen one, seemed a greater danger than the experimenters. After Antietam there was talk of the "butcher's" surgery of that battle. In denial Medical Director Letterman quoted no less an observer than the Medical Inspector General of the British Army to the effect that he had never seen wounded men better cared for. The formation of division hospitals and brigade operating teams, with the senior surgeon of each brigade as chief operator, seems to have removed the chief causes for complaints. Indeed, the subsequently famous Dr. W. S. Billings held that the surgery of the Army of the Potomac's 1864 campaign was "unprecedentedly good." The better men on the operating teams gained much experience, and improved their skill to such a degree that an elderly surgeon could write as late as 1914: "The experience of subsequent years has added comparatively little to the technique of operative surgery."

This may be conceded if by "technique" the author meant skill in use of knife, saw and forceps, and dexterity in the tying of ligatures. But the briefest review of surgical procedures in the dressing stations and the field hospitals shows such a gulf between the methods of that day and the aseptic routine of our own that centuries, not a mere two generations, might well have separated 1865 and 1914.

With rare exceptions the medical officers in charge of advance depots, or dressing stations, confined their surgical activities to the checking of hemorrhage and simple bandaging. Tourniquets were twisted on the limbs of bleeding men or compresses applied; in rare emergencies an artery might be tied. Liquor, in the form of whisky or brandy, was given to counteract shock— a prescription upon which modern science frowns. "Because they expect it" the wounded were usually given an opium pill, or from an eighth to a quarter of a grain of morphine. It was considered desirable that bandages be held to a minimum in all except fracture cases, because "they become dirty and stiff, and are usually cut away and destroyed without having become really useful."

There were two schools on the use of lint. One held that a wad of it should be plugged into the wound "to keep it open"; the other that lint was of use only as padding around a splint

With muskets for tent poles the Antietam wounded lay under temporary canvas waiting for ambulances.

Part of a field hospital at Gettysburg. Non-uniformed persons were probably members of the Sanitary Commission, a volunteer group that performed some of the functions of the present day Red Cross.

Campbell Hospital near Washington—Flowers and Female Nurses here.

Armory Square Hospital in Washington, often visited by Lincoln.

Dr. Jonathan Letterman, Medical Director of the Army of the Potomac, and his staff.

The two types of field ambulance—the two-wheeler nicknamed "avalanche," because of its jolting and the more merciful four-wheeler.

An ambulance train at City Point which served the troops in the Wilderness Campaign.

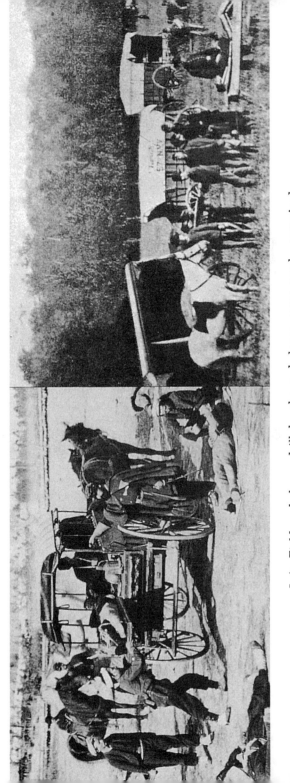

Left. Field ambulance drill by the ambulance corps newly organized after the Battle of Antietam.

Right. Removing the wounded from the Marye's Heights battlefield May 2, 1864.

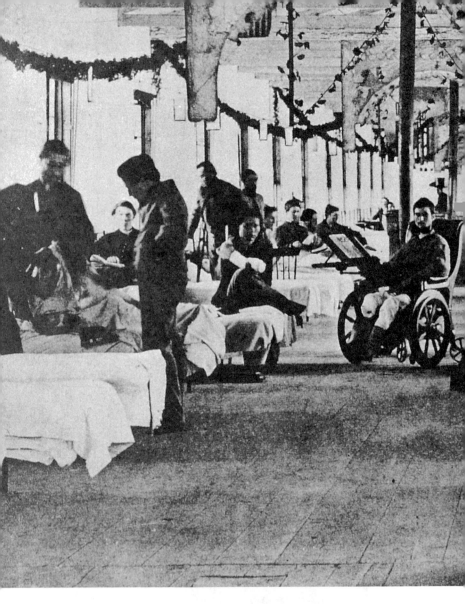

Carver Hospital (Washington) on a holiday, during visiting hours.

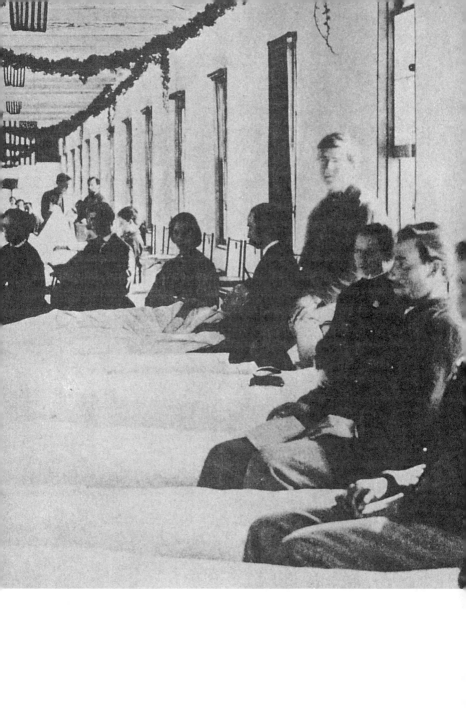

A field hospital at Brandy Station which served troops during Grant's campaign in Virginia.

The Jeffersonville, Indiana, Hospital, one of the famous "pavilion" type, with numerous wings radiating from a circular structure to facilitate segregation and ventilation.

Central office in Washington of the Sanitary Commission, volunteer civilian organization largely responsible for some of the major advances in military medical procedures.

A link with the people at home. Officers and nurses of the Sanitary Commission at Fredericksburg, 1864.

United States ambulance repair shop at Washington

or to wipe away pus—and had come into use on the mistaken theory that it is necessary to keep a wound from healing to permit the escape of humors.

Upon arrival at the field hospital the wounded man would find himself one of a large number of men lying on the ground or upon piles of straw and waiting their turn on the operating table. The less seriously wounded would be attended by the "dressing surgeon" and would then be let alone, except for a feeding of beef broth, or the administration of opiates or stimulants as required, until the seriously hurt had been attended by the surgeons. The operating team of each brigade would ordinarily pass over both the slightly and the mortally wounded.

Placing the patient upon an operating table, always a crude affair and sometimes merely a door torn from its hinges, the surgeons would begin what was expected to be a painful examination by the administration of a general anesthetic; but sometimes a simple bullet wound would be probed while the patient was fully conscious, and shrieks and groans would alarm those waiting their turn. Attempts would be made to stanch dangerous hemorrhages, and if the examination showed an operation to be necessary it would be performed immediately.

It was believed that major operations should be performed before the "irritative stage" (i.e., infection) began, which was usually from 24 to 48 hours after the wound was incurred. It was also felt that patients in a state of deep shock should be allowed to rally before being operated upon. But pressure of numbers led to operations regardless; if the irritative stage had begun, it was ignored and cases of shock were "rallied" with doses of liquor. Once foreign bodies had been removed from a wound and repairs effected, the management of a surgical case was "exceedingly simple," consisting "in the majority of cases, in the fulfillment of the following indications, viz., absolute rest, keeping down inflammation by cold fomentations, the relieving of pain by opiates, and the supporting of the system (by liquor and quinine) to enable it to go through the necessary process of suppuration."

These hurried, wartime operations violated every canon of modern asepsis, in which the surgeon's hands are scrubbed for ten minutes, he wears a sterile gown and mask and handles only boiled, or otherwise sterilized, instruments, dressings and sutures. Operations presented a frightening, gruesome sight to laymen, carried on as they were next to piles five feet high of severed arms and legs, and perhaps with black, swollen corpses nearby. General Carl Schurz described an operation at Gettysburg as follows:

> Most of the operating tables were placed in the open where the light was best, some of them partially protected against the rain by tarpaulins or blankets stretched upon poles. There stood the surgeons, their sleeves rolled up to their elbows, their bare arms as well as their linen aprons smeared with blood, their knives not seldom held between their teeth, while they were helping a patient on or off the table or had their hands otherwise occupied ... As a wounded man was lifted on the table, often shrieking with pain as the attendants handled him, the surgeon quickly examined the wound and resolved upon cutting off the injured limb. Some ether was administered and the body put in position in a moment. The surgeon snatched his knife from between his teeth . . . , wiped it rapidly once or twice across his bloodstained apron, and the cutting began. The operation accomplished, the surgeon would look around with a deep sigh, and then—"Next!"

And well might he sigh, for that cry of "Next!" would be repeated scores or even hundreds of times at each operating table after a major battle, and the surgeons might work on, using sperm candles at night, for days and nights together with hardly a respite. From a hospital on Spotsylvania field a surgeon wrote his wife that he had operated steadily for four days and two nights, and his feet were badly swollen. "It does not seem as though I could take a knife in my hand today," he concluded, "yet there are a hundred cases of amputations waiting for me. Poor fellows come and beg almost on their knees for the first chance to have an arm taken off. It is a scene of horror such as I never saw."

Unconsciously cruel though they may have been at times, the surgeons tried to cause as little pain as possible, using opiates freely and even administering general anesthetics when paint dressings had to be changed. Most wounds were not especially painful at the beginning, though pain and shock were both "usually present to some degree," varying according to the temperament of the patient. In severe wounds the pain was usually "lost in the anesthesia of the shock" that soon followed. Shock is a "sudden prostration of the vital powers due to injury or emotion," which shows itself in pallor, a cold and clammy skin and a weak pulse. Being mistakenly dosed with whisky, and having had the usual dressing-station opium pill, the victims ordinarily gave few signs of suffering, such as screams or groans, unless rudely handled by stretcher and ambulance men. Most of the pain of a wound comes after infection; it was after from 24 to 48 hours that opiates would be most needed.

Opium pills were the most widely used form of relief, but there was considerable experimentation, especially in the Army of the Cumberland, with morphine (one to three grains) scattered on or rubbed into the wound. Good results were reported by those who adopted the practice. The hypodermic syringe was quite rare early in the war, but, as it became better known, numerous surgeons discovered the advantages of injecting morphine with it.

Wartime anesthetics

Probably no wartime lesson was of greater value to the surgeons than their experiences with anesthetics. Ether had been used in surgical operations since 1846, and chloroform since 1851, but many doctors were poorly schooled in their use, particularly of the latter, which was to become popular with the postwar generation. This ignorance, combined with standpatism and reports of mishaps in their use during the Mexican and Crimean Wars, no doubt accounts for the rear-guard action waged by some prominent surgeons against them in 1861. Ether, used by the American army at Vera Cruz during a part of 1847,

ıdoned as too dangerous. Chloroform was used in
ıs in the Crimea, despite the fact that the British
:ral believed it to be dangerous in serious cases.
ents against anesthetics, as summarized in a New
York medical journal in 1861, went as follows: "(1) The ex-
citement of the soldier is often sufficient to carry him safely
through the severest operation (Guthrie); (2) The shock after
gun-shot wounds produces such depression that anesthetics
would prove injurious by adding to the depression (Velpeau);
Pain is a necessary stimulant in shock (Cole); Anesthetics re-
tard union by first intention (i.e., healing without suppuration),
and predispose to hemorrhage and pyaemia (Porter, U. S. A.)."
The editor's advice to his readers was that, in the light of favorable results in the Crimea they should not hesitate to anesthetize
their patients.

The chief anesthetic of the Civil War was chloroform. It was
preferred to ether according to some writers because of its
smaller bulk. Other writers point to its speedy action and its
nonimflammability as additional reasons for the preference. It
was not pointed out, and may not have been fully understood
at that time, that ether is a much more dangerous agent in cases
of shock, and that, by distending the blood vessels, it encourages
hemorrhage. Nevertheless, chloroform is considered a much
more dangerous anesthetic in civil practice. A sudden, strong
inhalation by the patient is likely to give him an overdose which
will paralyze his heart and kill him. A third Civil War anesthetic, a mixture of the two is frowned upon by twentieth-century surgeons.

Throughout the four years of war some 80,000 general anesthetics are supposed to have been given, of which 76 per cent
were chloroform, 14 per cent ether and 9 per cent the mixed
agent. The number of deaths attributed to the anesthetic was
very small: 37 from chloroform, 4 from ether, and 2 from the
mixture. Considering the tensions of anesthetists working under
battle conditions and their extreme fatigue at certain times, this
seems a remarkably low mortality, especially as **chloroform**

was almost the only anesthetic used in the field, the use of ether being pretty well confined to general hospitals. That there were not more deaths from chloroform may be due to the method of administration. The anesthetic would be dropped on a folded cloth or towel, or perhaps upon a paper cone with a sponge in its apex. The cloth or cone would be gradually lowered toward the patient's nose and mouth and withdrawn on full anesthesia. As most operations were performed out of doors or in tents, fresh air mixed with the sleep-inducing fumes. Whatever the cause, the mortality seemed very low to the surgeons of the day. They felt that anesthetics, by sparing the patient great anguish, had lowered the anticipated mortality rate and had earned a permanent place in American surgery.

Possibly because cutting weapons were so little used in battle, hemorrhage was not a major menace to life among the men brought into field hospitals. The dread of bleeding shown by recruits, and the increased shock it caused and the depletion of the patient's strength when continued for any length of time, caused concern to the surgeons. Since the tendency of most gunshot wounds is to stop bleeding with the approach of syncope (fainting), and as the usual wound bled rather little, surgeons took the attitude that tourniquets were unnecessary on the battlefield. Those applied by stretchermen, were often poorly done and resulted in much trouble through the stoppage of circulation. This led to the feeling that tourniquets in the hands of the even more ignorant fighting troops would do more harm than good.

A hemorrhage occurring within twenty-four hours of a wound was classified as "primary." Of 1,480 hemorrhages, the exact times of which were known, only 153 were primary. Some hemorrhages would begin during the "intermediary period," from the first day until "the establishment of suppuration on the fifth or sixth day." On the fourth day after the wound or operation the number would rise, reaching a maximum on the tenth day, and then fall, though some of these "secondary" hemorrhages, as those occurring during the period of suppuration were called, might not begin until more than three months had passed. There was some dispute as to whether the "intermediary hemorrhages" were caused by sloughing of the arteries or by increased arterial action. It was recognized that secondary hemorrhage was usually caused by "separation of a slough"; that is, the wound had become infected, the infection had killed the arterial tissue; as it disintegrated from the living tissue the blood would gush forth.

It was, then, the septic surgery of the pre-Listerian era which laid the base for such hemorrhages; and it was the technique of removing the ligature tied around an artery which precipitated them. In operative cases and in serious cases of primary hemorrhage the bleeding artery would be tied with a ligature of undisinfected silk thread, or if silk was not available, linen or cotton thread. One end of the thread would be left hanging out of the wound, and every day the surgeon would pull on it to see if the loop on the blood vessel had rotted loose. When it came away, if a blood clot had formed and closed the blood-vessel, well and good; if no such clot had formed, then a secondary and often fatal hemorrhage followed. Emergencies of this kind arose with "dreadful frequency" in Civil War hospitals. In the era of antiseptic surgery, and of ligatures made of sterilized and absorbable animal tissues, they have become rarities.

Faced with serious bleeding, the surgeon could choose among several measures ranging from the application of ice and cold compresses to the tying of ligatures. Where the flow of blood to an artery needed to be stopped only temporarily, as in an operation, it was a frequent practice to apply a tourniquet; though some surgeons preferred to use none, entrusting an assistant with the duty of holding the artery in his fingers. This practice was criticized on the ground that a nearby shell burst would force everyone to duck, and the excited assistant might release his grip. Ligatures, however, were regarded as the most reliable means of stopping the flow of blood, and were used in more than half the 2,235 cases in which bleeding "formed an important element." Indeed, understanding of ligatures and skill in applying them were considered among the leading surgical advances of the war.

It is hard to see how the surgeons could have felt very complacent about their work. The 2,235 cases of bleeding had a mortality of 61.7 per cent, which compares most unfavorably with the general mortality of 13.6 per cent in all gunshot wound cases, and seems appalling in comparison with the World War I hemorrhage mortality rate of 2.01 per cent! Undoubtedly the Civil War rate was much increased by the fact that pyemia, erysipelas, or gangrene developed in 20 per cent of the cases. Even without such complications the hemorrhage mortalities were still very high. The mortality in cases where ligature was used (59 per cent) was slightly lower than the general hemorrhage mortality, and the distribution of mortalities according to just which blood vessel was being ligated, and when, provided a guide for the future as to when ligation was worth trying. The few ligatures attempted in cases of primary hemorrhage proved "quite successful." It was found that deaths where ligatures were tied both above and below the wound were much fewer than where only one ligature was used—20 per cent as opposed to 63 per cent. Therefore it might be better to amputate a limb, injuries to which made two ligatures impossible, than to risk tying only one.

For hemorrhages from one of the smaller vessels, it was a frequent practice to pack the wound with what a modern military surgeon has described as "astringent, coagulant, and generally harmful drugs." The styptic most used was persulphate of iron, which was placed by the Medical Department in every hospital knapsack, but perchloride of iron, alum, nitrate of silver, gallic and tannic acids, and turpentine were also used.

When the location of a bleeding artery precluded the ligation of the vessel and the hemorrhage was too forceful for any styptic, it might be controlled manually. We are told of one case, in a Union hospital, where relays of nurses working in four-hour shifts kept their thumbs pressed on the offending artery for a week and of a Confederate case where similar relays performed that service for three weeks.

Deliberate bloodletting, by lancet or leech, seems a curious treatment to use for gunshot wounds, but it had long been a cardinal article of surgical faith and still had adherents in 1861. Gunshot wounds of the chest, lung hemorrhages, and abdominal hemorrhages were generally thought to demand "copious bleeding" until the British surgeon, Dr. Patrick Fraser. attacked the theory, as disproved by his Crimean War experience. Both Union and Confederate Medical Departments denounced the practice early in the war and it was seldom resorted to.

More dangerous than hemorrhages, and indeed responsible for many of them, were the infections which cursed the surgery of the time. The ordinary, pus-producing staphylococcus infection was not even considered to be such, but as a normal process of tissue repair. Wounds, it was thought, were lined with dead tissue which had to be thrown out of the body in the form of pus, and when a wound healed satisfactorily without suppuration, as they are now expected to do when properly handled, it was considered a freak. As the war went on, however, enough wounds healed by "first intention," i.e., without suppuration, to make some doctors feel that the classic theory needed reexamination. Septicemia and pyemia—infections of the blood stream—were recognized as abnormal, but were so frequent in the hospitals of civil life that they had come to be accepted as common though mysterious afflictions which would probably appear, along with "hospital gangrene," wherever large numbers of surgical patients were gathered together.

Pre-Listerian surgery at its zenith

The septic sins of the time, responsible for this harvest of death and suffering, make hair-raising reading. A great surgeon, W. W. Keen, has thus described them:

Wartime Surgery

We operated in old blood-stained and often pus-stained coats, veterans of a hundred fights. We operated with clean hands in the soci_ sense, but they were undisinfected hands. . . . We used undisinfected instruments from undisinfected plush-lined cases, and still worse used marine sponges which had been used in prior pus cases and had been only washed in tap water. If a sponge or an instrument fell on the floor it was washed and squeezed in a basin of tap water and used as if it were clean.

It remains to be added that at times even these standards could not be maintained. At Perryville water was so scarce that some surgeons were unable to wash their hands for two days. It was generally urged that the surgeon's finger made a better probe with which to explore the track of a bullet than any instrument, and it was held that the "cool surgeon" could readily control emergency hemorrhages by putting his finger ends "directly upon the mouths" of the injured arteries. When a surgeon recommended a syringe for draining the pus from a bone wound, he added that the appliance "should be kept clean by occasionally rinsing with clean water." To remain uncontaminated from the examination and operation, a wound had to run the gantlet of repeated washings from a communal basin and sponge. The same sponge and basin of pus-filled water might be used on every wound in a ward.

It is the purpose of dressings to protect a wound against contamination, but it is questionable whether those of the sixties served that purpose. The lint used, much as absorbent cotton is used now, was supposed to have been scraped from clean pieces of cloth, but was of course not aseptic. Frequently it would be applied wet, covered with a piece of gauze, and held in place by adhesive plaster. Raw cotton was introduced as a substitute during the war, and though it may have been cleaner than material scraped from old sheets and wearing apparel it was not the sterile article in use today. Nearly all dressings were applied wet, and were kept wet, often by directing a constant drip of water upon them. It was believed the water would keep the wound "clean and sweet." As the water was not sterile it may

that object; but it was unquestionably soothing.
sometimes used in place of the usual "cold water
their supposed value in "encouraging suppura-
ıe surgeons were already suspicious of them, and
one o… er men at Gettysburg listed their nonuse as a factor in the quick and satisfactory healing of the wounds from that battle.

The worst abuse in dressings was the tendency of some economical hospitals to wash old dressings for use on new patients, an abomination actually urged upon surgeons by an agent of the Sanitary Commission. A hospital washerwoman lost her finger from an infection incurred in washing such bandages, and some surgeons forbade the practice, on the suspicion that infections could be spread that way. The other great abuse was the government's failure to supply the soldiers with emergency dressings, which led to the wounded binding up their wounds in "dirty handkerchiefs" or pieces of "cloth torn from a sweaty shirt."

What about antisepsis? Because Lister published his first paper on antisepsis in 1867 it is sometimes assumed that the Civil War was fought without antiseptics. And because Lister gave carbolic acid its first great advertisement as an antiseptic it is sometimes thought that he invented it, or that, at least, he had been the first to use it in surgery. But the surgeons of 1861–1865 used not only carbolic but many of the other chemicals that rank high as antiseptics. The essential difficulty lay in the failure to employ them at the right time. An infection would be allowed to reach full and horrifying bloom before the antiseptic was applied. The greatest obstacle to using the right chemical, in the right way, at the right time, was ignorance of the nature of infection and of its method of communication.

Except for the "laudable pus" which appeared in healing wounds, the discharges and other signs of infection were regarded as undesirable and as having some external cause. There was no general agreement as to what this cause was, but the obviously communicable nature of many of the "surgical diseases," as observed in the wards of military hospitals, led to a fairly general suspicion that the agents of infection were airborne. "Noxious effluvia," unpleasant smells of all kinds, were highly suspect, and it was believed that absolutely pure air, or an approximation thereof, was essential if surgical diseases were to be kept down. A special committee of the American Medical Association, meeting in 1864, considered the value of ventilation "the great lesson of the war." It went beyond the theory of "noxious effluvia" by stating that air is full of "pus-corpuscles floating about as dust." These corpuscles, it was held, would carry erysipelas or hospital gangrene to every wound on which they might settle. This overemphasized the role of air as conveyor of bacteria: but the committee made a valuable contribution when they added that the air is also contaminated by expectorations and by contact with the "urine and feces of men unable to walk to the closet." The consequent injunction to leave no fecal matter exposed and to treat all latrines, bedpans, etc., with strong antiseptics was salutary.

The practical result of the ventilation theory was to place a premium upon hospital cleanliness and to enhance the value of antiseptics, which were valued as disinfectors of air, floors and chamber pots, and as deodorants. Of the long list of antiseptics recommended by the Sanitary Commission chlorine and charcoal were the most used. Sodium hypochlorite, which as Dakin's solution was to be the great antiseptic of World War I, was popular as a disinfectant, and as Labbaraque's solution it was used in treating noisome ulcers and suppurating, gangrenous wounds, a purpose for which permanganate of potassa was also widely used.

Carbolic acid was furnished by the purveyor, and if the surgeons kept up with current English medical literature they knew its value in gangrene and to "check the spread of slough," to put on ulcers, and to paint the throat in diphtheria. It was recommended in this country, however, merely as an "antiseptic and deodorant . . . of considerable energy and permanency," a label shared by the coal tar compounds.

Iodine was first used to "counteract the effect of certain animal poisons" by an American, Professor Daniel Brainard, in 1855; but it was not mentioned in the Sanitary Commission's pamphlet on antiseptics, and was seldom used otherwise than as a curative agent. An exception was the field hospital at Jonesboro, Georgia, where it was sprayed into the air as an antiseptic gesture. Bromine is not found in modern accounts of antiseptics, but was highly regarded and widely used during the war. Dr. Elisha Harris proclaimed it "the most prompt and efficient antiseptic known." Considered of great value in the treatment of hospital gangrene, it was sprayed into the air. Some surgeons and attendants who had experimented with it on small cuts and abrasions on their hands announced its success as a preventive.

Certain acids—sulphuric, hydrochloric, nitric and nitrous— were considered of antiseptic value for their power to absorb moisture and "recombine some of the elements of noxious effluvia." They were used in treating gangrene. Among other supposed antiseptic agents corrosive sublimate (bichloride of mercury) still maintains a respectable reputation, as does alcohol, which was used both in its pure form and as whisky.

Whatever the infecting agent in pyemia, gangrene, and erysipelas, it was recognized that certain factors influenced their development and their course. Exhausted, ill-fed men, who had endured the horrors of mismanaged ambulance transportation, fared much worse under surgery than well-conditioned men. The psychic factor was also recognized as important: the wounded man who wanted to recover stood the better chance. Wholesome food was generally considered a valuable curative agent, though some surgeons believed that seriously sick patients lacked the nutritive powers to assimilate food.

From the modern viewpoint the increasing realization that hospital cleanliness was a necessity appears to be the most important advance in the whole complex of factors called "war surgery." Therefore, it seems strange that no one bethought himself of the necessity of clean surgical instruments. The "antiseptic" value of heat was recognized; many powerful germicides were used to "purify" floors, bedpans and hospital air; yet no instrument was ever boiled or chemically treated. The new era of surgery toward which the Civil War doctors were fumbling could not be reached until the bacteriologists provided the guiding clues.

Paradoxically, one of the most strenuous efforts to secure wound cleanliness had the opposite effect. Maggots wiggling about in a wound tortured and worried the soldiers. Surgeons considered them an "infection of the worst type," and got rid of them, wherever possible, by injections of chloroform. A group of Confederate surgeons, tending gangrene cases in a prison stockade at Chattanooga, and denied bandages and supplies by Union surgeons who were husbanding their own short supplies, were compelled to leave their patients' wounds unbound and fly-blown. A miracle occurred: the maggoty Confederate wounds cleared up quickly, while the de-maggoted Union wounded died in large numbers.

The joyous Confederate surgeons continued to invite the attentions of maggots for the remainder of the war, while Northern surgeons continued to repulse them. Maggots perform a scavenging job, eating only the diseased tissue in a wound, leaving it clean and healthy. This had been observed during the Napoleonic Wars and then forgotten. Its rediscovery in the Civil War was, for all practical purposes, forgotten again. Its final rediscovery in World War I led to the breeding of maggots for use in treating osteomyelitis.

Operations

and

Infections

WRITING WITH A PERSPECTIVE OF FIFTEEN YEARS, SURGEON George A. Otis offered the following as the principal surgical advances of the war: (1) surgeons had learned "something" about head injuries; (2) how to deal with "ghastly injuries of the face without dismay," and to perform "restorative operations from which they would formerly have recoiled"; (3) thousands now knew how to ligate the great arteries where only a few had had that skill before the war; and the futility of tying arteries of the neck to stop hemorrhage from face wounds was well established; (4) information on injuries of the vertebral column had been "augmented"; and (5) "theory and practice" in regard to chest wounds had been revolutionized.

The melancholy feature of this modest array of accomplishments is that, with the exception of the tying of the major arteries, none could benefit any large group of wounded. As we have seen, arm and leg wounds made up the majority of the cases and bone fractures the largest category of serious injuries.

The great surgical controversy of the war was between advocates of "conservative" measures, who sought to save the injured limb, and those who believed in prompt amputation. Europeans leaned toward "conservative" surgery, because amputations in the Crimean War had shown a very high mortality. The British Surgeon General Guthrie went so far as to advise against amputation except where the limb had been struck by a cannon ball. Guthrie's pamphlet, which was reprinted by the U.S. Sanitary Commission, and distributed to the surgeons of the army, probably did much to strengthen the "conservatives." Perhaps thinking they were encouraging extremists, five months later in December, 1861, the commission brought out a pamphlet by Dr. D. D. Slade, of Boston. His more orthodox views on amputation seem to have won gradual acceptance by a majority of the military surgeons. Slade held that where the limb was badly lacerated, or had suffered a compound fracture (i.e., the bone had penetrated the skin) with much splintering it was best to amputate at once, especially where joints were involved. The rough conditions of wartime surgery precluded such attempts to save a limb as might be proper in civil practice. Injured soldiers, quite understandably, sought to retain their arms and legs and were prone to suspect surgeons of a callous desire for practice when they recommended amputation. Some tried to sway the doctor to the "conservative" treatment by bluster, bribery, or even the point of a gun.

Neither the general public nor the fighting men could be rid of their aversion to amputations. As the war went on, Army medical opinion, too, turned "conservative." Writing in 1864, the medical director of the Army of the Ohio reported the controversy still raging among his subordinates. Those who had done much reading but had seen little were ardent "conservatives," he said, while those who had done little reading but had seen much were the pro-amputation extremists. A public outcry against "excessive" amputation rang out after the battle of Antietam, but Medical Director Letterman believed that there had been too few, an opinion shared by those who have studied the situation from the vantage point of the twentieth century.

The advocates of conservatism might have fared better had they carried their conservatism to the length of letting the wound strictly alone. The routine of the time involved exploration of the wound with septic probe and undisinfected finger and attempts to withdraw the bullet. Frequently there would be further poking about in the wound to excise bone fragments or resect (remove a section of) the bone. As a Minie ball could shatter a bone, or split it for several inches, the area over which bone splinters might have been scattered could be large, and was often deliberately enlarged by the surgeon. The most dreadful result that might occur was pyemia, but other dire results might be osteomyelitis (chronic bone infection) with its years of misery, or the possession of a useless limb in which the broken bone had never grown together or whose injured joint failed to support the weight of the body. The mischief from this type of surgical meddling had become so evident by the end of the first year of the war that the surgical associates of the Sanitary Commission published a pamphlet advocating that resection and excision be limited under certain conditions. The belief gradually gained currency within the Army that excision of bone demonstrated that "however bad the wound may be, art can make it worse."

It was increasingly recognized that circumstances often compelled amputation. Men worn down by hardship and disease were poor operative risks, but even poorer subjects for resection or excision. Patients tainted with scurvy could stand little surgical meddling. The field surgeon's inability to maintain contact with the case, his frequently justifiable worries about the hygienic conditions of the hospitals in which the patient must lie, and the perils of transportation to the rear—the cruel jolting of army ambulances, and the rough handling in loading and unloading trains and hospital boats, provoked hemorrhages, were hard on the injured—and sometimes fatal to the compound fracture patients—all these considerations favored amputation.

As World War I experience was to show, many lives could have been saved and limbs conserved had better splints been available. There seems to have been little concern for the protection of arm fractures, since those patients could sit up in the ambulance and do something to protect themselves; but leg fractures, particularly those of the femur, offered a real problem. The Army furnished "Smith's Anterior," an extension splint in which the patient's leg could be suspended from the roof of the ambulance, but many surgeons never learned how to use it. The most generally used splint, made of a piece of board or fence paling, was unsuitable for many types of fracture. But it was easy to make, as were those splints formed from the bark of trees and bundles of straw, which were preferred by some doctors. The Sanitary Commission contributed and sought to promote the use of sheets of perforated zinc which could be shaped to the needs of the individual patient, but this device was largely ignored. Inventive surgeons took at least a short step toward anticipating the famous Thomas splint of World War days by making splints of heavy wire.

The one great orthopedic contribution of the war was the Hodgen splint, invented in 1863 by Surgeon John T. Hodgen, of St. Louis. This still used device, by providing a better extension of the limb, prevented contraction. It did this without pressure or injury; it gave maximum comfort to the patient; and it was constructed in such a way that the wound could be dressed, and drainage maintained, without disturbing the fracture.

All through the war surgeons argued the merits of the two fundamental amputation operations. The "flap" operation, devised by William Cheselden in the eighteenth century, was preferred by about six surgeons out of ten. Its advantages over the older "circular" operation were its speed and the fact that it left a better stump; its admitted disadvantages were that it sacrificed more of the limb and made a larger wound. There was disagreement as to which operation was more subject to infection and sloughing of the flesh, which of the two involved the greater risk of hemorrhage, and which would best withstand the rigors of transportation. Advocates of the flap operation sometimes charged their opponents with preferring the circular because they were afraid to attempt the arterial ligatures necessary, and were retorted to with the accusation that they sacrificed their patients' interest to speed. The onlooking layman was tempted to mutter "a plague on both your houses." Modern surgery makes use of both operations and of others as well, letting the circumstances of the case determine. What was more to the point was the bungling of some inexperienced Civil War surgeons who provided insufficient flap, or left a conical stump with the bone protruding, or who began an operation by the "flap" method and carved away tissue until they had to end it as "circular."

The desire for speed was mainly dictated by the enormous work load after a battle and was consistent with the generally held view that an amputation should be "primary," i.e., should be attempted within twenty-four hours of the time the wound was received. Many patients must have been operated upon before they had properly rallied from the shock of their injury, which is dangerous; experience, however, showed that mortality increased sharply if the operation was postponed to the following day. The object of most amputations was to avoid septicemia, and delay gave the invading bacteria a fatal head start. An additional argument was the psychology of the patient: the soldier's mood on the day of battle would help him withstand surgical shock. Some surgeons still held the old theory that by amputating immediately—just as soon as the patient was brought from the firing line—they could complete the operation before the shock of the wound began to be felt. Medical Director Frank H. Hamilton, a celebrated professor of surgery, sought to check this rashness by dividing the "primary" period (the first 24 hours) into two periods, "immediate" and "primary," the first, six hours long, representing the period of wound shock, the other the period in which amputation was advisable.

As in earlier wars, abdominal wounds were highly fatal. They kept the surgeons humble, since no earthly intervention seemed to help. Little could then be learned about them because the patients died so quickly. The overall mortality was 87 per cent —100 per cent when the small intestine was involved. In the latter case peritonitis quickly set in, and in two or three days the patient died. When the wound was in the large intestine the survival rate was 59 per cent. It was the received opinion that "when balls are lost in the capacity of the belly one need not amuse himself by hunting for them." This axiom was hotly debated during the war, as was the desirability of suturing, or sewing up, injured intestines. A majority adopted the view that tradition might be defied and the intestines repaired if exuding fecal matter indicated perforation of the intestines. With the patient facing almost certain peritonitis there seemed little to be lost by operating. Ordinary medical treatment included administration of opium by suppository, to stop peristalsis, coupled with absolute quiet and the withdrawal of food. That protruding bits of omentum (peritoneal layers supporting the stomach and other organs) should be replaced in the abdomen was questioned by many surgeons, but it was standard practice to stuff protruding intestines into the cavity and sew up the wound.

Peritoneal wounds proved less dangerous than those of the other cavities. Recoveries were about 75 per cent. Fractures of the pelvis bones, however, were most serious. Four-fifths of the patients died, and those who recovered might suffer protracted periods of recurring suppuration and pain from bone infections. Arterial and bladder injuries seemed beyond aid.

Little was learned in observing injuries of internal organs. Liver wounds usually brought death from hemorrhage. If that peril was escaped death frequently followed from peritonitis or liver abscess. Penetrating wounds of the stomach were all fatal. Splenitis was not found to be the invariable sequel to a spleen wound, as had been thought. Supposedly, there had been 26 recoveries from kidney wounds; but these were dubious, the injuries having been diagnosed solely by external signs.

Wounds of the chest cavity were only a little less dangerous than those of the abdomen, but they were simple to treat. Luckily, more than half of all chest injuries were flesh wounds and had an extremely low mortality rate (1 per cent). Chest wounds made by cutting weapons had a mortality of 9 per cent, but were few in number. Penetrating gunshot wounds, 8,700 in number, proved fatal in 62 per cent of the cases. This was a little poorer than the record of the British army in the Crimea, but much better than the French. The treatment involved the then revolutionary step of abandoning bleeding. Foreign bodies were removed, finger or rubber catheter usually being preferred to the probe. A simple dressing would be applied, topped with a broad chest-bandage intended to keep the chest immobile. Broad strips of adhesive became popular as a substitute for the bandage. Rest and light diet would effect a cure unless there were complications. Contrary to European expectations, pneumonia was an infrequent complication, and there were remarkably few cases of erysipelas, gangrene, or tetanus among the chest-wound cases. The great menace was empyema, a suppurative pleurisy caused by the pneumococcus, which was treated by the insertion of drainage tubes through incisions cut for the purpose. Hemorrhage, another major difficulty, was stopped by arterial ligatures if its source could be determined; otherwise, by ice or compression. At least such was the approved practice: "heedless surgeons" would merely plug the wound with lint and monsel's salt.

Surgical controversy in this field centered about the advisability of the hermetic sealing of chest wounds. Surgeon Benjamin Howard, proponent of this practice, had begun by sealing an abdominal wound in 1861 and by 1863 was advocating the procedure for chest wounds. He argued that the extreme and frightening breathlessness (dyspnoea) suffered by many chest-wound patients would be relieved by a plug of charpie and lint held together and made airtight by coatings of collodion. Being a field surgeon he had always lost sight of patients he had thus treated after they were evacuated to the rear. Surgeon General

W. A. Hammond ordered that special facilities for follow-up study should be afforded him after the battle of Gettysburg. In six cases, whose wounds were sealed upon that occasion and then left strictly alone, the mortality was 100 per cent. Autopsies upon two of the patients showed one to have had empyema, the other pleuropneumonia. The surgeon who performed the autopsies believed that later patients treated by the Howard method survived only because the general-hospital surgeons who received such cases from the front removed the seal and allowed the wounds to drain. Although opposed by the majority of army men Howard's treatment found admirers, and was adopted in one of the division hospitals of the Army of the Potomac. It was obviously of value in making the patient comfortable by relieving dyspnoea. Since the mortality rate in those cases for which full records were available was no higher than in cases receiving the standard treatment, it did not deserve the harsh censure of its critics. The chief drawback was the tendency of men treated by hermetic sealing to remain semi-invalids through damage to the respiratory apparatus.

Disappointment in hermetic sealing was more than offset by brilliant pioneer work on nerve injuries. This field, virtually unknown to prewar medical literature, attracted the interest of a trio of Philadelphians: S. Weir Mitchell, George R. Moorhouse and William W. Keen. Mitchell was soon to earn recognition as America's pioneer neurologist and one of the great neurologists of the world.

The three were granted the privilege of operating the small Turner's Lane Hospital in Philadelphia as a center of clinical research in nerve wounds and nervous disorders. Shock, paralysis, and referred pain were the usual immediate effects of a nerve wound. Though usually temporary, in some cases these lingered on, the paralysis seeming permanent or the neuralgia so agonizing that the general health of the patient seemed seriously affected. Mitchell, Moorhouse, and Keen, unguided by precept, worked out treatments. Electric shocks proved of diagnostic value in the paralysis cases. A muscle that showed reaction proved likely to recover if given a long series of treatments by "faradization," i.e., mild electrical shocks. Electricity was also found useful as a counterirritant in quieting painful nerves, but was excelled for this purpose by leeches placed along the track of the nerve. Hypodermic injections of morphine and atropin were used to quiet the patient during the treatments. Mitchell, much impressed with the value of morphine in neuralgia cases, urged its use hypodermically, and scolded the medical profession for its reluctance in using this mighty painkiller, pointing out that some patients' agonies were so severe the choice must lie between morphine and amputation. Some of the more baffling Turner's Lane cases would probably be diagnosed today as "shell shock," or psychoneuroses.

Surgical "fevers" and their treatment

Painful as neuralgia was it could not compete as a cause of suffering with staphylococcus aureus, the organism of common suppuration. This bacterium infected so many wounds that the pus it created was considered by most surgeons of the time an evidence of normal healing. They were less complacent toward the "surgical fevers": pyemia, tetanus, erysipelas, osteomyelitis, and hospital gangrene, which accounted for the great majority of wound fatalities. The belief gradually gained currency that they were infections, but no one could determine the causative agents, or the means of transmission, let alone devise a reliable treatment. The mystery was deepened by the fact that some groups of wounded, in some places, escaped major infections almost entirely, while groups at other places were scourged by them. Experience suggested that hardship and exposure, chronic malarial and dysenteric troubles predisposed a wounded soldier to "surgical fevers." Some believed that the complex of dietetic deficiencies lumped together by that generation as "scorbutic diathesis" not only thinned the blood, making coagulation bad, but opened the door to pyemia, gangrene, and erysipelas. The close connection between general health and surgical infections is now sound doctrine.

Pyemia was the bete noire of surgeons. One of them thus expresses his reaction to it:

Many a time have I had the following experience: A poor fellow whose leg or arm I had amputated a few days before would be getting on as well as we then expected—that is to say, he had pain, high fever, was thirsty and restless, but was gradually improving, for he had what we looked on as a favorable symptom—an abundant discharge of pus from his wound. Suddenly, over night, I would find that his fever had become markedly greater; his tongue dry, his pain and restlessness increased; sleep had deserted his eyelids, his cheeks were flushed; and on removing the dressings I would find the secretions from the wound dried up, and what there were were watery, thin, and foul smelling, and what union of the flaps had taken place had melted away. Pyemia was the verdict, and death the usual result within a few days.

The dreaded pyemia struck 2,818 men, of whom only 71 recovered, a mortality of 97.4 per cent. Approximately one wounded man in a hundred contracted it, but it accounted for 6 per cent of wound mortalities.

Pyemia means literally "pus in the blood." As used in the Civil War reports, it included all cases of blood poisoning, although the more precise might differentiate between septicemia and pyemia, the former meaning infection of the blood stream, the latter the same thing accompanied by secondary abscesses. In modern terminology the name "bacteremia" is used to cover them both. Bacteremia is not considered a "disease," strictly speaking. It can be caused by a number of pyogenic organisms, streptococcus pyogenes predominating.

In the 1860's pyemia was beginning to be regarded as a "contagion." An English authority believed that it "may arise spontaneously in any putrefaction of wound products." Surgeon J. A. Liddell, an American, held it to be "closely allied to erysipelas and hospital gangrene"—which was at least partly right, inasmuch as erysipelas is a streptococcal infection and hospital gangrene may have been. Writing in 1863, Professor William Detmold made the acute observation that pyemia was the same thing as "puerperal fever" (puerperal septicemia). This led him to the belief that the infection might be spread by the surgeon's hands, as had been demonstrated in the case of puerperal fever, and caused him to recommend greater cleanliness in surgery, particularly that instruments and sponges used in post-mortems be kept in the mortuary and that surgeons clean themselves vigorously after autopsies. There is no evidence that Detmold's precepts were followed.

Nothing the doctor prescribed seemed of value once pyemia developed. It was agreed that the treatment should be "tonic and stimulating." This meant a diet of milk, eggs, and beef tea, and dosage with "stimulant drugs,"—dilute sulphuric acid or quinine, the latter sometimes given in quantities as large as forty grains a day. Occasionally iron preparations were pre-scribed; and opium was recommended by Detmold. Liquor, usually in large quantities, was regarded as essential, and along with most of the other elements of this treatment it retained credit well into the twentieth century. The modern treatment is, in contrast, simplicity itself: the bowels must be kept open and a maximum of fluids given the patient by mouth, by rectum, and by subcutaneous effusion. If there is a focus of infection the surgeon is to remove it, by amputation if necessary.

Alcohol was the sovereign remedy of the Civil War, rivalled only by quinine. But even at that time a few doctors questioned its value, and as the years passed alcohol lost ground, some of which it has recently regained in certain diseases and as an appetizer for convalescents. Today even its champions consider it positively harmful in bacteremia or any other acute infection. Alcohol is fatiguing; and the patient needs all his strength to fight the infection.

Alcohol was customarily prescribed in small and frequent doses, usually in the form of punch or eggnog, made of brandy or whisky, but was sometimes given undiluted. A very ill sixteen-year-old soldier in a St. Louis hospital was "kept alive" by 36 ounces of brandy a day. In a Virginia hospital one patient was given 48 ounces of eggnog and two or three bottles of porter every day for several weeks; another got a half-pint of egg and brandy every two hours; a third was to have as much of this mixture as he could take.

With a mortality of 89 per cent, tetanus was only slightly less fatal than pyemia, but was much rarer. As there had been little or none of it in the Mexican War, American surgeons were unfamiliar with it and generally tried experimental treatments when it appeared. The first Civil War cases were interpreted by many surgeons as infection by poisoned bullets. The 505 cases of tetanus had an uneven distribution. A "considerable number" of cases appeared in one of the field hospitals at Antietam, and later in the year 1862 among the wounded from Stone's River. The Battles of Chancellorsville and Gettysburg and the whole Atlanta campaign seem to have been free, or almost free, of it, but numerous cases turned up in the Army of the Potomac depot hospital at Fredericksburg after the Battle of the Wilderness.

Tetanus then was attributed to many causes: exposure to excessive heat or cold, night air and drafts; neglect of thorough and early cleansing of a wound; pressure upon nerves by missiles, bone splinters or bandages; or injuries to nerves while the surgeon probed or operated. The disease is now known to be caused by the widespread bacillus tetani, which is frequently found in the soil. Since the bacillus can be carried in the intestines of horses, ground fertilized by horse manure is very likely to be contaminated. The bacillus tetani is anaerobic, i.e., it cannot survive in air; but if it gains entrance to a deep wound, away from air, it gives off toxins which affect the victim's muscles, causing convulsions and the horrible fixed smile and locked jaw which had given the disease its popular name.

It is significant that the field hospital at Antietam where the disease flared up alarmingly was an old stable, the floor of which had been two feet deep in manure; and that many of the Wilderness wounded were bedded on the floors of Fredericksburg stables. The Army's relative freedom from tetanus was attributed by the surgeons to prompt removal of the wounded from the field and to their subsequent protection against exposure. After Stone's River the idea that exposure and night air were major causes of the disease was called in question by at least one doctor. He noticed that tetanus developed more frequently among patients treated in houses than among those in tents. The modern explanation of the low tetanus incidence is that most of the battlefields were on virgin soil untouched by the plow and unmanured.

By twentieth-century standards the handling of the many cases of erysipelas during the latter part of the war was sensible and fairly successful. High as is its one per cent annual incidence the figure should be higher, numerous cases having been given another diagnosis. With those cases counted in, some believe that the erysipelas mortality rate would have been lower than the officially listed 8 per cent. Inasmuch as the mortality today varies from 5 per cent to 9 per cent, we may say either that the Civil War surgeons were very good or that there has been no appreciable progress in the treatment of this disease since 1865. The vast majority of cases were "idiopathic," that is, spontaneous, appearing independent of any wound. In the relatively few instances (1097) of "traumatic" erysipelas (erysipelas arising in a wound) the disease was dangerous. Their mortality reached 41 per cent, terminating frequently in a fatal "pyemia" or a hemorrhage.

Erysipelas is a highly contagious streptococcal infection. Its principal symptom is a characteristic rash accompanied by fever and evidences of toxemia. It can be communicated by touch of dirty instruments, dressings, and doctor's hands, etc., or by dust particles in the air. Civil War cases were at first treated in the general wards. Epidemics followed, the wards being filled with exhausted men rendered more susceptible by their condition. This converted medical men to the contagion theory. Later erysipelas patients were customarily segregated into wards or tents of their own, and those articles which had touched the patient were disinfected. The fact that most of the nurses in these wards contracted the disease dealt an additional blow to the theory of its spontaneous generation. It was also observed that erysipelas spread through a ward, and from ward to ward, in the direction of the prevailing winds. The resulting theory that it was air-borne was buttressed by a report from a Louisville hospital. This institution reduced incidence from half-a-dozen new cases a week to none, after spraying bromine vapor into the air. The appearance of isolated cases in the army continued to be a mystery. The guess was that erysipelas might be caused by "reabsorption of the putrid substance of a wound."

The old standard treatment, of bleeding and calomel, was discarded. The patient was treated much as he would be today, though drugs were more freely used. Mild cases were given laxatives and diaphoretics. Serious ones were purged "freely," and were given tincture of iron or chlorate of potash internally. The principal reliance was upon careful nursing, stimulants and good food. Painting the inflamed areas with silver nitrate or tincture of iodine does not seem to have been successful, but their use on the skin around the inflammation, in an attempt to check its spread, presumably was of value, since it is still being done. In modern practice the emphasis is placed upon prevention of erysipelas by prompt disinfection of wounds.

Osteomyelitis, the most common acute inflammation of bones, was a frequent result of the excision of bone wounds. The acute form of the disease caused severe fever and prostration, and chronic cases might suffer pain and exude pus for many years. The infecting bacteria are streptococci, staphylococci, or a number of other microorganisms, introduced directly into a bone injury or reaching it via the blood stream from some distant focus, such as a boil. During the Civil War it seems to have been confused with similar tuberculous and syphilitic bone involvements. In the modern treatment pus is drained from the center of infection, entrance being effected with a drill, after which the wound may be irrigated with Dakin's solution. If the focus of infection is not found immediately, the modern surgeon is warned against poking around and injuring tissue.

The old treatment was vastly more complicated and interfering. Medicines included quinine, liquor, iodide of potassium, along with enough morphine or opium to relieve pain. Some physicians prescribed mercurial drugs, which others considered harmful. The "local treatment" was to keep the infected part quiet, apply cold compresses, and perhaps resort to local bleeding by leeches or cups. Dr. J. A. Liddell advocated repeated applications of iodine to the skin over the inflamed area. The growing conviction that the disease was caused by air contaminated from "soiled linen, dressings, or any other form of filth" led to a salutary injunction that everything about the patient be kept scrupulously clean. Three operative procedures might be used. Incisions might be cut down to the bone, or if a chronic cone abscess were found it might be sawed out with a trephine. And if the difficulty lay in a limb, amputation might be resorted to.

From the patient's point of view no "surgical" disease was more horrible than "hospital gangrene," though it was far less fatal than pyemia. The gangrene patient might see a black spot the size of a dime, appear on his healing wound, and watch with horrified interest its rapid spread until his whole leg or arm was but a rotten, evil-smelling mass of dead flesh. The death (necrosis) of tissue may be caused either by the stoppage of blood circulation or by bacterial infection. Some Civil War cases reported under the heading "Hospital Gangrene" were of the noninfectious variety, but the overwhelming majority seem to have been bacterial.

Hospital gangrene is now an extinct disease and there is no agreement as to its nature. Surgeon W. W. Keen, who survived into the nineteen-twenties as a prominent Philadelphia surgeon, considered it a streptococcus infection. Another veteran regarded it as a "diphtheria of wounds." Woods Hutchinson, writing in 1918 about the recently discovered gas bacillus, ventured the opinion that hospital gangrene may have been "a mixed infection, a gas-bacillus combined with a pus germ, Streptococcus or Staphylococcus, though we shall never know with certainty." The symptoms of hospital gangrene seem distinct from those of gas gangrene, and it may have been that the latter disease was rare, or absent entirely, for the same reason that tetanus was rare: namely, that the war was fought over uninfected, unmanured land.

In July of 1861 the Sanitary Commission published a British statement, based on Crimean experience, that hospital gangrene was "contagious and infectious" and must be treated in isolation. Since there were only four cases in all during 1861 there was little interest in the disease until two epidemics flared up in the last months of 1862. The first broke out in the hospitals at Frederick, Maryland, among the Antietam wounded. The early cases were not isolated immediately and the contagion went on until 50 men were afflicted. The second flareup at the West Philadelphia general hospital in December was quickly checked after Surgeon W. W. Keen ordered that separate sponges be used for each case, no re-use of bandages and dressings, and that nurses dress gangrenous wounds last, and wash their hands carefully in dilute chlorinated soda afterwards.

A serious outbreak occurred among paroled prisoners at Annapolis in January 1863, and was followed in April by one at Hospital Number 8, at Memphis. There a special survey was made by Surgeon Middleton Goldsmith, who had developed a successful treatment for hospital gangrene at Louisville. Finding that all the original cases had developed in Ward L, that the patients all occupied beds on the side of the room nearest the windows, and that the windows opened upon an alley full of "emanations" from the leaky hospital sewer, Goldsmith attributed the disease to "sewer effluvia." By far the largest number of cases occurred at Fredericksburg in 1864, following the Battle of the Wilderness, and at the Georgia field hospitals. By that time, however, the disease was no longer a nightmare to the surgeons, who had found effective means of coping with it.

Goldsmith's experiments with bromine as a remedy were made in 1862 in the face of considerable opposition. The treatment was used in 1863 by two of Goldsmith's former associates at Memphis and ultimately won general, though not universal, adherence from Army surgeons. The procedure was as follows: The sloughing tissue would be dissected with forceps and scissors, while the patient was under an anesthetic, and was left nearly clean; the surgeon would then apply pure bromine beneath the undermined edges of the gangrenous wound, using a small syringe, and would fill up the entire cavity with lint moistened with a weak solution of bromine. A period of three to ten days, during which there was apparently little or no result, would be followed by a sudden healing of the wound. Sometimes seemingly miraculous results were achieved. John H. Brinton describes one patient who was gangrenous from the hips down, and nearly dead. The morning after the bromine treatment the man was sitting up in bed "howling" for more breakfast. Some surgeons prescribed bromine internally. Goldsmith himself suggested putting bromine-filled dishes in various parts of a ward, apparently with the idea of combating the "effluvia."

The bromine treatment was a great victory, if the statistics are reliable. In a series of 334 cases those treated with bromine had a mortality of 2.6 per cent; those treated with nitric acid, the remedy recommended by the British Surgeon General, had a rate of 61.5 per cent; and those treated by all other methods a rate of 38.4 per cent. Investigators appointed by the Medical Department and the Sanitary Commission gave enthusiastic support, and the medical director of the Army of the Ohio not only hailed bromine as the sovereign remedy for gangrene but hazarded the guess that it would prove equally useful in "a large class of septic and contagious diseases."

But doubters remained. One of these thought it valuable only in superficial wounds, another objected that bromine's suffocating fumes prevented close examination of the wound, and a third held that the treatment seemed successful only because some surgeons tended "to regard every slough as gangrene." And it might have been added that the treatment was torture to the patient. A modern textbook writer holds that the disease has a tendency to spontaneous recovery, and adds that "local antiseptic dressings do not influence it to any noticeable degree." If Dr. Goldsmith were allowed a rebuttal he might point out how odd it was that the spontaneous recoveries should appear so frequently among the bromine-treatment cases and so seldom among the nitric-acid ones. And apropos of these twentieth-century dicta it must be remembered that we are discussing a malady which has for all practical purposes been extinct since the dawn of the antiseptic era.

The surgeons of the sixties were not entirely satisfied with Goldsmith's "sewer effluvia" explanation and his consequent insistence upon good ventilation. It was called in question when the tent patients in Columbian Hospital at Washington developed gangrene and those in the permanent buildings did not. Numerous Confederates thought that the contamination was spread by flies, which was perspicacious of them, as the role of the fly in transmitting disease was not generally understood until a generation later. It occurred to a few that bacteria might be responsible, but bacteriology was too little developed to give the answer. Microscopic examination of gangrenous matter revealed only "the ordinary bacteria which are to be observed in every decomposing animal substance." With the definite cause of hospital gangrene unknown, the idea gained currency that its general cause was filth, and that it was transmitted by touch. At Memphis a hospital surgeon established a new record in Civil War sanitary precautions by insisting that each gangrene patient have individual sponge, cup, utensils, etc., and if he had two wounds, one gangrenous and one not, he must have two sponges. When the nurses and attendants in the gangrene ward of this hospital began to develop gangrenous sores on their hands, they were told to paint any abrasion with bromine as a precaution. It is worthy of record that no more such sores appeared.

When the major epidemics of 1864 produced 1,600 of the war's total of 2,600 cases, enough surgeons took sanitary precautions and isolated their patients quickly enough to stop the disease in its tracks. There was no gangrene epidemic in 1865, and the scattered cases were fewer than in 1862. During the last six months of its existence there was not a single case in the great base hospital of the Army of the Potomac at City Point.

8

The

General

Hospitals

AS SOON AS A SICK SOLDIER, WHOSE ILLNESS WAS RECOGNIZED AS serious, could be conveniently evacuated from the field hospital, he was sent to a "general" hospital, so called because admissions were not confined to men of any particular military unit or post. Throughout the first year of the war, these hospitals were often improvisations. One at Washington had originally been a jail; others had been hotels, girls' schools, churches and warehouses. In Philadelphia they included a railroad station, a coach factory, and a silk mill; and at Newark and Elmira they were converted furniture factories. The same kind of hurried adaptation went on throughout the West. Almost all were badly equipped; some even lacked beds, bedding, medicines and dressings. Some were so badly managed as to defy comparison with any other hospitals "in the civilized world." It is not surprising, therefore, that wounded men sometimes went to private institutions, hoping the government would pay their bills.

The sanitary commissioners, who first looked into the matter in June, 1861, were clamorous over it by December. Their agitation, along with the efforts of the new surgeon general, W. A. Hammond, who was appointed in the spring of 1862, led to the creation of a hospital system which became one of the wonders of the medical world. During the four years of the war, the general hospitals cared for 1,057,523 white soldiers with a mortality of only 8 per cent, the lowest ever recorded for military hospitals and lower than in many civil institutions. They far out-distanced the hospitals of Europe, those of the Prussians in 1870–1871 seeming dirty, badly organized and "twenty years behind us" in comparison.

Except for some small log-cabin hospitals during the War of 1812 the United States Army had no practice in hospital building. In the Mexican War, churches and convents had been considered good enough. Furthermore, European opinion was divided upon the advisability of concentrating the sick in large infirmaries. Sir John Pringle had pronounced them one of the "chief causes of mortality in armies," a dictum which the first year of the Crimean War and the experiences at large civil hospitals seemed to support. But the amazing drop in mortalities, after Florence Nightingale showed what the cleaning of hospitals could accomplish, had reopened the argument. The French, whose unhappy experiences in the Napoleonic Wars had been capped by similar tragedy in the Crimea, went through the War of 1859 in Italy (against Austria), on a basis of a multitude of small "lazarets." The results were highly gratifying; both the mortalities and the incidence of "surgical fevers" being lowered.

We know now that the high mortality was due to septic surgical and nursing methods; but a current idea attributed it to mysterious concentrations of "poison" or "effluvia" which gained in potency in direct ratio to the number of patients gathered together. Yet large general hospitals had advantages. They permitted better administration, more efficient kitchens, laundries, etc., separation of the sick and wounded on the basis of their ailment, and specialization of function on the part of the medical staff.

If the "poison" of the hospitals could be appreciably checked by fresh air as Crimean experience indicated, tent hospitals seemed an obvious solution. Conservatism and the dearth of suitable tents postponed a trial in the field until the Battle of Shiloh, April, 1862. There was no general hospital under canvas until September of that year when overcrowding of buildings in Frederick, Maryland, compelled the creation of two for the hordes of South Mountain and Antietam wounded. Similar needs led to the creation of Harewood Hospital at Washington, where tent accommodation was provided for 3,000 patients. The relatively rapid recoveries of men cared for in these institutions convinced numerous surgeons of the advantages of open-air treatment. Field hospitals were "housed" in tents or small huts throughout the remainder of the war; but general hospitals seldom used tents except in emergencies. The refusal of the authorities to heed the preachings of the tent enthusiasts was due partly to the rigors of winter weather and partly to the counter-enthusiasm for the new "pavilion" hospitals.

The Army's pavilion hospitals seem to have been suggested by British experience in the Crimea and French experience in Algeria. Other prototypes were four permanent buildings: the *Lariboiserie* (Paris), the Blackburn Hospital (England), the Boston City Hospital, and the Episcopal Hospital (Philadelphia). All had long wings branching out from a central edifice, on the theory that this would permit better segregation of the various categories of cases and would inhibit the concentration of hospital "poisons." To these advantages the army structures added another, fresh air—ventilation was an obsession of that generation.

The general hospital situation remained chaotic throughout 1861. The Quartermaster General, who saw to all army construction work, was slow to see the need for special hospital buildings. The first to be completed, at Parkersburg, West Virginia, early in 1862, consisted of two long sheds, 130 feet by

25 feet, with 14-foot ceilings. They owed their existence to Asst. Surgeon W. A. Hammond, soon to be Surgeon General. Their chief feature was the open "ridge ventilation" which kept the air fresh but made these buildings, and duplicates erected soon after, very difficult to heat in the winter. "Ridge ventilation" became a feature of American pavilion hospitals, but in its perfected form it provided for ridge-shutters which could be closed when warmth was desired. The intention was to give a building the advantages of a tent without the disadvantages: the air circulated, but there were no drafts and, in theory, the room was warm.

Profiteering by contractors joined with official lethargy to delay hospital building at Washington. Late in 1861 the Sanitary Commission approached Medical Director Charles Tripler, of the Army of the Potomac, with the suggestion that pavilions be built to accommodate 5,000 patients. Dr. Tripler, foreseeing the carnage ahead, insisted that the proposed structures provide 20,000 new beds. The sanitary commissioners returned after several days with a proposal that the War Department build on a 15,000-bed basis. At this juncture Tripler discovered that not he but the Surgeon General was to be in charge of the general hospitals at Washington.

After an appeal to General McClellan had saved his authority, he resumed conversations with the commissioners, proposing simple shacks which could be built for $25 a bed. The commissioners sent in plans for elaborate buildings estimated at $75 a bed. At McClellan's objections to the high cost, the program was reduced to 5,000 beds, although 20,000 were needed. But the contractors' bids ranged from $120 to $400 a bed, and Tripler felt able to build only two, of 200 beds each, which were not completed until April, 1862. Preparations for the expected spring offensive were made by converting private houses, stores, etc., in Alexandria, Baltimore, and Philadelphia. The fact that five large and excellent hospitals were built in 1864–1865—none at Washington—at an average cost of $31 a bed bears out Tripler's charges of profiteering.

Additional hospitals were built in 1862 in all parts of the country, and as the enormous numbers of sick and wounded poured in from the Peninsular campaign, the second Bull Run, Antietam, Shiloh, and Stone's River, it became obvious that construction in 1863 must be on a much greater scale. The 28,000 patients in general hospitals on August 1 had increased to almost 56,000 by November, to be still further augmented by great battles before the year was over. The building program increased capacity to 84,000 beds in 182 hospitals on June 30, 1863. Between that date and June 30, 1864, the number was increased to 120,521, but only eight more hospitals were added to the roster. In the last fiscal year of the war there were 204 hospitals and 136,894 beds, the maximum for the whole four years.

The pavilion hospital program

A survey of the system as of December 17, 1864, shows that it embraced every part of the North and the occupied South. The institutions ranged in size from the giant "Satterlee" at Philadelphia, with 3,500 beds, to the pygmies, "Number 6" at Kansas City, with 102 beds, and "Number 20" at Tullahoma, Tennessee, with 100. The average had 614 beds of which only 434 were then occupied. Many were still converted buildings, but the numerous large ones were vast pavilion-type structures.

So much was learned in the building program of 1862 that the hospitals of 1863 were noticeably better. They were lighter, warmer, and better ventilated; their pavilion wards were usually 150 feet long, 25 feet wide, with a 12- or 14-foot ceiling. The various "offices" such as a steam laundry, kitchen, dispensary, "dead house," food-storage cellars, ice room, baggage room, guard room, operating room, records room and female nurses' quarters were all better planned and better located.

Circumstances made Washington the principal hospital center. Its geographical situation was in its favor, and it was said that proximity of the Surgeon General made for better hospital administration than prevailed elsewhere. But it remained a dirty, sickly town, despite efforts by the military authorities to keep it clean. It was soon learned that Washington hospitals, because they were so near the front, must be always ready for inundations of wounded, and must evacuate their patients to other centers as soon as possible.

The sick and wounded from the Peninsular campaign soon filled the hospitals at Fortress Monroe to overflowing and began moving northward. It became obvious that the 6,000 beds Tripler had provided at Washington, Baltimore, and Philadelphia were inadequate. When the second Bull Run campaign added its thousands the shortage became acute. Cots were set up in the halls of Congress and among the exhibits of the patent office; Georgetown prison was emptied and converted into a hospital; newspaper advertisements begged citizens to take convalescents into their homes in order to make hospital beds available. During September old barracks were used, tent hospitals were set up, and existing hospitals were greatly enlarged, two being increased to 2,000 beds. By the end of the month, when the Antietam wounded arrived, there were 20,000 beds prepared, almost ten times the number available at the end of 1861. From August 31 to the end of 1862, 56,050 cases were treated in Washington, 44,253 of which had been admitted during the period. Nine thousand were sent elsewhere; otherwise, this great number could never have been handled. However, this solution created new problems since some of the hospitals and camps to which these men were sent were unprepared.

By the spring of 1863 benevolent visitors, the poet Longfellow among them, found the Washington hospitals improved and almost empty. Better distribution of the wounded throughout the country and the increasing number of new pavilions prevented any such crisis as that of the previous year. In September there were only 8,000 patients in the capital. As the hospitals were practically cleared before the campaign of 1864 opened, it was supposed that ample provision had been made. But Grant's tactics at the Wilderness and Spotsylvania created a new emergency: within a few weeks 26,000 sick and wounded poured in from the Army of the Potomac. Fortunately the creation of the great "depot" hospital at City Point cared for many of the wounded in the later phases of the campaign and by September there were 6,000 empty beds at Washington. At the end of 1864 the city contained sixteen hospitals, many of them large and fine; there were seven at nearby Alexandria and one each at Georgetown and at Point Lookout, Maryland. Outstanding was "Harewood," which was said to resemble "an English nobleman's estate," with professionally landscaped grounds, flower gardens, and a large vegetable garden. Its buildings consisted of fifteen big pavilions in addition to the appropriate service buildings and some tents.

Although the East had scores of general hospitals by the end of the war, scattered in large cities and small, Philadelphia was the only hospital center to rival Washington. On March 1, 1865, there were 27 hospitals and 25,000 beds in or near that city. Soldiers preferred to be sent to Philadelphia, for the food was good, the inhabitants generous and the Quaker doctors kindly and efficient.

The Western cities never got their share of new pavilion hospitals, probably because the Western troops penetrated so deeply into the South that it seemed wise to build the hospitals in Memphis, Nashville, and Chattanooga, or in the Louisville area which could be easily reached via the Cumberland and Tennessee rivers. In 1864, during the Atlanta campaign, these were the hospital bases of Sherman's army. Their combined capacity of 24,500 beds proved adequate, as only 100,000 soldiers participated in the campaign and many of the less serious cases were treated in the "traveling" general hospital which followed the army southward from Chattanooga.

The showpiece among Western hospitals was the "Jefferson," at Jeffersonville, Indiana, in the Louisville region. Built in the winter of 1863–1864 at a cost of $250,000, it provided beds for 2,000 patients, later increased to 2,600. Had the war gone on a little longer it would have been enlarged to 5,000 beds and would have been the largest hospital in existence. Its most interesting architectural feature was a circular corridor, 2,000 feet long, from which projected 24 pavilions, each 175 feet long. Grass and flowers occupied the spaces between the pavilions.

Throughout the first half of the war nothing connected with hospitals was more vexatious than their systems of admission and discharge. Patients might arrive in small groups of ten or a dozen each day for months at a time, and then suddenly, and often with no warning, by hundreds. A too-frequent result was the hauling of worn-out and suffering men from one hospital to another in the attempt to find empty beds. Another evil was the ease with which malingerers and mild cases could worm their way into the security of a general hospital during mass admissions. This loose system justified field surgeons in retaining dangerously sick patients on the claim that they could not start the men north without assurance that beds awaited them.

The situation was improved when medical directors in the field paid better attention to the administration of the hospitals within their own jurisdiction. It was clarified as regards hospitals further north when a general order of June 12, 1862, forbade medical directors to transfer patients to hospitals outside their departments without orders from the Surgeon General.

The system of hospital discharging was criticized because it provided no assurance of the patient's return to his regiment. This created friction between the Medical Department and commanding generals who saw their armies dwindling away. Early in the war many volunteer surgeons discharged men on their own authority, though they were only permitted to sign a certificate of disability, which the military authorities might or might not make the basis for a discharge. The great majority of improper discharges were innocently intended; but such laxity encouraged venality and favoritism and made things easier for malingerers. The Medical Department sought to mend matters by making the officer in charge of all hospitals in a city responsible for certificates of disability issued there, and by instructing surgeons in the field that discharge papers must be signed by the general in command. This was attacked in the Senate as "dilatory." Shortly thereafter a compromise was reached. It was provided that Regular Army surgeons must sign a discharge after the military commander had "endorsed the authority to discharge the soldier upon the usual certificate of disability."

"Sick" furloughs raised another vexatious question. Surgeons argued that many cases, particularly chronic ones, were clogging the hospitals without benefit to themselves or to the service, and urged that they be sent home. There they would thrive upon home food and loving care. But military officers hated to see men leave the Army's control. They argued, justifiably, that some men would play sick in order to get home; others would find home too attractive to leave, and would prolong their illnesses.

With hopes of an early end of the war given up in 1862, a host of politicians, benevolent ladies and state agents began lobbying to have general hospitals established in their home states and to have as many as possible of the wounded sent to them. The state agents considered it their duty to secure transfers, particularly if the patient did not like the institution in which he was. As the New Hampshire agent put it: "I frequently find a New Hampshire soldier with some disease that requires the tender treatment and pure air of home in order for his recovery."

This political pressure and certain features of the administration of general hospitals, alienated the surgeons in the field. General hospitals were said to be characterized by "elegance in appointments" and "luxury in living," where "the surgeons dress in full feather and prance about on horses" and women's societies rivalled one another in pampering the patients.

The field men glorified field hospitals as safer and better than general hospitals. Tripler had begun the policy of retention in 1861 because of a fantastic theory that the number of sick in a field hospital would remain constant. The beds cleared by evacuating patients to the rear would be quickly filled by new patients, who presumably would not sicken if there were no beds ready for them. However, there was something to be said for treating a man among his friends and sparing him the torture of transportation. Many soldiers preferred staying with the army to being sent to a general hospital, among strangers. This was especially true during 1861–1862, when some of the hospitals were bad enough to frighten anyone.

Critics of field hospitals thought that many sick could not recover in them because the surgeons gave priority to the surgical cases, the nursing service was poor, and the diet available in the field was limited and poor. These objections were pertinent, especially in 1862 when the field-hospital system had not yet been perfected. The typhoid or dysentery case could hardly thrive upon a diet of pork and beans. The negligence of some attendants and the entire absence of night nurses in a number of the hospitals occasioned accounts of field-hospital experience which read like descriptions of hell. Later in the war, better organization and the establishment of hospital gardens by the Sanitary Commission changed matters. Even then these hospitals presented few advantages for intestinal-disease cases, particularly the chronic kind.

Problems of hospital administration

The looseness of the hospital administrative system was responsible for many difficulties. In reality, there was no "system" at all. The Army medical regulations, governing both field hospitals and general hospitals, laid down a few brief injunctions, and let it go at that. The senior surgeon present was to take charge; he was to be aided by assistant surgeons; he was to visit the wards daily as long as "the state of the sick may require it"; the hospital was to be clean, well-ventilated, and uncrowded. It was suggested that one assistant surgeon be made responsible for the records and another for the equipment. In the absence of clear lines of control the hospital head was subject to both the Surgeon General and the general commanding the Military District with no rule as to who was to be obeyed when the orders conflicted. When a number of hospitals were located in the same city they might be placed under the control of a single medical officer responsible to the general commanding in the area; but for the most part the surgeons-in-charge, as hospital heads were called, were a law unto themselves, checked only by what the Sanitary Commission inspectors, and later the army medical inspectors, might report about them.

As a hospital was an army post the surgeon-in-charge was military commander over his staff and his patients. One was so impressed by this that he marched through the corridors with fife and drum when he made his visits to the sick. There was some dispute as to who should command the hospital guard in case the military officer detailed to it outranked the surgeon. This grew acute when a line officer claimed that his superior rank gave him authority over the convalescent soldiers who were doing most of the work of the hospital. To avoid such problems contract surgeons, who had no military rank, were seldom put in charge of hospitals.

The internal administration is difficult to describe because it varied so widely from place to place. Indeed, what system there was is said to have been brought about through the pressure and advice of the Sanitary Commission inspectors. The surgeon-in-charge was usually assisted by an "executive officer," a surgeon, who took charge of the records, controlled the clerks and orderlies, distributed the new patients, and left the chief free to give general supervision. There was usually a ward physician for each 75 to 100 patients. A chaplain, who acted as morale officer, operated the library, supervised the cemetery and distributed the mail. A handful of medical students, serving as medical cadets, dressed wounds and made themselves generally useful.

In some respects, the most important members of the staff were the three or four hospital stewards, usually druggists in civil life, who carried on a large part of the institution's routine. At the Hampton Hospital, Fortress Monroe, which seems to have been better organized than most, a steward and two or three assistants ran each of the three departments into which the hospital was divided. The "general steward" was responsible for the condition of the patients, clothing and hygienic state of the wards. He inspected every ward of this 1,800 bed hospital twice a day. The "commissary steward" attended to food and cooking. The "dispensing steward" operated the hospital pharmacy. Aside from the surgeons, the stewards were the only men skilled in their work and permanently attached to the staff. The wardmasters, one of whom was in charge of the nursing and cleaning in each ward, were, like a majority of the male nurses and many of the cooks, merely convalescent soldiers who might be recalled to their regiments at any moment. Most hospitals had a few female nurses or light diet cooks and a varying number of washerwomen and women kitchen-helpers. Men civilians were oftentimes hired as "contract nurses" in the latter half of the war.

A typical hospital of 1,000 beds would have twenty wardmasters, from forty to a hundred nurses, five or six cooks, eight or ten assistant cooks, from ten to fifteen carpenters, blacksmiths, etc., from ten to fifteen storeroom workers, three or four "dead-house" attendants, ten clerks in the headquarters office and library, and three attendants for the officers' quarters and mess. The staff ordinarily varied from 120 to 200 men, and in the big hospitals reached larger numbers. The "Mower" hospital at Philadelphia, the "largest hospital in the world," had a total staff, commissioned and otherwise, of 622. After the formation of the *Invalid Corps* large hospitals always had a guard in charge of one or more line officers. It was remarked that much smaller staffs would have sufficed had the government permitted the enlistment of a regular hospital corps instead of using feeble, untrained and rapidly changing convalescents. The continual complaint about most hospitals was the need for more medical men, and that as soon as an attendant learned his duties he was returned to his regiment.

The high spot of each day in the hospital wards was the morning visit of the ward physician. He would return briefly in the afternoon, but the real work was done in the morning. As the doctor entered the ward he would be met at the door by the wardmaster. Every patient able to stand was expected to leap to his feet, salute, and stand at attention until he had the surgeon's order to sit down, a command which young officers were sometimes callously slow in giving.

Looking about him, the doctor would see two rows of beds, two between each pair of windows, placed four feet apart and extending down 125- to 175-foot-long pavilions. Two kinds of beds were in use: one a wooden folding cot with a canvas cover, the other a light iron bed, with wooden slats running lengthwise. The iron bed is said to have been quite comfortable. Accompanied by a nurse and by the wardmaster, a notebook in hand to take the great man's orders, the surgeon would move from man to man down the ward, examining wounds, changing dressings, prescribing drugs and changes in diet.

The surgeon was aided by record cards which war experience had developed. Each patient wore a tag on his chest, bearing his name, rank, and unit. At the foot of each bed were two cards: one indicated by its color the particular standard diet now prescribed for the patient, the other recorded the diagnosis and treatment. When all the patients had been visited and the new orders written down the doctor would depart, leaving the wardmaster in charge.

A still greater event would be the inspection tour of the surgeon-in-charge, which in many hospitals occurred every Sunday. Its imminence tended to make Saturday the weekly cleaning day in most places, though some cleaned twice a week. Daily floor scrubbing, considered objectionable because it made the room too damp for the lungs of sick men, was unnecessary; more deplorable was the tendency of some wardmasters to leave patients in soiled garments and bedclothes until just before weekly inspection. The inspection itself was a glittering affair, with the medical officers clad in full-dress uniforms and the patients expected to appear very military.

Hospital life and morale

Such visitations helped vary the monotony, and if the surgeon-in-charge showed interest in the men, morale benefited. Once past the climax of pain the typical patient was usually in good spirits, and often even gay, though a death in the ward could plunge the whole group into deepest gloom. The chaplain, formally charged with the maintenance of good morale, could not succeed unless the attendants, and particularly the "female" nurses, were friendly and cheery.

The statement that hospital patients were easily pleased by "little comforts and pleasures which ordinary eyes can hardly see with a magnifying glass" underestimates the amount that was done for the men. The chaplain, aside from holding services and comforting the despondent, was at their beck and call as a letter writer, sometimes writing twenty-five or thirty a day.

He operated the hospital library, usually furnished by the Christian Commission. Devotional tracts were "cheerfully accepted and often faithfully read," especially Dr. Newman Hall's *Come To Jesus;* but magazines and novels were more in demand. *David Copperfield* was the most popular book in an Alexandria hospital, with Shakespeare and other classics in demand.

For those who sang, some hospitals organized choirs, and at least one institution had a dramatic society directed by the chaplain's daughter. Campbell Hospital at Washington combined beauty with occupational therapy by organizing a competition among the convalescents to see which ward could grow the best flower garden outside its windows. Hospital patients in New York and New England were entertained by free "lyceum" lectures.

This whole brighter side of hospital life is quite unimaginable without the women. In addition to their formal duties, they led singing in the wards, or played the piano to soothe the men to sleep. They hung bright window drapes, twisted garlands to hang from the rafters, wrote letters ad infinitum, baked cake, or smuggled in pickles and pie. They readily sympathized with the sick soldier in contests with authority, and were all too quick to criticize the shortcomings of surgeons. In short, being untrained, they behaved like women rather than nurses.

Under their heartening influence "the boys" became such gay dogs that amputation cases cracked jokes about buying shoes together, or gloves, or tried their hands at verse:

> Oh the weather is bad and the whisky bad,
> Bad luck to the mud and the drizzle,
> Though they chop us up like sausage meat,
> The war is a murthering fizzle
>
> The Rebs have taken the best of me legs,
> Bad luck to the chap that hit it,
> If Uncle Sam gives me a cork for me stump,
> I hope 'twill be one that will fit it.

"Hospital visitors" in the wards of the Northern hospitals, brought delicacies to tempt appetites, and would often write letters for the sick. The best of them, Walt Whitman, believed that too many came out of curiosity, and bored the men or brought them the wrong things. After depressing a patient by inquiring if he was ready to die, a religious lady presented him with a tract on the "evil effects of dancing." He threw back the covers and showed her two amputation stumps.

Probably the most humane and least military feature of Civil War hospitals was the relative ease with which mothers, wives, and sisters gained entrance to nurse their sick. Some were permitted free board at the nurses' table.

Until the Invalid Corps was formed and guard details were added to hospital staffs, there was considerable trouble, at Washington and other large cities, about the convalescents' practice of slipping out of the ward after dark to go cn a spree. Lapses of discipline were punished, the relation of doctor and patient being that of officer and enlisted man. Offenders were sent to the guardhouse, made to wear derogatory placards, or to march about carrying logs.

Good food is recognized as a curative agent of great importance. Miss Katherine Wormeley, a nurse of wide military experience, stated that she never saw food of inferior quality in an army hospital. This statement is recorded here with due solemnity because it stands alone among much contradictory testimony. Surgeon General Dale of Massachusetts, always cooperative toward the Medical Department, reported in 1862 that poor food was retarding recoveries. That same year Sanitary Commission inspectors declared the ration in hospitals of the Washington area to be generally adequate in bulk but poor in quality. Later in the war, with hospitals less crowded and better administered, things improved; but rations were too heavy by modern standards, and vitamin-bearing fruits and vegetables were dangerously inadequate.

From almost every hospital came lamentations about ill-cooked and monotonous fare. Considering how many cooks were convalescent soldiers, it is surprising that even some of them proved satisfactory.

The monotony of hospital fare was due not only to the limited range but also to the carelessness of medical officers. Standard diets would be prepared for men suffering from various complaints or in different stages of recovery, and these would be persisted in until the patient despaired. A common arrangement was "low diet," "half diet," and "full diet," to meet the respective needs of the very sick, the sick, and the convalescent patient. Typical menus not supplemented by outside gifts or purchases from a hospital fund follow:

Full Diet	**Half Diet**	**Low Diet**
Breakfast	*Breakfast*	*Breakfast*
Coffee	Coffee	Coffee or tea
Cold meat	Bread	Bread or toast
Bread	Butter	Butter
Dinner	*Dinner*	*Dinner*
Pork and beans	Mutton soup and meat	Farina gruel
Bread pudding	Boiled potatoes	Bread
	Bread	
Supper	*Supper*	*Supper*
Tea with milk	Tea with milk	Tea or cocoa
Bread and butter	Bread and butter	Bread or toast
		Butter

As time went on, women "special diet" superintendents were introduced, some from the Army Nurse Corps as agents of Dorothea Dix, others from the Christian Commission's diet-kitchen service, established in 1864. With the jellies and other delicacies offered by the Sanitary and Christian Commissions they were able to improve the "low diet" of the seriously sick, and sometimes the "full" and "half" diets as well.

But the type of foods available and the dietary ideas of that generation produced some bizarre meals. A man suffering from "inflammation of the stomach" was fed hot cakes, cheese, and molasses candy. Potatoes and plum pudding were the only non-meat additions to the government rations offered to a typhoid case.

Gardens furnished additional vegetables for many hospitals during the growing seasons, but cabbage and potatoes were the staples. Women sent canned tomatoes and canned fruits. Canning, however, was in its infancy, with condensed milk its chief contribution to the hospitals. In 1864, institutions located in regions where eggs were hard to get were furnished a new triumph of science, desiccated eggs, or "condensed eggs," as the Army called them. These dried eggs, put up in cans, were found useful in cooking. Another modern boon was ice, furnished to both field and general hospitals at a rate of one pound per day per patient for hospitals south of Washington, and half that allowance for those to the north.

A sarcastic nurse charged that hospital surgeons were deliberately opposed to good food because of their fear that the patients would become "wedded to hospital life." This was hardly fair. Surgeons might justly be charged with not varying the diet sufficiently, but they tried hard to operate their kitchens on the budgeted pittance. The standard Army ration or its commutation value of eighteen cents a day was all the government provided. The only way a hospital could acquire the money to buy provisions not specified in the ration was through the accumulation of a "hospital fund" made up of the difference in money value between the amount of rations drawn and the amount allowed. The theory was not a bad one from the standpoint of Army bookkeeping. After all, many men were too sick to eat anything like the quantity of bread, pork, and beans the Army allowed for a well man. It was supposed that "delicacies"— eggs, milk, fruit, vegetables, etc.—could be provided by spending the value of the uneaten food. This was estimated at $650 a month in a hospital of 500 beds.

But there were many unforeseen difficulties. No unit could start out with a "fund"; it had to be laboriously accumulated, which inexperienced surgeons, ungifted for business, found difficult. In at least one case a hospital accumulated a deficit instead of a fund. Some well-to-do surgeons-in-charge contributed their own money in lieu of a "fund," or while one accumulated. The problem was aggravated by rising prices. And often "fund" money had to go for other needed articles—window curtains, brushes and combs, extra liquor, and a long list of other desired items. Large city hospitals were customarily lighted by gas, but received only a small candle allowance; so the money had to be taken from the fund. The Chester Hospital, in Pennsylvania, used gas at the rate of $225 a month, but had a candle allowance of $59.

The purchase of perishables for a large institution of varying population was a great worry to some commanders. Operating on a small grant, and personally responsible for any losses by spoilage, it is not surprising that some were reluctant to purchase fresh fruits and vegetables and preferred to draw tapioca, farina, and the other dry staples from the commissary's stock.

Realizing the need for better food, Surgeon General Hammond drew up an experimental diet table based upon those of the British Army and three leading American civil hospitals. This was tried for several months in 1862 in a number of "our best" general hospitals. Recoveries were faster but all the hospitals using the new diet went into debt. Legislation permitting a larger ration allowance seemed the only answer, and Hammond persuaded Senator Henry Wilson to introduce a bill raising the commutation value of the hospital allowance from eighteen to thirty cents. But the bill was never passed.

Hospital heads tried various expedients to save money. One hired a cook at $80 a month and found that the diminished waste saved much more than the man's salary. Others resorted to cheese-paring by issuing only food enough to the cooks to meet the total of that day's diet prescriptions as computed in ounces, pints, etc. The discovery that garbage could be sold to contractors, furnished money for additional food, library books, band instruments, and other desirable things. Dr. Middleton Goldsmith, who held that the food wastage of a 1,000-bed hospital could run as high as $2,000 a month, was strongly opposed to the sale of garbage for fear that venal contractors would bribe the cooks to secure maximum waste. Careful supervision of the use of food, and insistence upon the "re-use" of left-overs, would save the hospital much more than it might get for "swill," he claimed. Goldsmith was assured by the Surgeon General that as a last resort medical purveyors were authorized to purchase anything really needed by a hospital. But Goldsmith never found a purveyor who knew he had such powers, and they do not seem to have been used. Naturally, gardens became increasingly important.

Luckily, the civilian commissions were able to supplement

the hospital diet and to furnish such "necessities" as night-clothes, rockingchairs, games, books, and cooking utensils. But the need for such aid lessened after 1862 because of the greater efficiency of hospital administration. The Sanitary Commission found that underwear, nightclothes, bandages, and liquor were most in demand. Hospitals located in the South were especially likely to need quantities of vegetables, which the commission tried to supply. Sometimes they were badly in need of milk. The day of the refrigerator car had not arrived, and milk could be supplied only by sending cows—which was sometimes done.

The sad consequences of the improper diet were lowered resistance to disease and surgical infection and a poorer battle against them after they had taken hold.

If cleanliness had been as highly esteemed as ventilation, all would have been well. Considering the publicity given to Florence Nightingale's accomplishments with soap and whitewash, it is astonishing that so much dirt was permitted. The progressive Middleton Goldsmith was one of the few surgeons who emphasized the new cult of cleanliness. "The cry of the hospital builders," he wrote, "is air, air!, ventilation, ventilation! If such people had seen as much of great hospitals as they have of books, the cry would be water, water!, cleanliness, cleanliness!"

The general inspections of hospitals which took place under Sanitary Commission auspices in 1862 and in 1864, with a few special visits interspersed, produced plenty of evidence on hospital filth. The subject is scarcely mentioned elsewhere. Only "bad" hospitals, poorly administered in nearly every respect, were outwardly dirty to the naked eye. Those at Cumberland, Maryland, or "Carver Barracks," "Emory," and "Columbian" at Washington may have had filled bedpans sitting about in the wards or on the stairs, used dressings lying about in the wards, and piles of trash on the grounds. But most hospitals kept things picked up, and cleaned the floors regularly, using the "dry" method of scouring with sand so that their patients might be spared the risk of tetanus that "wet" cleaning was thought to entail. Even in 1862, when conditions were much worse than in later years, the majority were dirty in only one particular: their plumbing.

Since intestinal diseases were more common than any others no fault could have been worse. New hospitals ordinarily had water closets, but frequently lacked the water to flush them regularly. The Central Park hospital at New York City occupied a building so tall that pressure would not raise the water to the toilets on the upper floors.

A good many buildings were equipped with a type of latrine especially admired in Philadelphia—a long zinc trough covered by a row of seat holes, with a water faucet at one end and a sewer-pipe hole at the other. In theory the water ran all the time and kept the trough clean, but not in actuality. To save water the tap was sometimes turned off entirely until a great quantity of ordure had collected. In a number of instances excellent toilets were provided, but these had to be flushed by water carried some distance in buckets—which put a premium upon infrequent flushing.

To come a step lower in sanitary arrangements, the Harewood Hospital at Washington, which began in tents, was unable to enforce the use of the trench latrines provided and, as a consequence, was soon surrounded by a wide area of ground covered with excrement from the intestines of the sick. Nauseating examples of this sort of thing could be multiplied. Suffice it to say that these conditions were almost universal in the first half of the war.

Typhoid, the dysenteries, and malarial fevers were the leading diseases of the war. The first two are spread by contamination from the excrement of patients or by carriers, and the third by infected Anopheles mosquitoes. Since the typhoid bacillus is frequently carried on the feet of flies on their way from the dirty latrine to the kitchen or the patient's tray, the presence of myriads of flies in the Washington hospitals, and in most of the others, is significant. The juxtaposition of latrines and kitchen, as at the Union Hotel Hospital in Alexandria, merely gave the winged hordes an additional advantage. Protection was offered against both flies and mosquitoes by mosquito nets draped on frames over the beds in most hospitals, but without any realization of the role of these insects in carrying disease. The patients usually felt stifled by the netting, and it could not be kept in place once they were well enough to get up and remove it.

A small percentage of recovered typhoid and dysentery patients continue to be carriers for months or years afterwards. Such people would be especially dangerous if assigned to kitchen duty, as some convalescents were. Slack methods of dish washing sharpened such dangers—and sometimes methods were very slack.

Though hospital water supplies came from every source, they seldom roused the suspicion of the surgeon. Large-city institutions usually had city water, which was untreated and unfiltered; some had wells, some used river water; and at Memphis and New Orleans they had rain water. The hospitals in the northern part of Washington, D.C. had to be supplied by water carts. Those at Camp Dennison, Ohio, and Hendersonville, Kentucky, used sources which had probably been contaminated by excrement, though no exceptional results were reported. The situation of some hospitals near open public sewers, as in Washington and Nashville, was recognized as an evil. Malaria and dysentery were believed by some doctors to be unusually prevalent in institutions so located; but nothing was done.

Kitchens and laundries were not severely censured in the commission's reports. Few, however, were singled out for praise.

The prodding of the Surgeon General and the Sanitary Commission brought earnest efforts for improvement. These were observed in a number of special inspections late in 1863 and in another general inspection in 1864. The Sanitary Commission quite rightly claimed a large share of the credit, but the Medical Department had also made contributions. The publication of Hammond's *Hygiene* and Woodward's *Hospital Stewards Manual* in 1863 established official standards to which surgeons and attendants could be held. These were supposedly enforced by the Army medical inspectors, commissioned, in 1862, who must have performed a useful function despite charges that they showed more interest in military punctilio than in dirty bedclothes.

Some attention should be paid here to the numerous specialized infirmaries which took shape as the war progressed. London hospitals avoided segregation of contagious-disease patients in order that the "poison" might not become concentrated and thus more malignant. Tested at Bellevue in New York this scheme worked badly. When measles and other "eruptive" fevers swept through the unsegregated sick of the army in 1861, isolation hospitals were established throughout the country. Some were crude and depressing at first, but they improved until, in 1864, the 750-bed "smallpox hospital" at Memphis was cited as an especially attractive institution, and its low mortality rate was attributed to its pleasant environment. Although most of these "pest houses" were called "smallpox" or "eruptive" hospitals they frequently treated patients suffering from other communicable diseases.

Other types of special hospital included "eye and ear infirmaries" at St. Louis and Washington, an institution for cripples at Wheeling, and, of course, the famous Turner's Lane Hospital at Philadelphia, all of whose 400 beds were devoted to sufferers from nerve wounds or nervous disorders. It was found necessary to establish a venereal hospital at Nashville in 1863. St. Louis seems to have had the first "distributing hospital," a small building near the railway station where incoming patients might rest up until appropriate hospital accommodations were found for them. Another of this type was located at Philadelphia, and also served as headquarters for the medical director of transportation who had charge of routing patients to the various general hospitals of the East.

The care of wounded officers proved a complicated problem. Because they were salaried men and paid for their food they were kept out of Army hospitals, which were thought of as paternalistic refuges for the underpaid enlisted men. Ordinarily, if he were not down for long, the sick or wounded officer was treated in quarters, his "dog-robber" orderly acting as nurse. In case of prolonged illness he usually asked for and obtained sick-leave home. But some officers were too sick to travel; and some had no home to go to and lacked the means to stay in a private hospital. For these a floor was set aside at "Armory Square" in Washington and a special hospital opened at Philadelphia in the winter of 1862–1863. The officers' hospital opened at Memphis about the same time has been pictured as a squalid place. The government furnished only medicine and medical advice. There were no beds, no bedclothes, no night clothes, no pillows, and no nurses—only a hundred melancholy "officers and gentlemen," dependent upon their "stupid" colored servants. This establishment was soon taken over by the Western Sanitary Commission, though charity for officers had not been included in its plan.

The War Department placed things on a sensible basis in March of 1864 by ordering that one officers' hospital be established in each military department, to be operated by the medical director of the department. The officers were charged $1.00 a day, and thirty cents extra if a personal servant boarded there. By December, ten had been established, ranging in size from an institution of 409 beds, at Annapolis, Maryland, to the tiny twenty-bed affair at Beaufort, South Carolina. Altogether, they provided 1,058 beds, of which 653 were then occupied. The officers were irritated by the $1.00-a-day fee, and when kept longer than they considered necessary they attributed it to the desire of the surgeon-in-charge to get his hands on their money.

With all their flaws the Civil War hospitals may be considered a credit to the nation. A country which lacked experience with military hospitals, and had had very little experience with large civil hospitals, had created a vast system with a capacity of 136,000 beds. This had been done in less than four years and in the midst of the confusion of a war which had not been prepared for. The hospitals had not fed their patients well, some had faulty plumbing, and complaints indicated neglect of the individual ego; but their mortalities were low.

As Samuel Johnson remarked apropos of a dog walking on his hind legs, the significant thing was not whether it was done "well or ill," but that it was done at all. Yet many hospitals performed very well indeed, like the great 3,500-bed "Mower" in 1864. Even in 1862 the Sanitary Commission inspectors found some like "Mount Pleasant," at Washington, where latrines were clean, diet was good, books were well kept, the hospital fund was adequate, the laundry excellent,—and there were "no cases of contagious fever or dysentery." Speaking in 1905, the great S. Weir Mitchell praised the hospitals as they were by the third year of the war and doubted that they had "even yet been excelled."

Nurses,

Staffs,

and

Convalescents

THE DOCTORS OF THE MEDICAL CORPS HAVE ALREADY BEEN discussed at length. The contract surgeons, however, who made up the great majority of hospital surgeons, were enough different to warrant separate treatment. Although they might, and sometimes did, wear officers' uniforms and were called "acting assistant surgeons," they held no commission but worked under contract. In the course of the war 5,500 were engaged. Many, however, served for only three or six months; the number on duty at one time averaged 1,500.

Candidates were expected to be medical school graduates and had to pass examinations before boards established by the Medical Department or departmental medical directors. Yet it was often charged that unfit persons were employed—not only such "irregulars" as botanics and homeopaths but some who had never seen the inside of a professional school. Those whose education could not be criticized were the "lame ducks" profession, who had failed in private practice through inc petence or drunkenness. Considering the efficiency of most hospitals and the need of reformers to find villains it would probably be unfair to conclude that the majority of contract surgeons were bad. But they were complimented so seldom and complained of so much that one suspects they averaged lower in quality than the profession at large.

There were good reasons for this. Until 1864 pay for fulltime service was only $80 to $100 a month. For part-time appointments—and many worked on that basis—it might be as low as $30. They had no military rank or authority and no opportunity for promotion. Commissioned men, on the other hand, ranked as majors and drew $165 a month, if full surgeons; assistant surgeons were captains or first lieutenants and received $100 or $130. Furthermore, commissioned men assigned to hospital duty received an extra $40 to $60 allowance for quarters. Assistant surgeons could become surgeons; surgeons could rise to administrative positions that made them lieutenant colonels or colonels.

It must also be remembered that the absence of thousands of doctors from civil practice left a golden harvest for those who remained at home. Consequently, it took fervent patriotism or sheer inability to build up a practice to draw physicians into government service. The efficient and patriotic man would be likely to try for a commission with its prestige, higher pay, and opportunity for field service. It was mainly the poorer sort who became contract surgeons. Some of the incompetents merely neglected their patients; others were drunkards; a few defrauded their hospitals or their patients.

Luckily there were enough good commissioned men and competent contract surgeons in the hospitals to make such conduct the exception. Even during the confusion of 1862 the Sanitary Commission's inspectors could praise the medical staffs of half the hospitals visited. In 1864 a larger proportion of commis-

st of whom had field service, were placed on

ies start a new profession

The outstanding contribution to hospital morale made by women nurses has already been mentioned. Their presence in hospitals was not only one of the outstanding novelties of the war, but an event in American social history. The war opened the gates of a great profession to women at a time when their economic opportunities were scarce.

As the president of the Sanitary Commission put it, "the month of April, 1861 was distinguished not more by the universal springing of the grass, than by the uprising of the women of the land." To put this horde of eager women to effective use in the hospitals required special experience and understanding. When Dorothea Dix, renowned founder of insane asylums, appeared in the office of the Secretary of War on April 19, she must have seemed Godsent. She was acquainted with the work of the British Sanitary Commission, and had visited the hospitals reformed by Florence Nightingale on the Black Sea. Having persuaded politicians to reform jails and establish insane asylums, she presumably knew how to deal with practical men.

Her services were accepted almost immediately. At first she was restricted to providing nurses for the hospitals in and near Washington, but in June she became "Superintendent of Female Nurses" without territorial limits. It remained for Congress to make "female" nurses legal and provide for their pay. This was done in August, the act providing that women might be substituted for men "in general or permanent hospitals when it seems desirable to the Surgeon General or the surgeon-in-charge." The salary was set at 40 cents a day and one ration.

Meanwhile the wisdom and propriety of permitting women to nurse became a subject of public controversy. Some objected that women nurses would faint at the sight of blood and disturb the wounded men with their hysterics. Others felt that women would only get in the way of the doctors, and be no help through lack of physical strength to lift their patients. Others worried over the affronts to modesty involved in nursing. Others feared that girls were drawn to the hospitals by the hope of finding love there, as in some contemporary romances about the Crimea. But Henry W. Bellows of the Sanitary Commission suggested that the volunteer soldiery were of such different clay from Regulars that they would benefit greatly from women's care.

An anonymous writer who showed familiarity with the Nightingale epic took a middle position. He granted that the feminine touch would make "all the difference" in some cases, but he urged that the women appointed be few in number, mature, and thoroughly trained to their duties—conclusions much like those of Miss Dix. To the editor of a medical journal the irrefutable argument in favor of the women was that they would keep the hospitals clean.

Conservative men and "womanly women" had their doubts; but they could not check the flood. That summer so many would-be nurses poured into Washington that the government had to beg Miss Dix to try to stop them at the source.

With "thousands" of applicants to choose from, the new superintendent established rigid standards of fitness. These seem curious to the eye of a later generation, unfamiliar with the Victorian canons of propriety. The candidates, each of whom was personally examined by Miss Dix, had to be past thirty, healthy, "plain almost to repulsion in dress, and devoid of personal attractions." Further requirements, as we are informed by a successful applicant, included knowledge of "how to cook all kinds of low diet" and renunciation of "colored dresses, hoops, curls, jewelry, and flowers on their bonnets." They must "look neat themselves, and keep their boys and wards the same. Must write and read for their boys, but not from any book or *newspaper;* must be in their own rooms at taps, or nine o'clock unless obliged to be with the sick; must not go to any place of amusement in the evening; must not walk out with any patient or officer in their own room except on business; must be willing to take the forty cents per day that is allowed by the government, to assist them in supplying what the rations . . . will not furnish in food," and be ready to spend what was left of their salaries on the welfare of their patients. These regulations were to prove the superintendent's undoing. It developed that age and homeliness did not guarantee good nursing.

Since Western women would not come to Washington to be examined, Miss Dix delegated powers of appointment to Mrs. D. P. Livermore of Chicago and James E. Yeatman of St. Louis. The latter, an officer of the Western Sanitary Commission, was considerably less rigid than Miss Dix in his requirements.

The exact number of women nurses has never been established. They included many whose appointments were irregular or illegal. Samuel Ramsey, former chief clerk of the medical bureau, estimated the total at around 3,200. They were rare early in the war, especially in the West. Yeatman licensed as many as 100 in only two months, late in 1863, but in May of 1864 it was reported that only 273 appointed by him were in service. The ratio of women nurses to men averaged one to about four or five, with the proportion varying from hospital to hospital.

The role of women "nurses," and the friction between them and the surgeons, cannot be understood unless it is realized that there was not a single trained nurse, as we use the term, in all America. Some, however, were partially trained, in special short courses.

The active phase of the war had hardly begun before it became apparent that Miss Dix, of whom so much had been expected, lacked administrative talents, while her obstinate and over-scrupulous sense of duty kept her continually at loggerheads with medical officers. When she was needed at Washington, she might be away on one of her long trips through the country. When she was in Washington she would spend much of her time distributing relief goods sent in response to her appeals. She would drive from hospital to hospital to learn what they lacked, and supplied it from stores she kept in a house she had rented. When a likely nurse candidate arrived in town, she might give up half a day to conducting the newcomer through the hospitals and finding a niche for her. She spurned a salary and with her own money rented a house where nurses could live while awaiting assignment, and to which they could return for rests. She sent food to nurses who found it hard to feed themselves on the twenty cents a day allowed them for rations. If one displeased the hospital chief under whom she worked, Miss Dix took her part, sometimes insisting that she stay in her position after the chief had discharged her. When bills to give soldiers land grants were introduced she sought, unsuccessfully, to have her nurses included. In four long years she never took a day off.

Creditable as these activities were to her heart, they show her as a muddled executive, too ready to champion her subordinates and unwilling to compromise with faltering human nature. She must have seemed to some like a mother hen who folds her chicks beneath her wings and cackles defiance at a hostile world. Although she clung to her post to the end, Miss Dix knew she was unequal to the task. "This is not the work I would have my life judged by," was her melancholy confession.

Trouble began when the first semitrained women arrived at Washington in 1861, with the idea that they were to be "head nurses," supervising the work of the men. Naturally they were affronted when assigned to menial tasks such as dishwashing. They found themselves "objects of continual evil speaking among coarse subordinates" and "looked at with a doubtful eye by all but the most enlightened surgeons." Miss Dix's injunctions to stand on their dignity and to assert their rank as "second only to the ward surgeon" led to clashes in which the women were threatened, snubbed, starved and, in a number of cases, sent back to their indignant superintendent.

This prompted the Surgeon General, in the fall of 1862, to consider the advisability of a "different management system" for the women. Since Miss Dix's medical enemies were too numerous to be removed, the Gordian knot might have been cut by her own removal. But War Secretary Stanton's resolute support made this impossible. Miss Dix wanted to fill out her monopoly in appointments with a rule that her nurses could not be discharged without cause, while the surgeons wanted the right to use or dispense with Miss Dix's appointees as they saw fit.

General order No. 351, issued on Oct. 29, 1863, presumably as a compromise, was in reality a victory for the surgeons. Superficially it seemed to give Miss Dix what she wanted: if a nurse was discharged the hospital commander had to offer specific reasons; no female nurses were to be carried on the muster roll except those of Miss Dix, "unless specially appointed by the Surgeon General." The "joker" in this last provision was readily apparent to the superintendent of female nurses, and in the words of her latest biographer it "broke her heart." Joseph K. Barnes, Acting Surgeon General, showed his attitude when he assured a young girl who had failed of regular appointment that henceforth he would enroll any woman requested by a hospital head "irrespective of age, size or looks."

Now nurses who had been employed by Miss Dix but disliked working under her asked for special appointments, as did the many women who had been serving without official status. These last included not only girls whose youth had barred them from consideration but also such famous older nurses as "Mother" Newcomb and "Mother" Bickerdyke, whose personalities had won them the devotion of the soldiery. Mrs. Newcomb felt so assured that she declined appointment when the superintendent offered it. The use of colored women in hospital wards was legalized in 1864, though they had been so employed earlier. State relief societies, like that of Indiana, sent an increasing number of women to the hospitals. Once they had attained official status, the younger women were able to take a more kindly view of "Miss Dix's nurses"; and now that they need have only women of whom they approved the surgeons complained less.

Every type of woman was to be found in the hospital, from a "drunken, swearing" English nurse at Alexandria to the gently bred Emily Parsons at St. Louis. Some were eccentric, others old and crochety; but most were self-sacrificing. A number of those who had been too young for Miss Dix were conspicuously successful, among them Cornelia Hancock, a spirited Quakeress, and Helen Gilson, of Lynn, Massachusetts, a beauty who wore a picturesque short-skirted costume and charmed her patients with her singing. Walt Whitman, however, thought the older, more maternal women made the best nurses. Some proved negligent, and some, like the "funereal lady" described by Louisa May Alcott, were temperamentally unfitted for hospital sights and smells. A few proved implacable toward their Confederate patients.

A half dozen were the wives of generals; one was the widow of a governor. Katherine Wormeley was the daughter of a British admiral; the three Woolsey sisters were the daughters of a president of Yale; Mary Husband was the wife of a prominent Philadelphia lawyer and a granddaughter of Robert Morris.

Most of them were the wives or daughters of substantial middle-class citizens, accustomed to obedience in the home and to polite, respectful masculine attention. A number were teachers or home missionaries. "Mother" Bickerdyke, the most famous of them all, was a hired housekeeper when the war began.

Fears for the virtue of women exposed to life among rough warriors were not borne out. Almost without exception the men were respectful; and all but a handful of the women behaved with decorum. Despite stern official disapproval, some nurses did not discourage sentiment in their patients. To the disgust of Miss Dix a number married and left the service, among them a nun who renounced her vows in order to marry an officer patient.

Considering the variety of women nurses and their lack of training, it is not surprising that many vexed the surgeons. The usual attitude of medical officers was that they were "permitted nuisances," especially at hospitals near the front. Their greatest failing was self-righteousness. All too many ignored Florence Nightingale's prime rule, "silent obedience." They came to the Army convinced of their moral superiority and of the vileness of men who smoked, drank, and swore. The insubordination they permitted themselves could hardly win the regard of their superiors. Those who kept quiet and did as they were told, behaving like modern trained nurses, had few difficulties; the other kind had plenty. A few unusual women, with "Mother" Bickerdyke as the best example, managed to combine "executive temperaments" with good sense in a way which permitted them to expose the Medical Corps' black sheep and defy military procedure without forfeiting the good will of the doctors.

A major grievance of surgeons was the tendency of women nurses to ignore prescriptions of medicines and diet. Some would not only slip forbidden foods onto a patient's tray, but would go so far as to substitute some home remedy of their own for the doctor's drugs, or even give cold drinking water to dangerously sick men for whom it was forbidden. "Mother" Newcomb was especially independent. She ignored curfew regulations for patients; she made trips home when the spirit moved her; she dosed men with her own "syrups," and she even prevented an amputation by shouting, "I don't care who sent you, nor what authority you work under. . . . I wear no shoulder-straps, but that boy's arm shall not come off while I am here." At Washington, Rebecca Pomroy allowed a patient to slip out of the ward for a night of gaiety, furnishing "beefsteak money" to brighten the expedition. He came back drunk; but his nurse was willing to arrange and finance a second excursion, from which he likewise returned drunk. Mrs. Mary Husband outraged the military authorities by making it her hobby to review court-martial cases and to attempt to win executive clemency for the culprits. These were good women, performing acts of kindness; but armies decry and doctors deplore such behavior. To the surgeons they were "fussy female notoriety seekers," . . . "quarrelsome, meddlesome, busybodies."

Another grievance was an alleged insistence upon "comforts."

A nurse's baggage, it was said, "exceeds that of the field and staff of a regiment." As John H. Brinton put it,

To him (i.e., the surgeon-in-charge) at last these wretched females would come. They did not wish much, not they, simply a room, a bed, a looking glass, someone to get their meals and do little things for them, and they would nurse "the sick boys of our gallant Union army." "Simply a room!" Can you fancy half a dozen or a dozen old hags, for *that* is what they were (our modern trained nurses were unknown), surrounding a bewildered hospital surgeon, each one clamoring for her little wants. And rooms so scarce and looking glasses so few! And then, when you had done your best, and had often sacrificed the accommodations of the sick to their benefit, how little gratitude did one receive. Usually nothing but complaints, fault-finding as to yourself, and back biting as to companions of their own sex.

This unhappy doctor solved his problem by sending the ladies packing, and replacing them with nuns, who were content with one room for the entire fifteen.

But there were surgeons who appreciated women as nurses, and there were more still who were pleased to have them supervise the light-diet kitchen and the laundry, or take the responsibility for the hospital's liquor stock. The patients preferred the women nurses, especially when they violated Miss Dix's regulations and brightened the wards by wearing light-colored dresses. Their tenderness with the dying was appreciated, as was their usually cheering conversation, which was in marked contrast with the gloomy, matter-of-fact toughness of male nurses. Their true role was that of Mother-substitutes, and unquestionably their presence made hospital life more bearable.

One of Dorothea Dix's oddities was the resolute anti-Catholic feeling which made her refuse appointment to a Catholic woman "if a Protestant could be substituted." It grieved her to see hospital heads ridding themselves of her nurses and substituting nuns. The Sisters were highly commended by the surgeons who worked with them, chiefly because they had been trained to obedience. Soldier patients liked them, and scornful but envious Protestant nurses had to concede them the virtues of "order and discipline," though sometimes questioning their "neatness" and intelligence. It was suggested that Protestant nursing orders be established.

Nuns seem to have been used first in the West, where by the fall of 1861 groups from convents in Indiana and Michigan had taken over the nursing in hospitals at Cairo and Paducah. They replaced regular women nurses in the large general hospital at Mound City, Illinois, in 1862, and were soon installed at Memphis. A number from Bardstown, Kentucky, took charge in several Louisville hospitals. In the East, a group of 60 nursed on the hospital boats plying to the York peninsula in the spring of 1862. Later on, two very large general hospitals, the Satterlee at Philadelphia and the Cliffburne at Georgetown, D.C., were staffed by them, and soon Sisters were established in a number of other good-sized institutions.

The soldiers commonly referred to all these women as "Sisters of Charity." Actually, three other orders participated: the Sisters of Mercy, Sisters of St. Joseph, and Sisters of the Holy Cross. Some lacked prior hospital experience, having been schoolteachers; but the proportion with previous nursing experience appears to have been much higher than among the Protestant nurses. As to their technical competence, a distinguished surgeon, writing forty years after the war, remarked: "We should not think them particularly skilled at the present day, but they were very good for that day."

Male attendants: the convalescent problem

The trump card of the advocates of female nurses was the uneven quality of male attendants. Little if any better than their counterparts in the field hospitals, these men evoked few compliments and many curses. At the start they were always soldiers of the line, sometimes detailed from nearby garrisons but usually convalescent invalids. If detailed men, they were likely to be of poor quality because no colonel wished to lose the services of a good trooper, even temporarily. If convalescents, they were so enfeebled, demoralized, and fretful that they might behave savagely to the helpless bed patients. In either case they lacked training and few showed natural aptitude. And they were nearly always called back to their regiments as soon as they had learned enough to be of any use.

The obvious answer to the problem was a regularly enlisted hospital corps, whose members would be chosen, trained and disciplined for the work. Such a body could have been recruited among civilians too old or too young for line service, or those with a tendency to hernia, or to imperfect vision, but who were educated and had an interest in the work. Nor would this deplete the fighting forces. But the conservative traditions of the Regular Army prevailed, and only feeble substitute measures could be adopted. One initiated in 1862 was a so-called "hospital corps" of civilians hired on short contracts at $20.50 a month. Its members were put into uniform and organized into squads of eleven under "squad chiefs,"—quite their sole resemblance to a military body. They were regarded as "a filthy, saucy lot," hard to hold for the duration of their contracts and apt to neglect or abuse their patients. Tales are told of their stealing money from patients, or selling them morphine. The government, preferring enlisted men, put obstacles in the way of engaging these civilians.

Getting work out of them was the responsibility of the hospital stewards, who had some background in medical affairs and were not subject to frequent transfers. They exercised their authority through ward masters who supervised the work of the wards. Experience suggested the value of specialization of responsibility. It was recommended that the routine duties of a ward be divided among eight attendants as follows: two waiters; two night nurses; one to sweep and clean walls, floors and windows; one to keep up the fires and manage the lights; one to clean the bathroom and toilets; and one to dispense medicines. In addition all were to tend the sick, bathing those too ill to bathe themselves. Sometimes they were asked to assist in wound dressing, but usually proved poor at it. Some of these "nurses by accident" did their clumsy best to make the patients comfortable, but they seldom understood the importance of cleanliness, hated cleaning as "women's work," and thus contributed to higher mortalities.

All that can be said in favor of the use of convalescents as nurses is that it saved some men from premature return to the line and gave them something to do. The convalescent not put to such work was the Army's "forgotten man." A little more concern was shown him in the East than in the West, but in both regions he received little attention and his morale suffered. He showed little interest in the language and mathematical courses offered him and shunned hospital work. To relieve their boredom a few pulled wires to rejoin their regiments, only to suffer relapses or crawl through months of unhappy semi-invalidism.

Colonels often complained that hospitals held patients too long, but the evidence points to the opposite. The overcrowding of the hospitals early in the war led to overhasty discharges. The results of this seem to have prompted an order of the Secretary of War that patients who would be unfit for duty within thirty days be discharged from the service at their own request. But events after April, 1862, when the order was issued, created such a demand for men that every effort was made to retain them.

Special commissions were sent to the hospitals to determine which patients might be returned to duty, which should remain in hospital, and which be discharged. These commissions included surgeons but for the most part were controlled by ignorant or callous line officers. Some men with unhealed wounds or pulmonary consumption were ordered to the front. Hospital attendants usually being the least feeble, they were the most frequently chosen to return to the line. Their departure sometimes disorganized the whole hospital administration and some boards tried to bear the hospitals' needs in mind.

What happened may be seen in the proportions of examinees retained in hospital by two commissions. Commission "A," headed by a medical inspector, left 23 per cent in the hospital; commission "B," headed by a line officer, only 3 per cent. But surgeons-in-charge soon learned how to fight back. They simply "forgot" to send back a patient whose health might be endangered by removal. And attendants whom they valued were simply hidden when the examiners appeared.

The unfortunates pulled back too soon might die at a Sanitary Commission lodge on their way to the front, or might suffer a relapse which landed them in another hospital. The insatiable need for both men and hospital beds in the campaign of 1864 accelerated hospital purges. In one week in June more than 10,000 men were pulled back to their regiments from institutions in Washington alone.

The Invalid Corps, established in April, 1863, represented an attempt to keep disabled soldiers in the service and to provide a better system of hospital guards. It was formed on a territorial basis, the men from the various states being proportionately distributed among the 161 companies of the Corps. There were two battalions, one made up of men physically unfit for field service but capable of garrison duty; the second of amputees able to act as watchmen or, occasionally, as attendants. Men might be transferred to the new unit directly from regiments in the field upon the order of a general commanding an army corps. But the great majority were "recruited" directly from the general hospitals and from the convalescent camps, the examining commissions having indicated which patients were "eligible" and for which battalion. In its eleven months' existence the Invalid Corps grew to 28,000 men, about three-fourths in the first battalion. Before the end of 1863 its members in Washington and vicinity, 9,000 strong, passed in review down Pennsylvania Avenue, dressed in new, distinctive, sky blue uniforms.

The new organization proved unpopular and brought many complaints. Good soldiers who felt strong enough for duty wanted to return to their regiments; if they felt weak they wanted to be sent home. They shrank from joining a group the members of which were, to their minds, neither soldiers nor civilians, and stigmatized as cowards. For, according to gossip, the corps was being filled with men the officers wanted to be rid of, and healthy men whom the surgeons got into the corps because they wanted to keep them on as attendants. Their officers were believed to be the undesirables of the active army and this belief persisted despite publication of denials by the War Department investigators. Men of the second battalion, on hospital duty, quailed before the quips and jibes of the patients, and the whole Corps resented being paraded about wearing "toy swords" and a gaudy uniform which proclaimed them to be either physical wrecks or "favorites averse to fighting."

To meet these reactions the Invalid Corps was reorganized into a "Veterans' Reserve Corps." A large number of physically sound soldiers whose three-year enlistments had run out and who did not want to reenlist for combat service were enrolled. Another change was designed to guarantee a satisfactory officer personnel by placing the appointive power in the hands of the Provost Marshal General, who commanded the corps. Commanders in the field now could not fob off their incompetent officers on the "Invalids." The Veteran's Corps was organized like its predecessor in two battalions, and grew to 60,000 men, not all of whom, however, were members at the same time.

The first battalion is said to have given valuable service in the defense of Washington during Early's raid and in the guarding of railways, bridges, and government property. The second battalion, both before and after reorganization, gave the Medical Department what it had long wanted—organized military companies, controlled by line officers, to guard the hospitals and care for the clothing and effects of the patients.

These tasks seem to have been reasonably well performed after Secretary Stanton had made it clear that the guard officers must take orders from the hospital commanders. But both "Invalids" and "Veterans" proved unsatisfactory attendants. Many were not physically capable of standing up to the work; others were shirkers and malingerers.

In October, 1862, President Lincoln wrote to Surgeon General Hammond:

A Baltimore committee called on me this morning, saying that city is full of straggling soldiers, half-sick, half-well, who profess to have been turned from the hospitals with no definite directions where to go. Is this true? Are men turned from the hospitals without knowing where to go?

A. LINCOLN.

Unknown to the President, the military authorities had already made the stumbling beginnings of a "convalescent camp" policy intended to end the straggling complained of by the Baltimore committee and to permit semi-invalids to recover their vigor without taxing the hospitals. As there were always men on leave, recruits, and stragglers who did not know how to find their units it was felt that they too might be allowed to stop briefly at a "distribution" camp before being escorted to the front.

The idea was a sound one in the case of patients actually convalescent. It was "discovered" in World War I that the latter stages of recovery were accelerated at such camps. In 1918 they were delightful places. One, under British auspices, was an attractive "village" of 3,000 men, living surrounded by flowers and amusing themselves with orchestras, a theater, billiards, golf, and cricket. Most of their Civil War counterparts were temporary, and because of their mixed population of convalescents and strays, were known only as "military depots." A few, housed in wooden barracks, developed into feeble foreshadowings of the British camp just described. Four of the more or less permanent convalescent camps were located in the West: Camp Chase, Camp Dennison, Camp Douglas, and Benton Barracks. The East had only the small and relatively unimportant one at David's Island, New York, and the very large one at Alexandria, Virginia, through which flowed patients from all the general hospitals east of the Alleghenies, for more than two years.

This great camp had its beginnings in the hectic last days of

August, 1862, when the hospitals of the Washington region over-flowed with the wounded from the second Bull Run, sent from the field hospitals of the Army of the Potomac which had to clear themselves of patients in order to follow the troops to Antietam. Miserable thousands from both general and field hos-pitals were herded together at a point two miles south of Wash-ington on the Virginia side of the Potomac. Their experiences there, and those of their successors for the next nine months, were a disgrace. The Medical Department, unfortunately, was not in charge of the camp, and the Army of the Potomac, which controlled it, underwent a rapid succession of commanding gen-erals none of whom bothered with what was regarded as a temporary camp.

As the autumn advanced and the nights grew colder, it won its nickname—"Camp Misery." It was "a sort of a pen, into which all who could limp, all deserters and stragglers, were driven promiscuously." There, huddled in torn and dirty tents, they dragged out a weary existence on the standard salt pork, beans, and hardtack of the Army ration. The arrival of winter made matters worse. The camp site was at the foot of a long slope down which water gushed after every rain, turning the ground on which the tents sat into a freezing quagmire. Men are said to have stood up all night rather than lie in it. The more sickly "convalescents" began to die off in December. Sanitary and Christian Commission agents passed out what comforts they could; one began "kidnapping" bad cases, and taking them to the hospital. The stronger men had been sent on to the Army, leaving only the weak to make out as best they could without enough clothing or blankets, without fuel, and without hope. There were many cases of pneumonia and intestinal diseases, and almost universal depression.

One night a group of Congressmen awakened General Samuel P. Heintzelman, commander of the Washington garrison, to in-form him that a number of men had frozen to death. The general sent out firewood and after an investigation ordered the camp relocated just north of Alexandria. The new site was occupied by

Christmas Day, and construction was begun on 50 wooden barracks, each to house 100 men.

But with convalescents as the laborers it took some time to complete the buildings, and conditions continued bad for months. At the new site the "Distribution and Recruit" camps were located on a ridge, but the convalescent camp proper was in a valley. Its drainage and policing were abominable. An inspection report of January 19, 1863, describes the drains as "mere ruts chiseled out around the tents, without outlets, and . . . already filled with bread, beans, rice, bones and other refuse indescribable in characteristics." The inhabitants of the distribution camp had littered the hillside with their excrement, while down in the valley the 7,000 convalescents—many with intestinal diseases—had been permitted to defecate where they willed. "Consequently," wrote the sanitary inspector, "we find about the grounds, an area of over three acres, encircling the camp as a broad belt, on which is deposited an almost perfect layer of human excrement." Since much of this area was on higher ground, the rain washed the ordure into the camp and into the spring and brook from which the drinking water was drawn. At the time of this inspection the food was good and the clothing plentiful, but the men begged to be discharged.

Congress took notice of "Camp Convalescent" in December when Senator Daniel Clark charged that its surgeons were embezzling the rations. A few weeks later Senator James Harlan defended the Army with a libel on the American standard of living. Ninety-nine per cent of the men out at Alexandria were living better than they ever had at home, he said. Some had to sleep on piles of brush, it was true, but he maintained that anyone who had ever gone camping knew that that was no hardship. A counter "eyewitness," Senator John C. Teneyck, painted a different picture. "Camp Convalescent," he concluded, should be renamed "Camp Relapse."

As late as April, 1863, the Connecticut state agents denounced it as "an unmitigated pest, destructive alike to the health and morals of the men and a nuisance which ought to be abated." But summer weather brought relief, and when autumn arrived the building program had been completed and a new camp commander had brought order out of chaos. Besides barracks for 5,000 convalescents there were cook houses and dining halls, a post office, a church with 1,200 seats, a library, a photographers' gallery, permanent quarters for the commissariat and the Quartermaster Department, and a row of houses for officers. A 300-bed post hospital was surrounded by flowers. The food was still heavy and monotonous but now included vegetables bought with the two-fifths of the regular ration which the men could not or would not eat. It had been found that the men were happier when occupied part of the day, and they were asked to do three hours' work, after which they amused themselves with a camp newspaper, plays and minstrel shows, and reading, as well as with "mechanical experiments" and "temperance or religious meetings." The Connecticut agents, returning in 1864, now sang its praises.

Despite these improvements the Surgeon General persuaded the War Department to discontinue the convalescent part of the camp in February, 1864, retaining the post as a "distribution depot" for healthy soldiers. Medical Department disapproval of convalescent camps run by line officers had been substantiated by the large numbers there found unfit for real duty. Of 7,727 men examined at Alexandria during 1863 only 30 per cent had been passed as fit to rejoin their regiments, while 22 per cent had been ordered back to general hospitals or retained for observation, and 43 per cent were declared fit only for the Invalid Corps. Five per cent were sick enough to win discharges. Such a record would indeed merit the name "Camp Relapse." It was the Medical Department's contention that sick men should stay in the hospital and well men did not require a special camp. Unfortunately, the new policy did not work as well as expected, for a constant 10 per cent of the men who passed through Alexandria after it became purely a "distribution" camp continued to be returned to the general hospitals. Evidently errors in judgment had led to that many premature dismissals from hospitals.

Small convalescent camps continued to operate at the rear of the field armies to hold patients who could be evacuated from field hospitals without being lost to their generals. They were small and poorly equipped, relying upon the relief commissions for delicacies. They attracted malingerers, who ignored discipline, especially in sanitary matters. An exception was the soldiers' home at Memphis, built and managed by the Western Sanitary Commission but aided by government rations and fuel. Beds were available there for 400 men, who could rebuild their strength in attractive surroundings while awaiting "distribution." In the summer of 1863 the large Chestnut Hill Hospital was serving as a concentration point for the convalescents of the Philadelphia area, but there is no evidence that it continued as such. Considered "a little too nice" by the idealists of the Sanitary Commission, it must have been a model of its kind.

The handling of convalescents was muddled for the same reason that hospital building and staffing were defective—the national genius for wishful thinking—or, as we like to call it, "optimism." Not wanting the war, the Northern people and their public officers did nothing to prepare for it; not wanting heavy casualties, they provided no suitable hospitals until the arrival of scores of thousands of sick and wounded. Hospital attendants were left untrained until the pressure of circumstances compelled makeshifts. No convalescent care was provided until the demand for hospital beds pushed the less gravely ill out on the street or into such extemporized camps as the scandalous one at Alexandria.

If people had realized how terrible the war would be and how long it would last, progress in all these matters would have been more rapid. Ultimately the United States achieved some splendid hospitals and at least one good convalescent camp: Americans can improvise successfully when forced to face reality; but the soldiers paid a heavy price for the delays.

10

Army

Sanitation

and

Hygiene

THAT TWO OUT OF THREE FATALITIES DIED FROM DISEASE AND that the surgeons treated 6,000,000 sicknesses as opposed to 400,000 wounds would imply to the twentieth-century reader that the Civil War was an unusually sickly conflict. But all things are comparative. World War I was the first in which weapons killed more Americans than did bacteria; and even that statement holds good only for the Expeditionary Force. The men of the "sixties," comparing past wars with their own, felt, justifiably, that they had succeeded in cutting down disease mortality.

The Mexican War count had been more than seven disease deaths for every battle death, and the annual mortality rate had been 10 per cent as compared to the Civil War rate of 7.2 per cent. Wellington's army in the Peninsular War had had fifteen times as many sick men as wounded men, and in the Napoleonic Wars as a whole the British ratio was 49 deaths by disease to six by death in battle or by wounds. In some peacetime years the French Army of the Second Empire had a disease mortality rate higher than that of the Union army in wartime. It may be conceded then, that the Civil War was a comparatively healthy one, as wars went in the 19th century; and since there had been relatively little advance in the art of healing since 1815, or 1846, the lowered mortality may be mainly attributed to improved sanitation and hygiene.

The sanitation scandals of the Crimean War were still reverberating. Of the 25,000 men who made up the first British expeditionary force sent to the Crimea, 18,000 were dead at the end of twelve months, all but a few of dysentery, cholera, scurvy or "fevers." They were the victims of dirty camps, dirty hospitals, bad food and bad nursing. To quiet the outraged British public, the Queen appointed a Sanitary Commission to go to the Crimea, and Miss Nightingale went out to revolutionize military hospitals. Their "clean-up" campaign wrought vast improvement and its lessons were heeded by the Civil War sanitarians.

Another factor was the public health movement, which had gathered momentum among the more enlightened physicians and laymen of Europe in the decade of the fifties, after the Westward spread of cholera, in the 1830's, rang the alarm. Then, under the leadership of English sanitarians like Edwin Chadwick, and the pathologists of the French school, and with the aid of the new science of medical statistics, governments began to assume responsibility for the public health.

The Americans were somewhat laggard. In Dr. Elisha Bartlett we had a prophet of the new scientific medicine; in Lemuel Shattuck we had a Massachusetts version of Chadwick. No state, however, could be persuaded to establish a health department in the prewar era; only four states made a pretense at collecting the vital statistics on which sound health programs could be based; and physicians and public alike received Shattuck's great sanitary report on Massachusetts with apathy and even with deprecation. Enough converts were made to hold annual "Sanitary Conventions" from 1857 through 1860.

Conspicuous among them were Dr. Elisha Harris and the other founders of the Sanitary Commission. Immediately after securing a semi-official status for the new commission they began to spread knowledge of "Sanitary Science" by circulating a series of pamphlets and by sending out inspectors. The latter had the threefold duty of learning the hygienic state of the army, putting the new pamphlets into the hands of surgeons and line officers, and persuading these officers to accept the commission's advice.

Medical theory did not comprehend the role of bacteria in disease, but it knew the "malarial miasms" of swamps, and the "mephitic effluvia" believed to hover about privies and unburied garbage, and the deadly "crowd poisoning" in camps where men slept packed together in stuffy tents. Against these evils the sanitarians counselled war on dirt and bad smells and faith in the hygienic qualities of fresh air, dry ground and sunlight.

An army sanitary program was dependent upon the enlightened cooperation of surgeons, line officers and soldiers; and this came hard. Many surgeons, having scant knowledge of the newfangled science of military hygiene, were touchy toward outside "inspectors." Others "seemed generally to regard them as of importance to every regiment except their own." Some accepted the new "preventive" ideal but shrank from applying it when the colonel disapproved. All too many line officers combined complacent ignorance with a lazy tolerance of their men's dirty habits, and would snub the surgeon who attempted to clean up the camp or improve its diet.

The majority of the rank and file had not learned good habits before they took to the field, with resulting high disease rates in the 1862 spring campaigns. It was remarked in the first year of the war that the discipline of a unit seemed to correlate with the sick rate, and later experience substantiated it. The Regulars, with their strict discipline and clean camps, proved healthier than the volunteers, "whose regiments fairly wallowed in abominable filth." Western troops, said to be less disciplined than Eastern, had a much higher dysentery rate. Discipline was repugnant to the free-born young Americans. To them orders were something to obey when they felt like it.

The great majority of recruits were in their teens or early twenties. All their lives women had cooked for them, cleaned for them, washed for them: now that they must perform these tasks for themselves they would do them in their own way, defying the "fussy" orders of surgeons and officers, and they were seldom checked by ignorant or popularity seeking officers.

In the East, dirty camps and dirty habits were blamed for the excessive sickness which, in the opinion of some medical-minded people, brought the Union forces to defeat in the Peninsular and second Bull Run campaigns. As a medical director put it:

When garbage lies everywhere in the company streets, and the air has a noisome odor both within and without the tents, we have found, also that the men are dirty, ragged and sickly—their muskets are rusty and out of order—they are insubordinate, mutinous, without drill and without discipline. They have no *esprit de corps*—no self-respect—no manliness—no courage; and they will not fight. These are the links which compose the chain. Dirt at one end, and cowardice at the other—commencing in the camp at Alexandria, and ending in the rout upon the plains of Manassas.

The sick and demoralized Army of the Potomac, huddled in misery at Harrison's Landing on the banks of the James, began a slow progress to recovery with the arrival of Jonathan Letterman as medical director, on July 4, 1862. He persuaded General McClellan of the necessity for better food and for new and rigidly enforced sanitary regulations. And he emphasized especially that latrines must be dug and used.

The military necessities of the Antietam and Fredericksburg campaigns, in September and December, and the addition of raw, inexperienced regiments, seem to have crippled sanitation efforts somewhat. Early in 1863, however, a determined effort was being made to keep the camps clean and the army well fed.

General "Fighting Joe" Hooker, the new Army of the Potomac commander, gave special attention to these matters. Although some officers withheld their cooperation, it could be said in February that improved sanitation had greatly reduced the number of "fever" cases and that the army had no greater mortality than a populous town. Surgeons were awakening to the importance of their "preventive" duties.

General Order No. 52, issued for the Army of the Potomac in May, 1863, formalized the best current sanitary practice of the Union army. According to its provisions camps were to be pitched upon new ground, and were to be drained by a system of ditches eighteen inches deep. Tents were to be struck twice a week to allow the sunning of their floors and contents. Cooking was to be done by company cooks. All refuse was to be burned or buried daily, while garbage was to be placed in a pit behind the kitchen. Sinks (i.e., latrines) were to be trenches eight feet deep, on which six inches of earth would be shovelled each evening. Personal hygiene was regulated by requirements that the men wear their hair cut short, bathe twice a week, and change their clothing at least once a week.

There was little complaint of hygienic conditions during the summer, and when the Eastern troops went into their winter camp of 1863–1864, at Brandy Station, Virginia, they had learned enough to make it a model of its kind. A rigorous system of inspections and reinspections by regimental surgeons, brigade chief surgeons and divisional inspectors brought results in the form of partly—and sometimes wholly—empty hospitals.

Meanwhile, in the West, other Federal armies were learning the same sanitary lessons in the same way. At Shiloh, in April, 1862, the sickness of the troops was appalling. When the troops shifted to the Corinth, Mississippi, region, typhoid and dysentery took such toll that the soldiers were described as "but the spectre of an army." Then Grant and Sherman undertook the enforcement of suitable hygienic regulations, the latter going so far as to pick the sites for latrines and instruct his men in the proper way to dig them. In 1863 the sloughs of the Mississippi bottoms around Vicksburg added the scourge of malaria; but improvements in sanitation continued, and with cool weather the sick rate sank to reasonable proportions.

Because reasonable success seemed to have been attained, and because the Army now had its own inspectors, the Sanitary Commission diminished the number of its inspections in 1862, and discontinued them entirely early in 1864.

Sanitary abuses continued but in the latter half of the war efforts at cleanliness were the usual thing among veteran regiments except when emergencies interrupted. New units were usually sickly, partly because their weaklings had not yet been winnowed out, but also because they had to learn from experience that cleanliness is next to godliness. The same generalization applied to new drafts of recruits in the old regiments, especially after substitutes and mercenary riffraff, who were difficult to discipline, became numerous. And finally, the medical knowledge of that generation was too limited for the surgeons to quite realize how important some precautions were.

This lack was nowhere more serious than in the field of intestinal diseases. The Civil War saw an enormous incidence of typhoid and "diarrhoea." Typhoid was the leading "killer" and "diarrhoea" was a universal ailment, its annual average being 73.8 per cent. The soldiers bore the latter bravely, nicknaming it "the Tennessee quick-step," and making grim jokes to the effect that "bowels are of more consequence than brains" in the Army.

"Tennessee quickstep": an account of the intestinal diseases

There was no agreement as to what "diarrhoea" was, or what "dysentery" was, or what caused either of them. Under the circumstances preventive measures would of necessity be fumbling. Ordinarily, a sick man with loose bowels was said to suffer from dysentery if there was blood in the stools, and the patient's symptoms included tenesmus, otherwise it was "diarrhoea." But some doctors thought bloody stools were of no importance in the diagnosis, and others, though they differentiated between diarrhea and dysentery in acute cases, believed that in chronic cases they were the same. The Medical Department lumped the two together for statistical purposes. As will be seen, confusion was twice confounded by serious misdiagnoses. The trouble lay in the fact that loose bowels is not a "disease" but a symptom which appears in numerous diseases. It is not strange therefore that a host of "causes" were given.

The more common were "defective diet," "exposure," "crowd poison" and "depressing mental agencies." Of these the first two had the greatest number of adherents among Army surgeons.

Among those who thought diet crucial there were three subdivisions: (1) those who blamed bad cooking, especially of fried foods; (2) those who blamed the food itself, the salt pork, hardtack, or beans; and, (3) those who laid the trouble to diet deficiencies, the lack of fresh food. The last two were, of course, obverse and reverse of the same thing. A few individuals had other dietetic views, such as overeating, or the eating of fresh meat by men habituated to salt. But the great majority thought deficiencies were the cause, and the evidence supported them. In numerous instances entire regiments recovered from "diarrhoea" as soon as they ate fresh fruits or vegetables. This led some physicians to the conclusion that the "diarrhoea" was really incipient scurvy. Yet if lack of fresh fruits and vegetables was a significant cause why should those diseases strike hardest in July, August, and September, when fresh food should have been plentiful? Possibly the answer was that these months usually saw the most active campaigning, when the troops subsisted mainly on "field rations"—salt meat and hardtack.

The surgeons agreed that diet was a factor but differed in their estimates of its relative weight among other factors. Many considered changes of weather, especially exposure to cold, the major factor, and urged the wearing of a flannel bandage, or "belly band." The disease so often accompanied other maladies —typhoid, Bright's disease, tuberculosis, malaria—that some surgeons thought the loose bowels merely a symptom of other diseases, as was no doubt frequently the case.

The suspicion that "acute dysentery" was often "continued fever" (i.e., an atypical typhoid) was based upon the belief that diarrhea is a typhoid symptom. This seems to be borne out by the World War I discovery that paratyphoid, unknown in the 1860's, is very likely to coexist in cases of bacillary dysentery. Those who considered diarrhea a malaria symptom argued from the facts that "diarrhoea or dysentery" often appeared in camps near a stagnant pond, that its seasonal incidence was often the same as malaria's, and that some patients had a good response to quinine.

The debate produced some bizarre theories. Overindulgence in coffee and breathing of "effluvia of putrefying corpses," were offered as cause. One surgeon attributed loose bowels to nervousness; another thought the diagnoses should be trichinosis, brought on by eating underdone pork. Some recruits had a theory of their own—that practical jokers were dosing their coffee with cathartics.

No clear answer can be given as to what the Civil War Army "diarrhoea and dysentery" actually was. The few autopsies made indicated a variety of causes. Frightened soldiers, chilled soldiers, and soldiers who had eaten unwholesome or badly prepared food could all develop loose bowels. The quite prevalent malaria, tuberculosis, and scurvy might well have produced "diarrhoea" which could not be properly diagnosed by the men and means available. And there is no reason to suppose that the true dysenteries, both bacillary and amoebic, were not present, even though the surgeons were not acquainted with them.

Bacillary dysentery is believed to have been brought to America in the slave ships, and is endemic in the South today, with the Flexner bacillus apparently the most common. Amoebic dysentery, caused by the protozoan parasite Entamoeba Histolytica, prevalent in the West Indies, is more common in the temperate zone than was once supposed, and is found in several Southern states. The dysenteries of the Civil War have been described as "relatively mild in character." The low mortality rate of the "diarrhoea and dysentery" category (2 per cent), would imply that either the bacilli involved were mild types, or that many of the patients did not have dysentery as we understand the word. The recorded clinical symptoms indicate that bacillary and amoebic dysentery must both have been present, and their prevalence in the United States in the present century supports that assumption. But it also seems reasonable to suppose that an indeterminate number of wrongly diagnosed cases went into the statistics. The presence of true dysentery on a large scale, however, is attested by the 48,000 deaths laid to "diarrhoea" or "dysentery." Furthermore, a good many more cases died at home, after leaving the Army. Such a number—larger than the total of those killed in action—cannot be accounted for by theories that Civil War bowel complaints were predominantly simple diarrheas of climatic or dietetic origin.

Dysenteric infections are commonly transmitted through water, milk, or food contaminated from the excreta of the sick. This contamination may be direct, as when the latrines drain into a camp water supply, or may be effected by flies. Human "carriers," who shelter the bacteria without suffering the disease, are a constant danger, especially when they are kitchen workers. A vague, centuries-old belief that dysentery was contagious, transmitted possibly through "emanations" from ordure, had become unfashionable among American doctors of the 1860's. Recent European experiences, pointing to contaminated water as a source of cholera, dysentery, and typhoid, impressed some American leaders of the profession, however. Further confirmation was offered by a few Army surgeons, whose wartime observation of the coincidence of bad latrines with high dysentery rates convinced them that at least the "more serious" varieties of the disease were communicable, and excreta was the probable cause. All this would have carried more conviction had a bacterial theory been produced, and the agency of flies and carriers made clear. But the dejecta theory of that time rested on "emanations," "privy gases," and gross contamination which seemed impossible to surgeons who had kept their regimental sinks "sanitary" within their understanding of the word, and had nevertheless been confronted with plenty of dysentery.

Typhoid fever is spread in the same ways as are the dysenteries, with flies as the chief carriers. The theory that it is transmitted through intestinal discharges was announced by Dr. William Budd in the *Lancet* in 1854, and confirmed in epidemics at Munich in 1860 and 1862. Americans continued to argue the possibilities of typhoid's spontaneous origin, without outside infection; even the minority who accepted the new idea admitted the likelihood of other explanations.

These were many and varied, including exposure, fatigue, and "lack of nerve force" and, above all, "miasms." It was thought that fires on the floors of the soldiers' tight little winter huts started fermentation in the ground, which rose as an unseen vapor and transmitted typhoid. Other explanations included: "malarial miasms," "odor of horse manure," "strong coffee and greasy food," "malarial odor from dead horses," and "decay of wood." A Sanitary Commission inspector saw the type of tents as a cause and thought a statistical study would prove his case. Surgeon General Hammond considered people of "choleric temperament" especially susceptible to typhoid, dysentery, dyspepsia, and hemorrhoids. Unfortunately, only a minority suspected contaminated water supplies.

Such diverse theories produced diverse ideas of prevention. One school advocated flannel "belly bands"; advocates of ventilation recommended the destruction of the close huts, mentioned above, as "plague spots." The "excreta" theory advocates, heartened in 1863 by the support of Elisha Harris and the consultants of the Sanitary Commission, laid great stress on the maintenance of clean latrines. Some followed Harris's advice and disinfected the regimental "privies" with carbolic acid or with chlorinated lime.

Considering the prevalence of intestinal diseases no subject in this study is more important than regimental sinks. It has been said that: "The first thing an army in the field does is to foul its own water supply and the second is to infect its food by the swarms of flies bred in its garbage dumps and manure heaps." In the first year of the war a good many units seem to have done their best to live up to these dicta, although the dangers of indiscriminate defecation had been known, vaguely, since the time of Moses. During the Peninsular campaign of 1862 the troops, being in motion a good part of the time, seldom thought it necessary to dig latrines. By the following spring, when sinks were common, the principal problem was to persuade the men to use them. Some soldiers wandered off into the bushes because of modesty alone. More often they did so, and imperiled the health of the whole neighborhood, because of the disgusting condition of the latrines. The ordinary kind was simply a pit, surmounted by a pole and possibly screened from view by a few pieces of brush. When its edges were clean, and earth was thrown into it once a day, it was considered adequate, even though it repelled its users, and would be condemned today.

It was in the West, where nonuse of latrines was notorious, that the only really good ones were introduced, probably as an incentive to civilized habits. These "Army of the Cumberland" sinks were covered with tight, board platforms, with kegs or cracker boxes on top, which served as comfortable seats.

At times of stress, such as the fighting near Chattanooga, or during the trench warfare around Petersburg, precautions lapsed, but in general there were few complaints about privies and their use after the middle of 1863.

Armies in motion were generally believed to be healthier than when stationary, because of the exercise and better morale, and because they "leave their dirt behind them." At such times slackness in using latrines might not cause much trouble, providing the troops kept on the go, did not recross their own trail, and did not come up with the filth of large enemy forces. Sherman's Army, which fulfilled these conditions during the last year of the war, had a low typhoid rate; but Grant's forces, maneuvering in a limited area were not so fortunate.

A Confederate surgeon suggested that flies might be the culprits in the transmission of hospital gangrene, but he seems to have been the only American of his generation to suspect that flies were dangerous. Their breeding may have been checked somewhat by orders requiring the burial of garbage and stable refuse, prompted by fears of "effluvia," but otherwise nothing was done about them.

Water supplies were as bad as they could be. Every kind of water was used. In Virginia, surface water was the usual source during the Peninsular campaign, and at the siege of Petersburg, until a drought forced the army to dig wells. On all fronts we hear of troops drinking from stagnant pools, puddles of rain water, and every sort of stream and river, even when they thought it was making them sick and when it was apparent that the pools and streams were fed from rivulets running down excrement-laden hillsides.

Sanitarians were confused as to what constituted "good" water, though they had various excellent methods of purifying suspected water. In general, water that was tasteless and colorless was presumed to be good. Fecal contamination was recognized as bad, but chemical impurities and the presence of decaying vegetable matter seemed equally alarming. Aeration and sedimentation were recognized methods of purifying, and a list of elaborate filters was brought to the Army's attention. The great value of distillation, or plain boiling, of dubious water was emphasized by both the Sanitary Commission and the Surgeon General, but there is no recorded instance of the advice being faithfully followed—except by a regiment which had to drink distilled salt water. Filters were supplied to numerous hospitals—where they seem to have gone unused. Early in the war they were occasionally sold to recruits—who soon threw them away.

Most of these water purifiers had some value. Their consistent use would probably have lowered the intestinal-disease rates. But that generation did not know about *Bacillus typhosus, Entamoeba histolytica,* and the dozens of dysentery bacilli. Filtering or boiling was a nuisance—so they took a chance.

Fortunately, the soldiers' passion for coffee at every meal and between meals meant that an important part of their water intake was boiled.

The Army's diet as a cause of disease

The only serious rival of camp filth as a health menace was poor and unbalanced diet. At the start of the war the legally established ration consisted of twelve ounces of salt pork (or one pound four ounces of salt beef), one pound two ounces of flour (or twelve ounces of hard bread), and one vegetable. The vegetable might be either navy beans or peas, at the rate of 64/100 of a gill per man per day, or 1.6 ounces of rice. This was recognized as a scurvy-producing diet, and an addition to the ration was voted by Congress in August, 1861. The Congressional act followed soldiers' complaints, the protests by Sanitarians, and the citations of the facts that bad food and resultant scurvy had made trouble for the British army in the Crimea and was in part responsible for the defeat of the Russian forces which had subsisted chiefly upon black bread and vodka.

The augmented ration, in effect from August, 1861, until June, 1864, increased the flour allowance by six ounces, added four ounces of hard bread, and, more important, three pounds of potatoes a week per man. It was stipulated that the meat be fresh rather than preserved "when practicable." Both before and after the reform coffee, sugar, salt, vinegar, candles, and soap were a part of the ration. Surgeon General Hammond boasted that this diet made the American soldier the best fed in the world. To foreigners it seemed prodigal and magnificent, for it was some 20 per cent above the rations of the British Army or Navy, almost twice as liberal as the French, and compared even more favorably with the Prussian, Austrian, and Russian diets.

If bulk and calories are the principal criteria these encomi-

ums were deserved. There were times and places when the subsistence officers found it impossible to supply the authorized
foodstuffs, and the men went hungry. The Army of the Potomac
nearly starved at Mine Run, in 1863. Western armies, covering
vast distances and being fed over long communication lines
stretching through enemy territory were more troubled with
"starving times." The Army of the Cumberland went hungry
when encircled at Chattanooga in the fall of 1863, being once
reduced to three ears of corn a day. In 1864 these same troops,
with the Army of the Tennessee as fellow sufferers, were on
short rations for months while they fought the Atlanta campaign.
The Army of the Mississippi went hungry, late in 1862, when
the supply base at Holly Springs, Mississippi, was captured.

But for the most part, so far as military necessity would permit, Union soldiers had enough to eat. Indeed, an idea took root
in high quarters that the ration was excessive, and in 1864 Congress reduced the quantities to those existing before August,
1861. Having robbed the soldiers with one hand the legislators
gave with the other by simultaneously raising the pay of enlisted men. This brought some complaints that Army food was
not adequate for active men.

The real difficulties were the poorly balanced character of
Army rations and their poor quality. Throughout the first two
years of the war, and occasionally later on, the staples, meat
and hardtack, were often nauseatingly bad.

Army "pickled" beef ("salt horse") was not the usual article
of commerce but a special product to meet government specifications. Prepared against decay for at least two years in the
hottest climate, it was so highly salted that it had to be soaked
in water before it could be eaten. This removed most of the
juices along with the salt. Despite efforts to render the beef
eternal it was frequently tainted when it reached the troops, and
was always tough.

Because beef-soaking required so much water and trouble,
salt pork was the preferred meat when the army was in the field.
The pork and the bacon were invariably fat. Frequently the

former was so bad that only a small portion could be used. "Much of it was musty and rancid . . . and much more was flabby, stringy, 'sow-belly,' as the men called it." On the outside "it was black as a shoe; on the inside, often yellow with putrefaction." Reformers inveighed against salt pork as indigestible, and as a producer of inordinate thirst for liquor; but it was useful, since it could be cooked in a variety of ways or eaten raw when circumstances would not permit a fire.

Inactive armies, especially in the East, were given fresh beef about half the time, supplied from great herds of Army cattle. It was usually tough, since the cattle had had much exercise, and it sometimes made the men sick, presumably because the meat moved too slowly from the slaughter pens to the frying pan.

Hard bread, or hardtack, was also inferior throughout the first half of the war. Called "worm castles" by the troops, these large, thick crackers were either so hard they had to be soaked to a mushlike consistency before they could be eaten, or wet and moldy from exposure. When moldy they could be replaced by a new consignment; but when infested with maggots or weevils, as was frequently the case, they were consumed. As a veteran put it, "eaten in the dark no one could tell the difference between it and hardtack that was untenanted."

Harrowing as this nasty food was to men of sensibility, it did not cause a tithe of the sickness and misery brought on by bad balance of food elements, and especially by the dearth of fresh vegetables. A Sanitary Commission expert commented that in an "almost tropical climate" Union soldiers were being fed a ration "which the Siberian might thrive on, and the Esquimaux consider a delicacy." "One pound of it," he continued, "contains enough carbon to raise the temperature of water to over 200 degrees of heat, and as if that were not quite warm enough, we add a modicum of beans, than which no vegetable is more heating or stimulating, and none more indigestible when hardened by age. Whilst potatoes and onions, the most healthful and palatable of vegetables are doled out with parsimonious hand, on semi-occasional periods, and green vegetables are totally ignored."

Whatever the official ration table might say, active armies oftentimes went without vegetable issues for weeks or months. For practical purposes, the field ration of the Union army was pork, beans, hardtack, and coffee. Since difficulties of transportation and preserving made even potatoes a luxury, the Western armies, with their long communications lines, were forced to endure more frequent and longer periods on "iron rations." In both East and West, soldiers developed a yearning for vegetables which sometimes amounted almost to mania. The lucky ones were those who garrisoned quiet spots, in undevastated country, where a well supplied local market provided good food for all soldiers who cared to buy.

Beginning in July, 1862, in the East, and about a year later in the West, commanding generals seem to have made more of an effort to secure vegetables. In this they were aided by gifts from civilian relief agencies. But a variety of reasons dictated that the Army ration should continue ill-balanced much of the time, with periods of few or no vegetable issues alternating with periods in which they were regular but small. The pitiful best that the well-situated Army of the Potomac could do during an inactive season is shown in the supply of "anti-scorbutics" distributed between January 1 and April 1, 1864:

Potatoes	2,229,000	pounds
Onions	399,000	pounds
Turnips	80,170	pounds
Dried apples	551,000	pounds

There were also small quantities of pickles, pickled cabbage and desiccated vegetables. This came to a weekly issue per man, of a pound and three quarters, or about five averaged-sized potatoes; four ounces or about two onions, and a little over one ounce of turnip. These troops received large supplies of fresh vegetables after midsummer of 1864, but during the following winter they received none at all from December 1 until the end of the war, because of transportation problems.

Sutlers roused the wrath of most Army doctors by selling the men food which sometimes upset their stomachs. But on the whole, the pies, cakes, cheeses, and other novelties provided were valuable supplementary foods, and a relief from the monotonous regular ration. With cheese at 50 cents a pound, condensed milk at 75 cents a can, and butter, often rancid, at a dollar a pound, the military clientele could buy little on their $13 a month. The sutler's molasses cookies, at six for a quarter, were his most popular goods, since they added to the government's two-ounce-a-day sugar ration. In some of the large Eastern camps men with money could always satisfy their hunger at restaurants and oyster houses.

The commonest and best way of supplementing the ration was foraging—in civilian language, "stealing." It might mean stripping a Southern family of all its foodstuffs, or it might involve only the surreptitious milking of cows, carried on at considerable risk to the foragers. Ordinarily, generals forbade it, George B. McClellan being particularly notable for his firm stand; but colonels and company officers, while pretending compliance with antiforaging rules, might actually encourage it.

Sherman's march to the sea, and the subsequent parade through the Carolinas, offered the war's best examples of the virtues of "living on the enemy," with the commanding general elevating foraging to an official policy. For a good part of the time, the regular ration issues were restricted to coffee, sugar and salt, and it was "root, hog, or die" for the soldiers. Some regiments fared poorly, but the bulk of the Army seems to have lived high, with plenty of vegetables, chickens, and turkeys for the first time in their military career. The resultant good health and spirits were described as remarkable.

But moral and legal considerations aside, foraging was no cure-all for the Army's vegetable deficiencies. Many Southern regions produced too little food and some localities were so stripped that the Army had to feed the civilian population.

Bad as the food was, cooking made it worse. Individual cooking by inexperienced soldiers is said to have prolonged the war by swelling the number of gastric invalids. During the summer of 1861 the Sanitary Commission crusaded for a professional cook hired for each company of volunteers. By autumn about half the regiments had gone over to cooking by companies rather than by individuals or squads. But the cooks were seldom professionals; often they merely made the coffee and boiled the beans, leaving further efforts up to the soldiers.

On moving into combat areas there was a general disposition to cease company cooking, replacing it with cooking by squads, each member taking his turn at the camp fire. As virtually the only utensil carried on campaign was the frying pan, meat was almost always fried. Beans were invariably boiled, but sometimes, due to pressure for time, not long enough to render them digestible. Ingenious ways of preparing hardtack were evolved. It might be crumbled in coffee or used to thicken soup. Some men preferred it fried in pork fat—and thus made thoroughly indigestible. Often it was toasted over the fire on the end of a stick. If it fell off, and was charred, it was eaten under the impression that carbon was "good for weak bowels." Sugar was spread on it by some, and those who could afford condensed milk sometimes made their "crackers" into "milk toast." Another triumph of military cookery was the flapjack, "tough as a mule's ear, about as heavy as lead, and very indigestible."

Distressed by such cooking, hygienists strove, early in 1863, to move the authorities to action. Company cooking was recommended, not only because men with some talent might then do the cooking, but also because soup-making and baking might be possible for the larger unit. In March, 1863, an act of Congress required cooking by companies, to be done by detailed men who might be assisted by specially hired Negroes. Under the act medical and line officers were made jointly responsible for supervision and instruction. There was less complaint during the remainder of the war, but squad cooking persisted in some regiments for a long time, and military necessity forced individual cooking at times. Had the "kitchen on wheels," introduced into the Army of the James in 1865 by the Christian Commission, been available earlier it would have simplified the problem of preparing baked and boiled foods in quantity. With boilers mounted on a pair of wheels, connecting with a provision cart like a cannon with a caisson, it must have resembled the modern field kitchen.

The inevitable result of the Army diet was scurvy. This wretched disease was so little seen in civil practice that many volunteer surgeons failed to recognize it. A number insisted that it never existed in the Army. It appeared at various times and places, usually when a force had left its base, found the foraging bad, and had lived for weeks or months on field rations.

More dangerous than this obvious scurvy, was the so-called "scorbutic diathesis," or incipient scurvy. This widespread ailment undoubtedly caused much sickness and death recorded under other headings, such as "chronic diarrhoea" and "debility." Many doctors realized that the strange new symptoms they saw, and the baffling changes in familiar diseases—the "rheumatism," and the poor blood coagulation—were due to dietetic deficiencies. As scurvy was the only deficiency disease known, these doctors lumped all the mystery cases together as "scurvy," though other deficiency diseases were probably present.

There was some argument and confusion as to exactly what caused scurvy, although the majority of Army surgeons came to attribute it to lack of fresh food. Where vegetable rations were wanting some doctors had the practical wisdom to urge men to eat weeds and wild berries or even to drink effusions of pine needles.

Great emphasis was placed upon potatoes because of a mistaken idea that they excel as an antiscorbutic. When it became apparent that the armies were not getting enough of them, the government heeded the advice of certain misguided scientists and introduced "desiccated potatoes" as a legal substitute. Tried by the British in the Crimea, the soldiers hated them, but medical officers thought them of value in balancing the ration. They ıı large, ugly slabs, and had to be boiled. When cooked, ᴊ product resembled "a dirty brook with all the dead leaves floating around promiscuously." Because they were so strongly loaded with pepper, as an "antiseptic," most men found them unpalatable and rejected them, though their consumption was commanded. To others, they were "something to eat," and were devoured with growing appreciation. Surgeons, unable to understand why scurvy should appear in their regiments when desiccated potatoes were plentiful, ascribed it to the men's recalcitrance in eating them. We know now that they were only additional bulk, for drying destroys vitamin C, the scurvy preventive. Experiments with desiccated meat, in the form of "beef essence" and stew won the approval of the soldiers upon whom it was tried, but they resented any attempt to substitute it for "natural meat," which could be chewed. It did not become a part of the ration.

One more attempt of science to provide a balanced diet remains to be recorded. This was the "horsford ration"—a worse failure than the dried potatoes. Invented by E. N. Horsford, a Harvard professor, it consisted of a "bread ration" and a "meat ration," which together were supposed to give the soldier everything he needed. The former was made up of nine parts of roasted wheat, coarsely ground, and one part of sugar and salt. It weighed eight ounces. The meat ration, or "sausaged meat," as it was called, weighed three ounces, and consisted of ground lean meat, heart, liver, tongue and kidneys, cooked by dry heat and "varnished" with gelatin. It was estimated that this ration would not only give the men a better diet but would save the government $10,000,000 a year. Having aroused public interest by his pamphlet, Professor Horsford succeeded in getting his invention before a special Medical Department board in June, 1864, which reported against it. To quiet protests it was submitted to a new board in the autumn, and it was decided to try it on one or two regiments. A test in Texas the following spring, had disastrous results. The bread spoiled, and became filled with vermin; the meat putrefied en route, and made the men sick.

Housing, clothing, and miscellaneous hygienic factors

Although conceding the hygienic importance of food, most Civil War surgeons were more concerned about ventilation. This was natural in an era when so many diseases were laid to "effluvias" and the dangers of carbon dioxide in a crowded room were exaggerated. The sometimes extreme insistence upon fresh air, was probably useful in checking the transmission of air-borne diseases. The alarming increase of tuberculosis in the nineteenth century contributed to the concern over ventilation.

Suitable objects of the attention of the ventilationists were the often overcrowded recruit barracks, filled with raw young volunteers sniffling with colds and falling prey to the "children's diseases." The debate veered to types of tents—the relative dangers from bad air in "wedge tents," "bell tents," and "wall tents." In the second year of the war the Army adopted the small "shelter" tent for summer use and recommended huts for winter. These "pup" tents, as the troops termed them, were merely pieces of canvas, five feet two by four feet eight, open at both ends, into which two infantrymen could crawl. In the winter they served as roofs for the huts.

Huts had their beginning early in 1862, and at that time were usually half-excavated, with a three- or four-foot-log wall. Hygienists found them damp and ill-ventilated, and kept up agitation against them until, by the winter of 1863–1864, little log houses had fairly generally replaced them. The iron stoves of some of the early huts were deemed most dangerous to ventilation and were replaced by small fireplaces. The fact that there was no less sickness in the approved type of housing than in the half-excavated type proved a minor medical mystery of the war.

Exposure to cold and rain probably caused much more sickness than did the dubious ventilation of the little two-man cabins. Sleeping on the bare ground, walking post, or doing picket duty in bad weather were recognized as causes of a "host of respiratory and rheumatic afflictions." New soldiers often suffered greatly in the conditioning process and in learning to make a blanket and a rubber poncho suffice for bedclothing. Soldiers who had lost their blankets far from a supply base, or had thrown them away during warm weather, sometimes suffered intensely. When proximity to the enemy made fires too hazardous the men could only grit their teeth and combat cold with exercise. Military criminals might suffer keenly from exposure, in addition to the barbarous punishments then in vogue, in the open "bull pens," in which they were confined.

The fumigation of transport vessels and barracks, a natural corollary of the "effluvia" theories, may have accomplished little as a bactericide, but was unwittingly useful as a destroyer of disease carriers—flies, mosquitoes, lice, rats and fleas.

The prescribed uniform and overcoat were warm and heavy, adequate for the southern winter's climate. There was criticism because the underdrawers were not all-wool. Complaints of the quality of material were often justified in the early part of the war, however, and regiments sometimes had shortages of clothing. In the fall of 1861, 11 per cent of the regiments at Washington had no overcoats, 7 per cent had inadequate supplies, and in 8 per cent a trouser shortage resulted in men being "frequently . . . seen . . . on duty and on parade in their drawers alone." In later years the principal complaint was the unsuitability of the uniform in summer. Its woolen blouse, trousers, and undershirt, weighed six pounds. In 1865, a few colored regiments were dressed in linen pants, lightweight blouses, and straw hats; but no white regiments appear to have been so well treated.

In 1861 there was a great rage for "Havelocks" (cloth cap covers which hung down behind to protect the neck), but they were thrown away in action. Considering the climate, it appears strange that only a few regiments were given straw hats. The Army was justifiably proud of the many sizes of shoes it had to offer. There were no complaints on that score.

Surgeons deplored the weight and distribution of equipment carried by the Infantry, attributing much kidney, heart, and lung trouble to it. The cartridge box, containing four pounds of ammunition, which hung from a waist-belt was held responsible for numerous hernias.

The medical director of the Army of the Ohio gave it as his "deliberate opinion based on three years of the most ample experience" that rapid and long marches, with full pack, had "more to do with depleting our armies than all other causes put together." Intelligent officers, like W. T. Sherman, insisted on frequent short rests for marching columns; but others, riding horses themselves, appeared oblivious of the infantry's weariness and sometimes pushed the men for as long as three hours without a rest.

Ordinarily a 15 or 20 mile march was no trouble. In case of necessity the men might go as far as 35 miles a day without breaking down. But strenuous exertion in unusually hot weather frequently proved too much for the wool-clad, heavy-laden warriors, who would keel over by the dozens with sunstroke and heatstroke. Such disabilities marked the rapid march of the Army of the Potomac from Virginia to Gettysburg, in June, 1863, 20 to 30 miles a day, under a broiling sun. The pursuit of Lee, after the battle, produced more sunstroke. Some units were so debilitated they had to go into rest-camp for as long as a month. Conditions were almost as bad the following summer in the marching and countermarching involved in Grant's attempt to outflank Lee. Western troops seem to have endured heat and fatigue better: possibly because more of them were outdoor men.

The squalor which characterized volunteer regiments in 1861–1862 abated somewhat as the war went on, but despite orders face washing and bathing were neglected by some men. Brushing the teeth, though in vogue in foreign armies and approved by hygienists as a preventive of "agues and disease," was rare. The wearing of clean clothes was oftentimes precluded by military necessity and was willfully dispensed with by incorrigibles. The practice of using mess kettles as washtubs detracted somewhat from the sanitary value of such laundering as was done.

World War I experience was to show that a large proportion of disability in the Army is traceable to infections admitted through small abrasions in dirty skin, often caused by scratching. In the Civil War scratching was as common as body lice, fleas and mosquitoes. Dirty clothing, carried into a bullet wound, was also a likely source of dangerous infection.

The influence of the Temperance movement of the 1840's and 1850's no doubt accounts for the presence of many nondrinkers among the Union recruits, and for the self-imposed rules against drinking in some regiments. Temperance was short-lived, however. From 1862 onward the army seems to have drunk all the liquor it could obtain. Drunkenness was the rule among soldiers on leave, and was frequent in the camps immediately after pay day. Since the sale of liquor was forbidden in most regiments, drinking was limited by the high prices charged for bootlegged goods. Sutlers did some of the bootlegging; and more liquor was supplied by camp followers or reached the men in packages from home. Officers were not restricted, and seem to have made liberal use of their privileges by ordering case lots, to be delivered by express, or buying from the commissary. Beer was permitted in some commands, under the impression that it was "good for the bowels."

There was, and still is, disagreement as to the hygienic results of moderate drinking. Surgeons noticed, however, that each pay day was followed by a rise in the sick rate. Suspicion of the value of alcohol as a "stimulant" for healthy soldiers had been increasing during the three decades preceding the war, and underlay the Sanitary Commission's recommendation of complete prohibition in the camps. The Army had given up the daily liquor ration in 1832, but the generals and the surgeons felt that special issues of whisky might benefit the troops in cases of unusual exposure or fatigue. Such issues, usually a half pint per man, were much more frequent in some commands than in others. The Army of the Potomac received them for a time in the summer of 1862, and again at the siege of Petersburg, in 1864. Whisky was sometimes prescribed for a whole command when its drinking water was brackish or was drawn from a stagnant supply. It was also widely used as "bitters," mixed with quinine, by troops in malarious regions. Observing the relative effects of liquor and coffee, a good many surgeons judged the latter to be the better stimulant, and some thought alcohol actually harmful.

With malaria present in every military department, and with an annual average incidence of more than 100 per cent in some, its control was a major sanitary problem. Preventive efforts were handicapped by a bewildering confusion of theories. These ranged from the belief that paroxysmal fevers were induced by "sleeping in damp blankets," rapid climatic changes, "bad drinking water," "exhalations of a crowded camp," "poisonous fungi in the atmosphere" and above all "gaseous emanations from the decomposition of vegetable matter, through the action of heat and moisture."

These erroneous ideas were compatible, however, with the various practical precautions evolved through the centuries. It was common knowledge that camps should be located far from stagnant water, and if that were impossible, to leeward of water or marsh. The digging of ditches and canals was considered an invitation to malaria. Bonfires, it was recognized, offered some protection against the disease. It had been noted that people who slept in closed rooms were less likely to get malaria than those who breathed "night air," and that those who lived on elevated ground, or the upper stories of buildings, were relatively immune. It remained for bacteriology to explain everything by discovering the malarial plasmodium in the anopheles mosquito, which has watery breeding-grounds, nocturnal habits, a tendency to follow the wind, an inability to fly high, and an aversion to smoke.

The value of quinine as a malaria specific was an old story, but its use as a prophylactic was recent. Late in 1861 the Sanitary Commission, after investigating the value of preventive doses of quinine, recommended the procedure to the Army.

In some regiments one or two grains a day, usually taken with an ounce of whisky, lowered the malarial rate. As the war went on many doctors became convinced of the value of such dosing, and resolved to introduce it into civil practice.

But the procedure was not followed consistently or universally, even in highly malarial regions, and a constantly rising malarial rate shows it to have been of little value in some instances. Many soldiers refused the dosage and the absence of systematic records clouded the issue. Twentieth-century experience has indicated that, although quinine will kill mature parasites in the blood stream, it cannot be relied upon to destroy immature types, and should be administered in ten-grain doses, rather than the one- or two-grain doses of Civil War days.

Against smallpox the Army had the mighty weapon, vaccination. Since almost seventy years had passed since Jenner conferred it upon a pox-ridden world, one might suppose that vaccination had become a commonplace. Physicians were well-nigh unanimous in their appreciation of it. But many of the laity still had doubts and a large part of the population had never been vaccinated. Epidemics raged in various parts of the country, and New York City stood out as "the grand depot of smallpox infection for the western continent."

Regulations required the vaccination of recruits, and revaccination "when necessary." The rule was followed closely enough to prevent large-scale infection, but neglect was sufficiently frequent to account for an annual average smallpox incidence of almost 5 per thousand. Vaccination was often neglected at the training camps maintained by the states, but the principal trouble seems to have been the general failure to appreciate need for revaccination, which had not been much practiced down to that time.

After a few lessons in the value of quarantine, segregation was generally observed. Carelessness in this respect, and failure to revaccinate, became unusual after the middle of 1862, except among colored troops, who suffered much from smallpox in 1863. The immunity of regiments whose surgeons had been scrupulous about vaccination ended all possible doubts of the value of the practice—where the virus was pure and the procedure correct.

Unhappily these conditions were not always met. Because it was cheap and easy, and because they did not realize the risks they ran, the doctors of that time used human vaccination scabs for vaccine, rather than animal virus. In 1862 reports began to come in from Western armies that whole regiments had sickened after vaccination. In many cases ulcers, sometimes called "chancres," appeared at point of vaccination and elsewhere upon the body, accompanied by mysterious swellings in the armpits and in the groin. When such reports grew more frequent, as they did in 1864, special investigations were set on foot to determine the nature and origin of the trouble. It was a grave matter indeed, since numbers of surgeons had diagnosed the disease as syphilis and blamed it on the vaccine which the Government had bought from contractors.

Many of the sick had been vaccinated from scabs obtained from children in the Louisville poorhouse. It does not seem likely that any large number of these tots could have had syphilis, at least in a transmissible form. But sometimes soldiers' scabs were used, and in one instance a large number of infected men had been vaccinated with a "crust" taken from "a young lady." The majority of the investigators decided against syphilis as the diagnosis, and tended to lay the difficulties to incipient scurvy. But this hypothesis would not fit all the cases, and Elisha Harris believed some were syphilitic. Considering the septic surgical methods of the day, and recalling that in some instances the men had vaccinated each other, using rusty pins, old penknives, or whatever was handy, these infections might have been almost anything. Today a majority of the more serious of these Civil War cases would probably be diagnosed as cellulitis.

Any attempt to draw a balance on army life as a conditioner of health and disease must put many items in the debit column.

Soldiers were badly fed, badly housed, overworked, and provided with unsuitable latrines. Imperfect knowledge was partly accountable but, still more so, military necessity, inadequate transportation facilities, and primitive methods of food preservation, along with bungling and the regrettable human tendency to take the easiest way.

Over against these were some "credit" items. Many men tried hard to utilize Crimean War findings and to profit from experience. Every phase of army hygiene improved as time passed, some remarkably. In the latter half of the war there was less complaint about camp cleanliness, and about the quality of food and cooking; such preventive measures as were then known were increasingly utilized, and large numbers of men began to realize that their mode of life and their collective cleanliness had something to do with continued health. And it might be noted that the soldiers led a vigorous, outdoor life in, for the most part, beautiful country. Battles were hard, but there were usually long, restful intervals between them.

Diseases

and

Treatments

IN THE SPRING OF 1862, WHEN THE UNION FORCES FIRST SERI-
ously attempted to penetrate the Confederacy, Southerners
were heard to boast that their "General Summer," would soon
come to their aid. By this they meant the summer diseases—
malaria, dysentery, and typhoid.

Thanks to the hygienic and sanitary precautions of the Army,
these adversaries proved less formidable than expected, and
showed no special preference for men in blue as opposed to
those in gray. Nevertheless, along with other maladies, they
took a terrible toll. Medical Department statistics show an annual average of 2,435 cases of sickness per thousand among
white troops. The average soldier fell sick more than twice each
year. The annual average death rate from disease was 53.4 per
thousand. There is reason to believe that large numbers of men
failed to "report sick" unless they were seriously ill, and that

the mortality was greater than the records indicate because of the thousands of discharged soldiers who died at home.

When the morbidity and mortality rates are examined by years it may be seen that the former fell constantly until the end of the war, but that deaths from disease increased sharply each year until 1864, when they receded to the 1862 rate. The dwindling sick rate may be due both to improved sanitation and the smaller proportion of recruits each year in relation to the number of seasoned men. The increasing mortality was no doubt partly attributable to the larger number of men campaigning in the lower south, where the more deadly malarias and dysenteries were found, and the constantly increasing deaths from typhoid may indicate that bacteria were gaining in virulence. The recession in mortalities after 1863 may reflect the increasing proportion of veterans who had acquired immunities. The greater attention given to sanitation and food was probably also an important factor.

Infectious disease was accepted as a commonplace of war, and responsible officials were pleased with the Army's health record. In his annual report for 1861–1862, a year in which 5 per cent of the men in the Army had died of disease, Surgeon General Hammond wrote: "During the past year the health of the troops has been remarkably excellent. No epidemics of any severity have appeared among them, and those diseases which affect men in camps have been kept at a low minimum." Two years later his successor boasted that only 9.3 per cent of the men in the Army were then sick.

A few comparisons will help us understand this optimism. In the European Peninsular War, almost a quarter of Wellington's army was continuously sick. That high proportion had been equaled at times in our Mexican War, and almost reached by the British force in Egypt in 1801. In the Crimean War the Allies had a disease *mortality* of 25 per cent, while the disease death-rates of the American army in Mexico, and during the peaceful years 1840–1846 and 1849–1859, were 11 per cent and 8 per cent respectively.

The contrast of the Civil War's morbidity and mortality rates (2,435 and 53.4 per thousand) with those of later times are even more striking. In the Spanish War and Philippine Insurrection, disease mortality was only 16 per thousand, despite the difficulties of climate. In World War I the annual average disease mortality was 12.58 per thousand, of which 9.8 per thousand was caused by the pandemic of influenza-pneumonia.

The influence of war upon health is shown most clearly in comparison with the sickness and death rates of male civilians of military age (i.e., twenty to forty). The tables of the New England health insurance companies indicated a constant morbidity of a little under 2 per cent for this group. Such comparison of civilian figures with Army rates in those days of poorly collected vital statistics may not mean much; but, if accepted, the Surgeon General was boasting of a morbidity four or five times greater than that in civil life. Comparative mortality figures showed that the soldier was five times as likely to die of disease as was the civilian.

Disease incidence varied from army to army, from region to region and from unit to unit. These differences were sometimes as striking as they were incomprehensible. In January, 1862, the 12th Massachusetts Infantry had a sick rate of only 4 per thousand and the 5th Vermont Infantry of 271 per thousand, yet both were reported to have clean camps. In March, 1864, of two Illinois regiments, occupying adjacent camps and belonging to the same division, one had but a single invalid, the other had ninety. Cavalry in the lower Mississippi Valley were reported to have peculiarly high rates, yet a cavalry regiment in the Army of the Potomac had very little sickness and a disease mortality of only 12 per thousand in 1862, the sickliest year of the war. What was probably the lowest disease mortality figure of the war was that of Sherman's 14th Army Corps, which had a rate of less than 2 per thousand in the winter and spring of 1864–1865.

In general, troops in the West were unhealthier than those in the East, and both morbidity and disease mortality tended to increase the further south the army went. In May, 1861, the sick rates in the two areas were substantially the same, but with the coming of summer those in the West rose disproportionately. By the spring of 1862 both of the principal Western armies, Grant's and Buell's, were stricken with the virulent dysenteries and malarial fevers which were to characterize the region throughout the remainder of the war. These difficulties continued throughout the summer, but the usual cold weather remission checked them, and only recruits were especially sickly; and then the summer and the siege of Vicksburg saw a return of the old complaints. The Atlanta campaign, of May to September, 1864, saw another rise in morbidity figures, due partly to incipient scurvy. This period was followed by the unusually healthy march to the sea.

The Army of the Potomac roughly paralleled the Western armies in its experiences with disease. From a condition in which about one-third of the force was constantly sick, in the summer of 1861, the morbidity fell until in some divisions there were only 6 per cent ill in October. It was noticed during the comparative health of the winter months, however, that the "malarial atmosphere" of the Potomac marshes had made the prevalent pneumonia and measles more virulent.

During May, 1862, in the earlier phases of the Peninsular campaign, the men were vigorous and well. But in June, and especially toward the end of the month, exhaustion and defeat as well as infections enormously raised the toll of disease. Malaria and dysentery were widespread; the killer, typhoid, was active; and scurvy added to the troubles. Six thousand sick were sent north in June, but early in July 20 per cent were on sick report. After spending most of July and August in improving its health through diet and rest the army took part in the September Antietam campaign. Another period of sickness followed, with malaria and "diarrhoea-dysentery" predominating.

The Army of the Potomac continued well, by its own standards, from January, 1863, until the summer of 1864. During this time "diarrhoea," rheumatism, colds and malaria, were the only common afflictions, with venereal diseases cropping up among groups returning from leave. "Fever" cases were only 11 per cent of the total in January, 1864, and were very light, with mortalities of only 2.28 per cent. The army's morbidity rate that winter and spring was only 4 to 5 per cent. With the coming of warm weather, and the neglect of sanitation during active campaigning, the rates shot up. In May morbidity was 11.41 per cent, but the army impressed observers as healthy. In June the rate reached 14.89 per cent, and in July, with the siege of Petersburg begun, and sanitation at its nadir, the sick rate jumped to 27.10 per cent. Cold weather brought relief, as usual. But the sickly summer had swollen the year's sick report to more than 173,000 cases, of which more than half were "diarrhoea-dysentery" or malarial.

In the last autumn and winter of the war the Eastern troops were healthier than ever before. The average daily sick report was only 4 per cent—then considered phenomenal—and most of the cases were relatively mild, with little "straight" typhoid or malaria present. The absence of fresh vegetables was blamed for the severe diarrhea and pneumonia of the late winter and spring.

Throughout the war the soldier's best chance of remaining alive was the fortuitous one of his not contracting one of the great "killer" diseases. Once sick, he could expect very little from the therapeutics of the time, and that little rested chiefly upon the individual management of his case by his doctor. If he suffered from a malarial fever the great specific, quinine, was at his disposal. Otherwise, the physician might use or abuse a considerable armament of drugs, but the good food, the good nursing and the clean tranquillity so badly needed were seldom available.

Diarrhea-dysentery, which averaged 711 per thousand annually, was treated in a variety of ways. Laxatives and opium were the most common prescription; epsom salts or castor oil were administered in the morning and opium in the evening. Before Surgeon General Hammond's ban of it, calomel was fre-

quently utilized. Ipecac, the old standby which had been super-
seded by calomel early in the century, began to come back
during the war years because of British experiments with it in
India. Believing that much of their "diarrhoea" was malarial,
some surgeons treated it with quinine. If the treatment worked,
they felt justified. Everyone believed in prescribing fresh foods,
fruit juices and so on, but these were often impossible to procure. With stubborn cases most surgeons tried to get a discharge
or a long furlough for the patient, realizing that otherwise they
would have him on their hands a long time.

Typhoid patients were treated according to their symptoms.
The accompanying diarrhea was frequently dosed with Dover's
powders or other opiates. Abdominal pain was treated with hot
fomentations, blisters, and cupping; fever was fought with cold
applications to the head, and frequent spraying of the body with
water. Small doses of turpentine were administered by mouth
to act upon the intestinal ulcers. Imminent collapse was the
signal for warmth and friction externally, for capsicum, am-
monia, or brandy internally. If the case was suspected of being
masked malaria, whisky and quinine were given. Bleeding,
an old treatment, was increasingly frowned upon, although the
Sanitary Commission approved the use of leeches, locally applied, in bad cases of headache.

Malarial fevers, which with their annual average rate of 522
cases per thousand were second only to diarrhea-dysentery in
their prevalence, were systematically dosed with quinine. Customarily, once the time of a patient's paroxysm was known,
the drug was given every two hours for six hours before the
paroxysm, in three to five grain doses. In severe cases the doses
might be as large as ten grains, and might be pushed until the
patient's ears rang or other signs of cinchonism appeared. In
at least one recorded case a soldier was given a total of 120
grains of quinine in seventeen hours. In the remittent forms of
the disease quinine would be administered during the fever as
well as in the intermissions. Malarial patients were also subjected
to mercurial remedies for control of their bowels, followed by

salts. Opium quieted the sufferer, pains in his umbilical region were treated externally with sinapisms and blisters.

From this it can be seen what a high regard that generation had for drugs. An increasing belief in the therapeutic value of food was hampered both by ignorance of biochemistry and by want of fresh meats, vegetables, and fruits. Some surgeons were also groping toward what is now called psychosomatic medicine. There is ample evidence of the psychoneuroses of war. When noted at all, they were dismissed under the rubric "nostalgia." Nervous cases usually had short shrift, the baffled doctors regarding most of such patients as willful malingerers.

The balance sheet

The medical and sanitary record of the Civil War was on the whole a good one. That this has not been generally realized is partly due to the fact that the Civil War took place at the very end of the medical "middle ages"—immediately before bacteriology and aseptic surgery made some of the war generation's triumphs seem piddling or irrelevant. Historians in general were uninterested in medical matters while medical historians preferred the biographical or "great man" approach.

From the standpoint of the man in uniform, the administrative reforms within the Medical Department were of great importance. In 1861, like all things military in the United States, that department was hopelessly amateurish, riddled with incompetence and thoroughly unprepared. By 1865 it was a large, smooth-functioning organization, spending more money than the Army had spent in the last year of peace, and controlling a system of hospitals more imposing than anything seen down to that time. The field-relief system had evolved from the near-anarchy of regimental hospital and ambulance units to the integrated division and corps hospitals and ambulance trains. The medical supply system had evolved from a single

distributing point and an annual issue, to a network of purveyors' depots throughout the country and a plan under which
every unit was kept constantly supplied.

Through the Army, American doctors, for the first time, had
the opportunity to organize and control large general hospitals.
They had discovered, to their cost, that cleanliness was important, and that surgical infections might be kept from spreading if sanitary precautions were observed. They had found
that women nurses could be of use; and the women, or at least
the more perceptive among them, had learned that training and
discipline are essential to the woman hospital nurse. Both
doctors and nurses had learned that attention to the patient's
morale is medically sound.

Through their work in the relief commissions, the civilians of
the country had made substantial contributions to the spread
of medical and sanitary knowledge, and to the distribution of
much-needed supplies. On that base were to rise the American
Red Cross and the other great voluntary associations which are
so characteristic of the America of our day.

Whether the kind of surgical practice which war gives the
already-competent surgeon is valuable, may be argued. But it
is impossible to deny that war experience made operating surgeons out of a large number of rural physicians who had in the
past referred surgical cases to city specialists. In the spread
of operational surgery which the "aseptic" era was soon to
usher in, this training with the knife was important.

The effect of the war upon the health of the men who participated was, on the whole, bad. Many a veteran carried with him
for years, or for life, the sequelae of his army diseases. The
population movements incidental to the war, and the return
home of infected soldiery, seem to have had a deleterious effect
on civilian health. Fortunately, however, the end result of the
war experience was a preparation of both the medical mind
and the public mind for the great era of sanitary reform. The
public health movement, which was to make such headway in
the last third of the century, was evoked by the pressing needs

of the fast-growing cities and was aided greatly by yellow-fever scares and cholera panics. But the men who led that movement were, in large part, the same men whose wartime experience as surgeons or Sanitary Commissioners had persuaded them of the interconnection of filth and disease. And the public with which they dealt was permeated with former soldiers whose recollections of the value of clean camps made them understanding cooperators in public health measures.

Sources,

Appendix,

and

Index

A NOTE ON THE SOURCES

(While not all of the sources used are mentioned below, it is believed that the more useful and more interesting ones are.—The Author)

Rich materials are to be found among the publications of the United States Government, the Confederate States Government, and the publications of the various state governments. Of overwhelming importance are the *War of the Rebellion: A Compilation of the Official Records of the Union and Confederate Armies* (128 vols., Washington 1880–1901) and the Medical Department's great contribution, *Medical and Surgical History of the War of the Rebellion (1861–65): Prepared in Accordance with Acts of Congress under the Direction of Surgeon General Joseph K. Barnes, United States Army* (6 vols. Washington, 1875–1888). The six elephantine volumes of this work reprint many reports in whole or in part, provide a statistical reservoir and contain extensive generalized discussion from the viewpoint of the technical medical mind of the period in which they were prepared.

Other valuable United States Government publications include *The Congressional Globe,* 2nd session of the 36th Congress through the 1st session of the 38th Congress; *Regulations for the Army, 1861;* and *Revised United States Army Regulations of 1861* (Washington, 1863); *The Annual Reports of the Secretary of War* for the war years, and *The Reports of the Surgeon General* for the same period. Pertinent publications of the Confederate States Government include the various editions of *Army Regulations* and J. Julian Chisholm's *A Manual of Military Surgery for the Use of Surgeons in the Confederate States Army, with an Appendix of the Rules and Regulations of the Confederate States Army* (Richmond, 1862). Of the various publications of the state governments, the most useful were the reports of state surgeon generals, especially the surgeon generals of Massachusetts, Pennsylvania, New York, and Wisconsin.

The United States Sanitary Commission issued many publications. The general reader will find most useful and interesting Charles J. Stillé's *History of the United States Sanitary Commission, Being the General Report of its Work During the War of the Rebellion* (Philadelphia, 1866). This excellent history—slightly limited by the circumspection necessary in an official account and otherwise limited only by the sources available and by the state of scientific knowledge in 1866— deserves to be more widely read. *The Documents of the United States Sanitary Commission* (2 vols., New York, 1866) consists of 95 separate, numbered publications, collected and bound after the War. Covering all aspects of the work of the commission, these documents were published in various cities throughout the years 1861 to 1865. Virtually all of them are valuable, many extremely so.

Frank Hastings Hamilton (ed.), *Surgical Memoirs of the War of the Rebellion, Collected and Published by the United States Sanitary Commission.* New York, 1870 and 1871. This collection represents the commission's attempt to pass along the surgical lessons of the war. Later this work was partially eclipsed by the more voluminous and better illustrated material in the gigantic official *Medical and Surgical History of the War of the Rebellion.* William A. Hammond, editor, *Medical and Surgical Essays; Prepared for the United States Sanitary Commission, edited by William A. Hammond, M. D., Surgeon General U.S.A.* (Philadelphia, n.d.), is a collection of numerous papers published individually throughout the war years. Each is written by an expert on the topic discussed. While the essays vary in value, all are useful as illustrations of the best contemporary thought of the time in medicine and surgery. Dr. J. S. Newberry's *The United States Sanitary Commission in the Valley of the Mississippi during the War of the Rebellion.*

1861–1866 (Cleveland, 1871) is a valuable specialized attempt by the man who was responsible for the commission's work in the West.

The most useful publication of the Western Sanitary Commission is J. G. Forman's, *The Western Sanitary Commission; A Sketch of its Organization, History, and Aid Given to Freedmen and Union Refugees, with Incidents of Hospital Life* (St. Louis, 1864).

The United States Christian Commission published reports in each year from 1863 to 1866. These are interesting and useful. The Reverend Lemuel Moss' *Annals of the United States Christian Commission* (Philadelphia, 1868) is in the main an undistinguished rehash of the four annual reports.

Memoirs and other books by war participants are numerous. However, the number of works in this category which bear more than slightly upon Health and Medicine is not overwhelming. A listing of the best of them follows:

Louisa M. Alcott, *Hospital Sketches and Camp and Fireside Stories* (Boston, 1899). An able description of hospital life by one of the most intelligent of the women hospital workers. John D. Billings, *Hardtack and Coffee, or the Unwritten Story of Army Life* (Boston, 1888). Probably the best of all descriptions of army life and manners. John Hill Brinton, *Personal Memoirs of John H. Brinton, Major and Surgeon, U.S.V., 1861–1865* (New York, 1914). A particularly useful, penetrating, and interesting book by a distinguished Philadelphia professor of surgery who was for a time General Grant's medical director. Sophronia E. Bucklin, *In Hospital and Camp: A Woman's Record of Thrilling Incidents among the Wounded in the Late War* (Philadelphia, 1869). One of the better nurse memoirs; written by a strong partisan of Miss Dix. Austin Flint (ed.), *Contributions Relating to the Causation and Prevention of Disease, and to Camp Diseases; Together with a Report of the Diseases . . . Among the Prisoners at Andersonville* (New York, 1867). An important contribution by one of the leading medical scientists of the period. Benjamin Apthorp Gould, *Investigations in the Military and Anthropological Statistics of American Soldiers* (New York, 1869). An interesting and valuable study prepared by a leading insurance actuary. Frank Hastings Hamilton, *A Treatise on Military Surgery and Hygiene* (New York, 1865). Crystallizes the war experience of a leading New York physician.

William Alexander Hammond, *A Treatise on Hygiene with Special Reference to the Military Service* (Philadelphia, 1863). The great Surgeon General's major contribution to the intellectual side of the movement for sanitary reform in the Army. Cornelia Hancock, *The South after Gettysburg: Letters of Cornelia Hancock From the Army of the*

Potomac, 1863–1865, edited by Henrietta Stratton Jaquette (Philadelphia, 1937). Useful. Too young and too attractive to receive appointment as a nurse from Miss Dix, this engaging girl entered the army by other means, proving her worth and writing a series of unusually perceptive letters. Solon Hyde, *A Captive of War* (New York, 1900). This book by a hospital steward is so interesting and so well written that it could probably be republished as fiction and become a best seller. Oscar L. Jackson, *The Colonel's Diary: Journals Kept before and during the Civil War by the Late Colonel Oscar L. Jackson of New Castle, Pennsylvania, Sometime Commander of the 63rd Regiment O.V.I.* (n.p., 1922). A useful diary by an outspoken, peppery officer. Jenkin Lloyd Jones, *An Artilleryman's Diary (Wisconsin History Commission. Original Papers, No. 8)* (n.p., 1914). Probably the best of the Civil War diaries kept by an enlisted man. The author, then in his teens, is naïve, painstaking, honest, intelligent, and observant. He later became an outstanding liberal clergyman in Chicago.

Joseph Jones, *Medical and Surgical Memoirs, 3 vols. in 4* (New Orleans, 1875). Represents the mature reflections of the most active medical scientist on the Confederate side. Dr. Jones deserves to be better known. Jonathan Letterman, *Medical Recollections of the Army of the Potomac* (New York, 1866). Valuable though circumspect memoirs of the most outstanding medical field administrator in the Union army. Mary A. Livermore, *My Story of the War: A Woman's Narrative of Four Years' Personal Experience as a Nurse in the Union Army* (n.p., n.d.). Recollections of an outstanding woman. Theodore Lyman, *Meade's Headquarters 1863–65: Letters from Colonel Theodore Lyman from the Wilderness to Appomattox,* selected and edited by George R. Agassiz (Boston, 1922). Presents a valuable view of how the "top brass" lived, and what they thought: it is an antidote to too many books by enlisted men and subordinate officers.

John Ordroneaux, M.D., *Hints on the Preservation of Health in Armies for the use of Volunteer Officers and Soldiers* (New York, 1861). One of the few things of its kind not published by the Sanitary Commission. It was inferior to the Sanitary Commission's pamphlets. John Gardner Perry, *Letters from a Surgeon of the Civil War,* edited by Martha Derby Perry (Boston, 1906). Contains interesting letters about the varied medico-military career of a young Harvard man who was allowed to acquire "war service credits" in the Harvard Medical School by work in the Army. Adelaide W. Smith, *Reminiscences of an Army Nurse During the Civil War* (New York, 1911), sheds light on the activities of state agents and on the deficiencies in nurse organization. Julia L. Wheelock's *The Boys in White; the Experience of a Hospital*

Agent in and around Washington (New York, 1870) was written by a dreadful woman who was the agent of the state of Michigan. The author is an example of how annoying a self-righteous woman can be to the military authorities. She illustrates, unconsciously, why both women and state agents were disliked by so many medical officers.

Walt Whitman, *The Wound Dresser: A Series of Letters Written from the Hospitals in Washington during the War of the Rebellion*, Edited by R. M. Bucke (Boston, 1898). Shows how the hospitals of Washington and Fredericksburg looked to the eyes of a poet and a lover of his fellow man. Joseph Janvier Woodward's *The Hospital Steward's Manual* (Philadelphia, 1863). An excellent attempt by a notable medical scientist to fill a long felt want. Invaluable on the functions and duties of medical enlisted personnel. The same author's *Chief Camp Diseases of the United States Armies as Observed during the War: A Practical Contribution to Military Medicine* (Philadelphia, 1863), was one of the first important attempts to learn from war experience. Katherine Prescott Wormeley's *The Other Side of War with the Army of the Potomac* (Boston, 1888). Excellent account of the chaotic period during which the sick and wounded of the Peninsular campaign were being evacuated. Miss Wormeley was an emergency nurse, a keen observer and a talented writer.

Jane Stewart Woolsey's *Hospital Days* (New York, 1870) is a charming book, little known and hard to find. Especially informing on the human side of hospital life, it is probably the best book about the Civil War by a woman writer. The author is intelligent, kind, perceptive, and restrained. John Allan Wyeth's *With Sabre and Scalpel; The Autobiography of a Soldier and Surgeon* (New York and London, 1914) is an excellent book by a Confederate who later became a prominent New York surgeon and founded the Polyclinic Hospital.

Secondary works useful for this subject are relatively few. George Barton's *Angels of the Battlefield, A History of the Labors of the Catholic Sisterhoods in the Late Civil War* (Philadelphia, 1897) is eulogistic and disappointing, but is virtually alone in its field. Louis C. Duncan's *The Medical Department of the United States Army in the Civil War* (Washington, 1914). A group of reprints of articles which appeared in the *Military Surgeon* bound in boards for distribution by the author. This is a careful, valuable work on field operations; but it scarcely notices most other aspects of the subject.

Two essential background works on medical history are Henry E. Sigerist's *American Medicine* (New York, 1934) and Richard Harrison Shryock's *The Development of Modern Medicine: An Interpretation of the Social and Scientific Factors Involved* (Philadelphia, 1936). The former work is by the world's greatest living medical historian and is unchallenged in its field. The latter is the only major attempt by a general historian to work in the field of medical history. It is an extraordinarily valuable book which should be much better known to historians and to the general public.

The medical journals of the war period provide good source material. All of the medical journals are worth reading. The *American Medical Times*, II–IX (May 18, 1861–July 2, 1864) was a rather "popular" medical weekly. It printed a vast quantity of correspondence from the field, brief articles, letters from surgeons, etc. *The Medical and Surgical Reporter*, IX–XII (Oct. 25, 1862–June 10, 1865) was a leading weekly of the same general type. Its specialty, from the standpoint of usefulness to this study, is its extensive regular correspondence and its serials by army surgeons, some of them running to book length. The *Sanitary Commission Bulletin*, I–II (Nov. 1, 1863–Aug. 1, 1865) was the commission's popular organ and "morale builder" for the home front.

In addition to the materials printed in the medical journals, a large literature of personal reminiscences and other articles by participants appeared in magazines of general circulation and in the collective publications of medical societies and veterans' organizations. The titles of a number of the best of these follow:

John Shaw Billings, "Medical Reminiscences," *Transactions, College of Physicians, Philadelphia*, 3rd ser., XXVII (1905), 115–121. Presents the recollections of a distinguished army surgeon who became a great librarian. Eben Hannaford, "In the Ranks at Stone River," *Harpers New Monthly Magazine*, XXVII (November, 1863), 809–815, is an unusually good description of getting wounded. The same author's "In Hospital after Stone River," *Ibid*, XXVIII (January, 1864), 260–265, is a particularly vivid account of a field hospital after a great battle, and of subsequent adventures in a general hospital. Elisha Harris, "Hygienic Experience in New Orleans during the War: Illustrating the Importance of Efficient Sanitary Regulations," *Southern Medical and Surgical Journal*, 3rd ser., I (July, 1866), 77–88, presents a striking early example of what military government can do for sanitation. Major Albert Gaillard Hart, "The Surgeon and the Hospital in the Civil War," in *Papers of the Military Historical Society of Massachusetts*, XIII (n.d.) 231–285, is a quite valuable and detailed account of its subjects. Berkeley Hill, "Sick Transport and Volunteer Aid in War," *Contemporary Review*, XVI (March, 1871), 600–618, is a valuable study, showing considerable research.

"An Inquiry into the Military Rights and Duties of Medical Officers in the Land Forces," *United States Service Magazine*, I (May, 1864),

478–489, ably examines a vexed, troublesome question. Edward Jarvis, "The Sanitary Condition of the Army," *Atlantic Monthly*, X (October, 1862), 463–497, is an important article by a prominent Boston medical man who was also a special inspector for the Sanitary Commission. W. W. Keen, "Military Surgery in 1861 and in 1918," in *Annals of the American Academy of Political and Social Science*, LXXX (November, 1918), 11–22, offers valuable recollections and comparisons by a distinguished Philadelphia surgeon. The same author's "Surgical Reminiscences of the Civil War," in *Transactions, College of Physicians, Philadelphia*, 3rd ser., XXVII (1905), 95–114, is likewise valuable—as is the similar offering of Dr. Keen's distinguished contemporary, S. Weir Mitchell, "Some Personal Recollections of the Civil War," *Transactions, College of Physicians, Philadelphia*, 3rd ser., XXVII (1905), 87–94. W. W. Potter's "Three Years with the Army of the Potomac," *Buffalo Medical Journal*, appears in sixteen installments, LXVI through LXVIII (July, 1911–November, 1912). While it contains much good material, its usefulness is not in proportion to its length.

Charles Smart, "Field Notes on Military Surgery in the United States," *Medical Times and Gazette*, is a serial appearing in fifteen installments between Feb. 7, 1863, and Apr. 23, 1865. These "field notes" are the valuable, on-the-spot observations of the medical officer who was later to become the editor of the medical volumes of the official *Medical and Surgical History of the War of the Rebellion*. James Tanner, "Experience of a Wounded Soldier at the Second Battle of Bull Run," *Military Surgeon*, LX (February, 1927), 121–139, presents the harrowing reminiscences of the "Corporal" Tanner of veterans' treasury-raiding fame. This material goes far toward explaining Tanner's political tendencies and his feeling that "nothing is too good for the wounded boys." The article is one of the best descriptions of the chaotic conditions that followed this peculiarly mismanaged battle.

Secondary articles which either bear directly upon health and medicine in the Union army, or which provided valuable collateral material, include:

W. Caldwell, "An Inquiry in the Condition of the Health of the Ex-Soldiers of the War of the Rebellion as a Class and to What Extent the Vicissitudes of the War Contributed to Stamp upon Them a More or Less Permanent Disability," *Cleveland Medical Gazette*, IV (1888–1889), 140–151, is a valuable survey of its melancholy subject. Lieut. Col. Louis C. Duncan, "The Strange Case of Surgeon General Hammond," *Military Surgeon*, LXIV (January, 1929), 98–114, and (February, 1929), 252–267, is an excellent account of General Hammond's court-martial and surrounding circumstances. The same author's "Evolution of the Ambulance Corps and Field Hospital," *Military Surgeon*, XXXII (March, 1913), 221–243, is the best short account of the subject. Lieut. Col. M. A. Reasoner, "The Development of the Medical Supply Service," *Military Surgeon*, LXIII (July, 1928) 1–18, presents useful material on an important facet of the subject. Rear Admiral E. R. Stitt, "Our Disease Inheritance from Slavery," *United States Navy Medical Bulletin*, XXVI (October, 1928), 801–810, is an extremely valuable and suggestive article regarding diseases introduced into the South via the slave trade.

Much the most important manuscript materials are those comprised in the archives of the United States Sanitary Commission. This archive, consisting of 1,200 boxes of papers, was placed in the Lenox Library shortly after the Civil War. When the New York Public Library was established, the Lenox Library was absorbed, and the Sanitary Commission archives were stored in a subbasement of the Library building. The boxes are now in poor condition, but the papers they contain are invaluable. Fortunately, a vast majority of these are canceled vouchers and financial materials of little interest. The pertinent documents are to be found in 125 boxes. Among the subsections of greatest value to this study are: The Papers of the Washington Office, The Papers of the New York Office, The Papers of the Army of the Potomac U.S.S.C. Office, and The Papers of the Historical Committee. The last named includes a valuable miscellany of scientific papers, special reports, observations on specific conditions and problems, and answers to questionnaires; all submitted to the commission because of their supposed historical value.

The following statistical materials, all of them copied from or derived from the statistical tables in *Medical and Surgical History of the War of the Rebellion,* are offered as supplemental to the material in Chapter XI.

(1)

GENERAL STATISTICS ON DISEASE AND THE MORTALITY FROM IT [1]

(A) Average annual rates per thousand of strength:

	Cases	Deaths
White troops	2435	53.4
Colored troops	3299	143.4

(B) Incidence by years:

		White Troops	Colored Troops
1861	Cases	3822	
	Deaths	10.8	
1862	Cases	2983	
	Deaths	49	
1863	Cases	2696	
	Deaths	63	
1864	Cases	2210	4092
	Deaths	48	211
1865	Cases	2273	3205
	Deaths	56	140
1866	Cases	2362	2797
	Deaths	42	94

(C) Average annual rates per thousand of strength arranged according to type of disease: [2]

[1] *Medical and Surgical History*, Med. vol. 3, p. 6.
[2] *Ibid.*, 13.

	White Troops		Colored Troops	
	Cases	Deaths	Cases	Deaths
Continued Fevers	40	11	22	12
Typho-Malarial	22	1	41	6
Malarial	522	3	829	10
Diarrhoea-Dysentery	711	15	839	35
Eruptive	46	4	92	18
Total Miasmatic	1414	38	1961	86
Venereal	82	0.06	77	0.17
Scurvy	13	0.16	88	2
Consumption	6	2	7	6
Diseases of the Nervous System	76	1	130	4
Acute Bronchitis	174	0.49	177	1
Inflammation of the lungs	41	6	127	28
Total Respiratory	261	7	354	32
Diseases of the Digestive System	252	1	295	5

(D) Confederate medical statistics are fragmentary. Consequently, overall statistical comparisons cannot be made between the armies. The following table on disease mortalities in each army to the end of 1862 attributed to certain diseases shows some striking similarities and dissimilarities: [3]

	Confederate Army	Union Army
	(Case death rate in %)	
Continued Fevers	33.27	22.28
Malarial Fevers	1.15	.95
Eruptive Diseases	5.12	5.27
Diarrhoea-Dysentery	1.48	1.25
Pulmonary Diseases	18.89	2.34
Rheumatism	1.26	.14
All other Diseases	0	1.32

(E) The following figures on disability discharges present an interesting picture not only of the diseases that were robbing the Army

[3] *Ibid.*, 31.

but of the diseases and disabilities which the soldiers were taking back to the civilian community: [4]

	Rate per thousand of mean strength, whole war period. (White troops only)	Mean annual rate per thousand of strength. (White troops only)
Discharges from all diseases	424	82
Specific diseases only	291	56
Diarrhoea-Dysentery	37	7
Debility	31	5
Syphilis	3	0.74
Rheumatism	25	4
Consumption	43	8
Epilepsy	8	1
Insanity	1	0.34
Paralysis	6	1
Heart disease	22	4
Asthma	2	0.50
Hernia	19	3
Piles	3	0.64
Anchylosis	3	0.76
Malaria	1	0.35
Typhoid	1	0.37
Ophthalmia	3	0.60
Deafness	2	0.48
Kidney inflammation	2	0.44
Bronchitis	8	1

(2)

SOME STATISTICS ON DIARRHOEA-DYSENTERY

(A) On mortality from these diseases the medical department statistics yield the following:

	Cases	Deaths
Acute Diarrhoea	1,269,027	4,291
Chronic Diarrhoea	182,586	30,836
Acute Dysentery	259,071	5,576
Chronic Dysentery	28,451	3,855

[4] *Ibid.*, 26.

However, the authors of the *Medical and Surgical History* believe these figures to be incomplete, since many deaths reported under enteritis, inflammation of the bowels, peritonitis, hemorrhage of the bowels, pneumonia, anemia, debility, etc., should, in their opinion, have been charged up to diarrhoea. These authors, after some statistical maneuvers, arrive at a grand total of 57,000 deaths; but they consider even that too low.[5]

(B) The following table shows the wide variation of mortality from diarrhoea-dysentery according to time and place.
(Mortalities per thousand of strength; white troops only).[6]

	Eastern Theater	Western	Pacific
Year ending 30 June 1862	1.10	9.56	0.70
Year ending 30 June 1863	8.91	23.00	0.85
Year ending 30 June 1864	8.06	20.80	0.67
Year ending 30 June 1865	19.59	23.25	1.10

(C) The constantly increasing deadliness of diarrhoea-dysentery is shown below (ratio per thousand of mean strength, white troops):[7]

May and June, 1861	Incidence (9,772 cases)	Mortality (4 deaths)	No. of Cases to Each Death
Year ending June 30, 1862	770	4.17	178–1
Year ending June 30, 1863	850	15.99	49–1
Year ending June 30, 1864	639	15.78	37–1
Year ending June 30, 1865	686	21.29	29–1

[5] *Ibid.*, med. vol. 2, pp. 2-3.
[6] *Ibid.*, 9.
[7] *Ibid.*, 6.

(3)

SOME STATISTICS ON MALARIAL FEVERS

(A) The following table shows the incidence and mortalities from the various malarial fevers (ratio per thousand of mean strength, white troops) : [8]

	1860–61		1861–62		1862–63		1863–64		1864–65		1865–66	
	I	M	I	M	I	M	I	M	I	M	I	M
Intermittent	126	0	252	.2	313	.4	463	.4	425	.4	685	.6
Congestive	5	.02	7	1.2	6	1.5	6	1.5	4	1.1	8	2.7
Remittent	43	0	143	1.3	140	1.8	114	1.3	127	1.9	159	2.6
Typho-malarial	—	—	—	—	38	1.8	18	1.7	22	2.3	16	2.5
Totals	174	.02	404	2.8	498	5.5	603	4.9	581	5.6	869	7.8
Totals on colored troops							889	26.	787	14.	981	13.

(B) Mean annual rate for malarial fevers as distributed geographically.

The four most malarious military departments and their mean annual rates per thousand were: [9]

Department of Arkansas	1287
Department of North Carolina	1035
Department of the Gulf	930
Department of Tennessee	865

The four least malarious departments were:

Department of the East	144
Department of the Northwest	238
The Middle Department	264
Department of the Ohio	265

(C) Relative incidence of malarial fevers in the two hostile armies is uncertain, although fragmentary statistics indicate that the Confederate Army had a greater incidence. The authors of the *Medical and Surgical History* believe that the Confederate death rate from malaria was lower than the Federal. The following figures on the incidence of malaria in the contending Armies of the Tennessee between June 1, 1862 and May 31, 1863 are of interest: [10]

[8] *Ibid.*, 82-83. For an explanation of the high rates among colored troops see p. 85.

[9] *Ibid.*, 86.

[10] *Ibid.*, 104. See also the discussion on pp. 105-107.

	U.S. A. of T.	*C.S. A. of T.*
June, 1862	62	141
July	62	179
August	70	125
September	92	69
October	80	75
November	62	47
December	45	43
January, 1863	46	45
February	44	44
March	48	65
April	45	80
May	39	100